LONGMAN CHILDREN'S
WORLD

Consultant editor Brian Dicks

EN'S ILLUSTRATED

O ATLAS

Longman

A QED BOOK

Longman Group Limited,
Longman House, Burnt Mill, Harlow, Essex, U.K.

First published in Great Britain 1982

© 1981 IBP Limited (assigned to Victoria House
Publishing Ltd) and QED Publishing Limited
Cartography © 1981 QED Publishing Limited

This book was designed and produced by
QED Publishing Ltd
32 Kingly Court
London W1

Art director Alastair Campbell
Production director Edward Kinsey
Editorial director Jeremy Harwood
Senior editor Kathy Rooney
Project editor Nicola Thompson
Art editor Heather Jackson
Designers Clive Hayball
Editorial Tim Healey, Keith Lye, Juila Kirk
Picture research Anne Lyons
Illustrators Marilyn Bruce, Chris Forsey, Gail Gibson,
Arka Graphics (maps), Elaine Keenan, Edwina Keene,
Abdul Aziz Khan, Elly King, Sally Kindberg (projects),
Susan Kinsey, Sally Launder, Gary Marsh, David Staples,
Perry Taylor, Martin Woodford

Filmset in Great Britain by Flowery Typesetting,
London
Colour origination in Hong Kong by Hong Kong
Graphic Arts Limited
Printed in Hong Kong by Leefung Asco Limited

Longman children's illustrated world atlas
I. Geography — Juvenile literature
I. Dicks, Brian
910   G133

ISBN 0-582-25059 5

FOREWORD

This book is designed to give the younger reader
a fuller understanding of our fascinating and
varied planet. The approach is strongly visual –
the maps, illustrations and photographs have
been carefully selected to show both the world's
exciting general features and the detailed
geographical characteristics of individual
countries, regions and continents.
The book is divided into two sections. The first
introduces the reader to maps, scales and
reference points, initially at the level of the
reader's own experience – their immediate
environment and area. Through successive
spreads, the context is broadened to include the
town, region, country and continent. In this way,
the reader becomes aware of ever larger areas
and scales of experience. Next, this section covers
the natural world – how it was formed, how it
moves, how immense forces of nature create
mountains, move continents and produce
earthquakes and volcanoes. The earth's land-
forms and scenery, weather and climate,
vegetation and mineral resources are all dealt with.
The second section examines the countries of the
world with the aid of maps and photographs.
Each map shows the main physical features,
economic and natural resources, as well as towns,
roads and rail communication. Picture symbols
ensure clear visual understanding. This type of
presentation enables the younger reader to learn
about his or her own country and, at the same
time, to compare and contrast it with other
countries in the world. For this purpose an
information panel provides such details as total
land area of the country, population, language,
currency and capital city.

Brian Dicks
Consultant editor

CONTENTS

YOUR WORLD

Your room

Where are you? Are you sitting in a room? How many windows does the room have? Where are they? Where is the door. How would you describe the room to someone else? Are you at school or at home?

One way of showing where things are in a room is to make a map of it. A map is a special kind of diagram of a place which shows exactly where things are. A map can be of a room or a house, but more often shows a town or a country.

A map of your classroom would show where the windows, door and furniture are. A map of your town would show, for example, where the streets and main buildings are. On a map of your country you would see larger features like rivers, mountains and towns. Maps can also include other information, such as where the political boundaries are or what a country produces. Such information is shown using signs which are called symbols. A map has a key which shows what the symbols and the different colours on it mean.

So that the map can show accurately where things are, it is drawn to scale. A scale is a system by which actual distances – for example one mile or one kilometre – are shown by much smaller distances – such as one inch or one centimetre. This means that many miles can be reduced to a size that will fit on a page, as well as still giving exact information about where places are. A collection of maps is called an atlas.

This picture and map both show the same classroom from above. It is easy to see what is in the picture, but the map would not make sense without the key. The key is very important as it explains what all the colours represent. For example, the chairs and desks would just be strange shapes on the map if the key was not there to explain what the different colours mean. Not everything in the picture is shown on the map. The people are not shown as they are not actually part of the room.

◀ If you want to be good at making maps you should try to remember everything you see in detail. For example, you often see your school but how well can you describe it from memory? Where are the doors and windows? What is the shape of the school? Is it made up of one building or many? Before you begin to draw a map you should note down as much information as possible.

◀ Maps are usually of large places — continents, countries or towns. However, if you want to make a map you could start with a small area like your classroom. A plan is another name for a map of a house or room.

▶ This is a simple map of the school illustrated here. The roof looks flat and none of the walls, windows or doors can be seen. This is because a map is like an aerial view. An aerial view means that something is only seen from directly above it. It is much easier to see what shape the building is from the map, which is like a diagram, rather than from the picture.

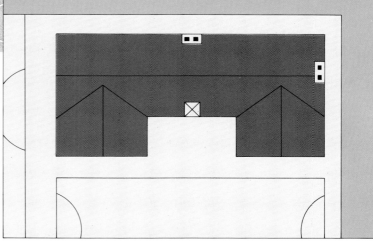

Key
- ◯ Floor
- ◯ Window
- ● Door
- ● Blackboard
- ◯ Wall
- ◯ Chair
- ◯ Table
- ◯ Other furniture

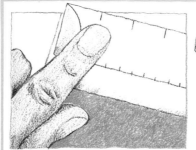 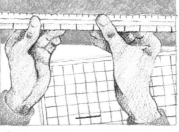 

Make a map of your classroom
1. Take a large piece of squared paper, a long tape measure, a ruler and some pencils. Measure your classroom with the tape measure and note down the measurements. Work out a scale for your map.

2. A scale is a way of showing a long distance by means of a shorter one. For example, one foot (25cm) could be shown as one square on your paper. Draw the scaled measurements of your classroom on to the paper lightly in pencil.

3. Next, measure where all the main objects in the room are. This should include, for example, the door, windows, desks and chairs. Draw the shapes in on the map to show their position in the room using the same scale as before.

 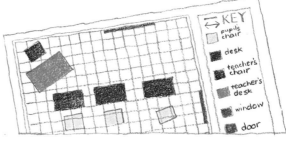

4. After drawing all the lines in pencil, go over the outline of the map in a coloured pencil or felt-tip pen. Then fill in the shapes of the objects in different colours. Use the same colour for all the chairs, another for all the desks and so on.

5. Next make the key at one side of the map. The key is an important part of the map, as it says what the colours or symbols on the map mean. Fill in one of the squares on the paper with the colour used for the desks and write 'desk' beside it.

Repeat for the other colours. Underneath the key write the scale you have used. When you look at a map, always look at the key and scale too. They help you to understand what the map means. You could also make a map of your home.

Your neighbourhood

Your home and your school are both part of a neighbourhood. If you live in a town, your neighbourhood will probably include streets, shops, houses, and perhaps parks, railway lines, churches and factories. This kind of neighbourhood is called urban. If you live in the country, your neighbourhood may include farms, hills, rivers, small towns or villages. This kind of neighbourhood is called rural. Roads, railways and rivers may link rural and urban areas. What kind of neighbourhood do you live in? Make a list of the main features of your neighbourhood.

In the past most people lived in rural areas; but today most people live in urban areas. Large towns and cities have two main parts – the inner city where there are offices and large shops for example, and the outer city or suburbs where most people live. Inner cities tend to be crowded with people and traffic. Roads and bus or rail routes link the inner with the outer city. The city is usually the centre of local government and administration which may cover both the urban and rural areas.

Town and regional maps
If you want to see on a map where you live, you could look at two different kinds of map. Maps of towns show detailed information like the names of streets and where parks and buildings are. Regional maps show a whole region so that there is not room for as much detail. The regional map on the opposite page shows only general information. You can see where towns are in relation to each other but you cannot see street names or where the roads go through a town. Regional maps are useful if you want to see how near one town is to another. Town maps help visitors find their way around the town.

Your town

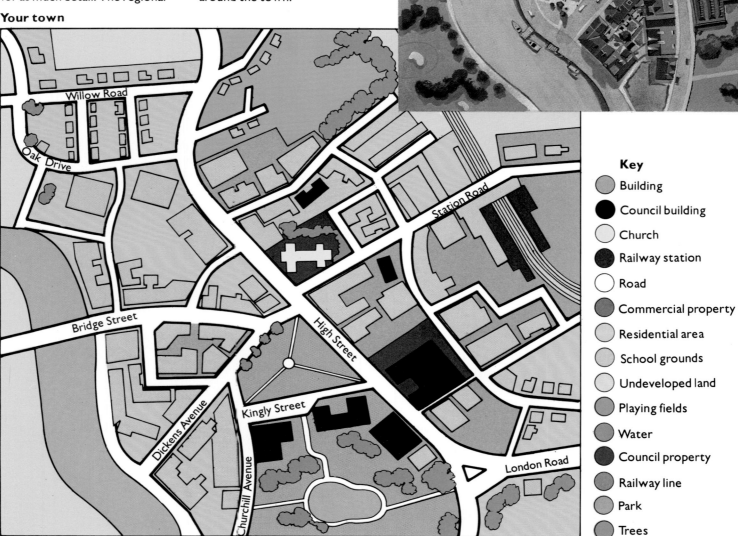

Key
- Building
- Council building
- Church
- Railway station
- Road
- Commercial property
- Residential area
- School grounds
- Undeveloped land
- Playing fields
- Water
- Council property
- Railway line
- Park
- Trees

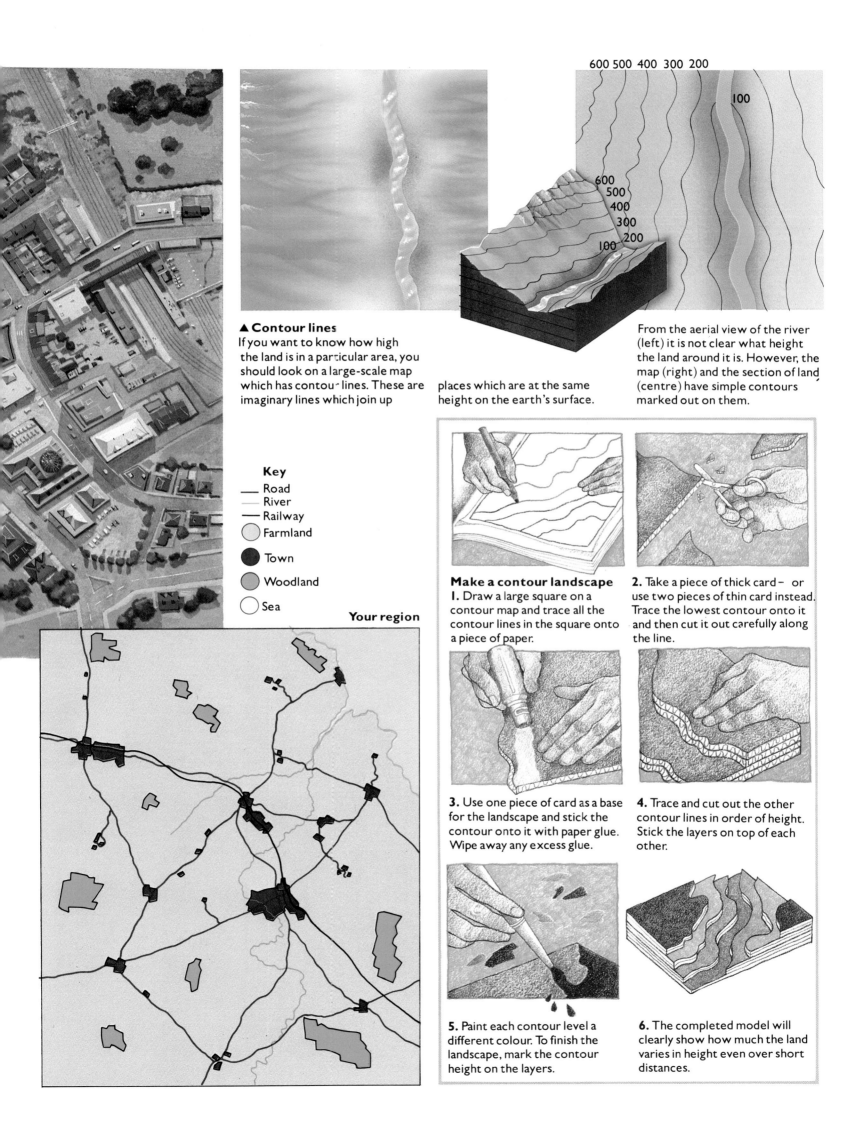

600 500 400 300 200

100

600
500
400
300
200
100

▲ Contour lines

If you want to know how high the land is in a particular area, you should look on a large-scale map which has contour lines. These are imaginary lines which join up places which are at the same height on the earth's surface.

From the aerial view of the river (left) it is not clear what height the land around it is. However, the map (right) and the section of land (centre) have simple contours marked out on them.

Key

— Road
— River
— Railway
⬤ Farmland
⬤ Town
⬤ Woodland
⬤ Sea

Your region

Make a contour landscape

1. Draw a large square on a contour map and trace all the contour lines in the square onto a piece of paper.

2. Take a piece of thick card – or use two pieces of thin card instead. Trace the lowest contour onto it and then cut it out carefully along the line.

3. Use one piece of card as a base for the landscape and stick the contour onto it with paper glue. Wipe away any excess glue.

4. Trace and cut out the other contour lines in order of height. Stick the layers on top of each other.

5. Paint each contour level a different colour. To finish the landscape, mark the contour height on the layers.

6. The completed model will clearly show how much the land varies in height even over short distances.

Your country

Your neighbourhood is part of your country. Your country may be large, like the United States and Australia, or small like Switzerland or Austria. A country is an area of land with its own people, government and laws.

Your country may join on to other countries. The dividing line between countries is called a boundary. Boundaries may follow natural features, such as the Pyrenees Mountains which separate Spain from France. Boundaries can also be straight lines which follow no natural features. For example, the boundary between the United States and Canada follows a line of latitude. Other countries, like Australia and Japan, are islands and have no land boundaries with other countries. What kind of boundaries does your country have? Does it border on any other countries?

All countries have a main city called the capital. Often the government and main administration are here. The capital is usually also the centre of the country's communications. What is the capital of your country?

Your country has many resources. These include soil for agriculture and farming and minerals, such as coal, oil and iron, which industry uses. All the things which farmers grow or industry makes are called products. A country with many farms and little industry is called an agricultural country, and a country with many industries and few farms is an industrial country. Is your country agricultural or industrial? What are its main products?

Scales
A scale is a system by which large distances on the earth's surface can be represented on a map as a short distance. There are three main ways of giving a scale. One is to write it in words — one inch to one mile, for example. Another type of scale uses numbers either as a fraction or as a ratio. 1/100 or 1:100 could mean that one inch (or one centimetre) on the map represents 100 inches (or 100 centimetres) in reality. This is a useful type of scale as it works with any measurement. The third way of showing a scale is to mark out distances on a line and put it under the map.

Your country

Key

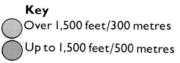

Over 1,500 feet/300 metres

Up to 1,500 feet/500 metres

◄ Contour map
The second main type of physical map is the contour map. Contours are lines drawn on maps along lines of height. On some contour maps, the lines themselves are shown. Others, as here, shade in the areas of the different contours. Contours are a good way of showing heights – they can vary between showing small differences in height (50 feet/20 metres) and large differences such as 1,000 feet/300 metres.

▲ Relief map
Maps which show the features of a country such as mountains and rivers are called physical maps. There are two main types of physical map. A relief map is like a picture of the country taken from above. It shows the mountains and rivers as on a photograph. The tops of mountains sometimes appear white, to indicate snow. The main mountain areas in the British Isles are in Scotland. Running down the centre of England like a backbone are the Pennine Mountains. Wales is also mountainous. Much of Ireland is flat.

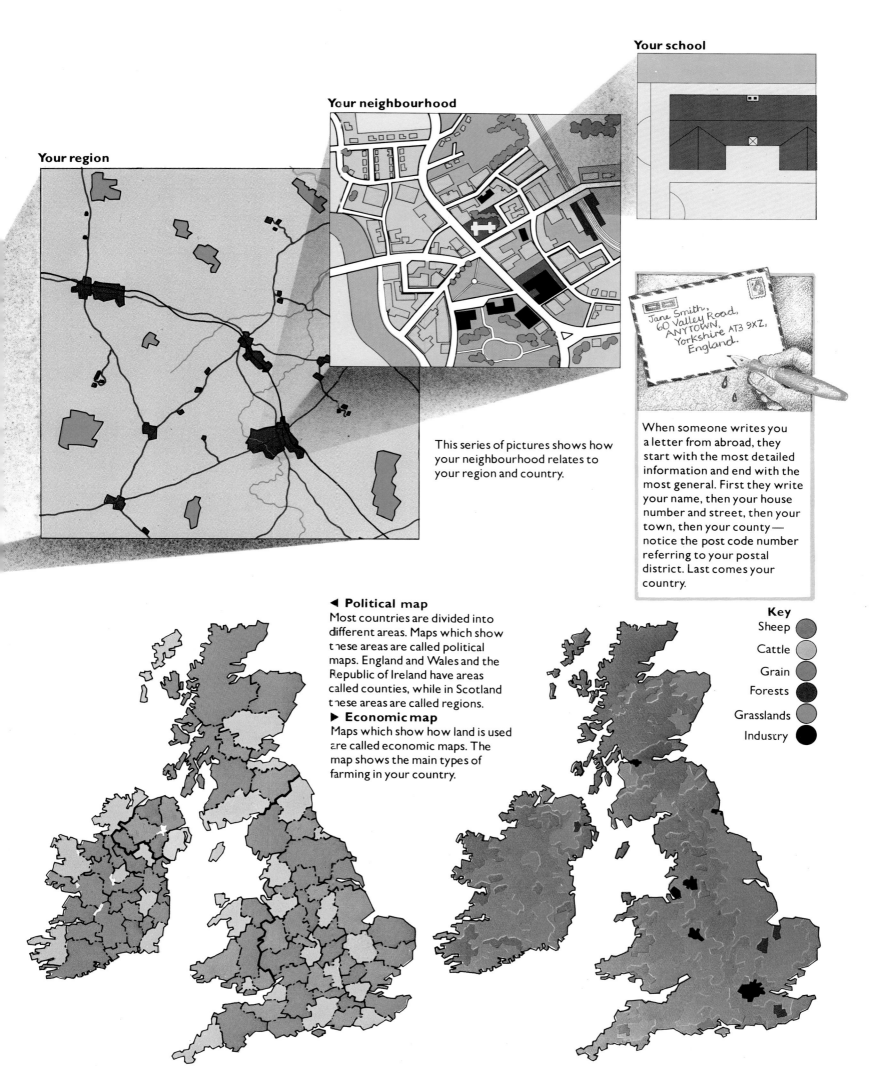

Your school

Your neighbourhood

Your region

This series of pictures shows how your neighbourhood relates to your region and country.

Jane Smith,
60 Valley Road,
ANYTOWN,
Yorkshire AT3 9XZ,
England.

When someone writes you a letter from abroad, they start with the most detailed information and end with the most general. First they write your name, then your house number and street, then your town, then your county — notice the post code number referring to your postal district. Last comes your country.

◀ **Political map**
Most countries are divided into different areas. Maps which show these areas are called political maps. England and Wales and the Republic of Ireland have areas called counties, while in Scotland these areas are called regions.

▶ **Economic map**
Maps which show how land is used are called economic maps. The map shows the main types of farming in your country.

Key
Sheep
Cattle
Grain
Forests
Grasslands
Industry

Your continent

Your country is part of a continent. The world has seven continents. Some, such as Europe and Asia, contain many countries. Others such as North America have fewer. How many countries does your continent have?

A continent is a large land area, one of the main sections of the earth's surface. The continents are Asia, Africa, North America, South America, Antarctica, Europe and Australasia. Most of the earth's land surface is in the northern hemisphere. However, only about one third of the earth's surface is land; the rest is covered by water. In the northern hemisphere about two fifths is land; in the southern hemisphere only about one fifth is land-covered.

Continents have many natural features which often cross country boundaries. These include many rivers and mountain ranges. What are the main features of your continent?

A continental island is an island off the coast of a continent which still is part of that continent. For example, Japan is a group of continental islands belonging to Asia. Newfoundland is a continental island which is part of North America. Does your continent have any continental islands?

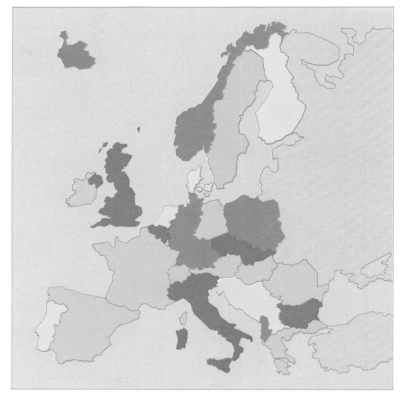

▲ This map is a simplified map of your continent — Europe. Europe is made up of many countries which are very small if you compare them with countries like Brazil in South America or China in Asia. Europe lies in the northern hemisphere to the west of Asia. Sometimes Europe and Asia are together called Eurasia. Part of the Soviet Union is in Europe but most of the country is in Asia. Turkey is another country which is also in Europe and Asia.

The countries in Europe have many different shapes. You can see how varied they are if you look at them as they are shown below — as separate countries. Some of the countries, Norway, Sweden and Italy for example, are like long fingers of land jutting out into the sea. These are large peninsulas. The British Isles and Iceland are called continental islands. This is because they are not joined onto the rest of Europe by land but are surrounded by sea.

Republic of Ireland

Norway

France

Italy

East Germany

United Kingdom

Sweden

Finland

West Germany

Spain

Rumania

Yugoslavia

Czechoslovakia

Greece

Iceland

Denmark

Portugal

Bulgaria

Hungary

Austria

Netherlands

Belgium

Poland

Albania

Switzerland

Luxembourg

▲ This map shows five independent states which are so small they are often not shown on maps. San Marino and the Vatican City are in Italy. Monaco has borders with France and Italy while Andorra borders on Spain and France. Liechtenstein lies between Austria and Switzerland.

Make a jigsaw of Europe
1. First you will need a map. You can use either the countries on this page or an atlas. Make sure that the map is large enough and the lines between the countries dark enough to see through a piece of tracing paper. Maps from large atlases are best. If it is a small book, it may be difficult to flatten out the page and keep the tracing paper straight.

2. Take a piece of tracing paper and place it over the map. The tracing paper should cover the entire map and not be too heavy or you will not be able to see through it. If the map you are tracing is one sheet of paper, you can secure the map and tracing paper with drawing pins. If the map is in a book, small pieces of masking tape can be placed on the corners to hold the paper steady.

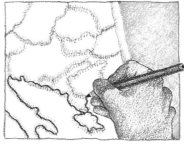

3. You are now ready to begin tracing the outlines of the countries. The country borders will be the darkest lines. Be careful not to confuse them with other lines. With a dark pencil trace over all the lines which you need to make the map. When you have traced all the country borders, turn the tracing paper over. Now scribble on the back of each line so that it is completely covered.

4. Once the country borders are completed, lift the tracing paper off the map. Take a piece of white paper the same size as the tracing paper and, turn the tracing paper over again so that the scribbled pencil marks are touching the white paper. Secure both sheets with drawing pins or pieces of masking tape. With a black pencil, draw over your outlines, pressing hard. Work carefully.

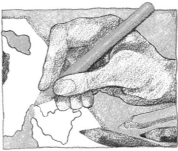

5. When you have finished tracing all the country borders (make sure you have traced all of them), lift off the tracing paper. You will have before you the continent of Europe! With five or six coloured pencils, carefully fill in the countries, making sure not to go over the borders. Try not to use the same colour for countries next to one another.

6. After you have coloured in all the countries, take a pair of small, sharp scissors and very carefully cut out each country, following the black borders. Take a piece of coloured paper (blue paper can represent the oceans and seas) and some paper glue, and stick down the countries as they are in the atlas. You can then write in the country names with a black pen.

The world's continents

The largest of the world's seven continents is Asia. It covers an area of about 17,000,000 square miles (43,000,000 sq km). Africa is the next largest continent, covering about 12,000,000 square miles (30,000,000 sq km). North and South America are near to one another in size – North America is slightly larger having an area of 9,400,000 square miles (24,300,000 sq km), while South America covers 6,800,000 square miles (17,800,000 sq km). The second smallest continent is Antarctica (5,500,000 square miles/14,250,000 sq km). Australasia is the smallest continent. Its land area is about 3,200,000 square miles (8,510,000 sq km).

Several of the world's continents are like triangles in shape. These are North America, South America and Africa, all of which become narrower towards the south. Europe is also triangular with the base of the triangle in the Ural Mountains and the top or apex in Spain and Portugal.

The continents are separated from one another by oceans and seas. The Mediterranean Sea, for example, lies between Europe and Africa. The longest land boundary between continents is along the Ural Mountains which separate Europe from Asia.

▼ The large, revolving globes show the earth as it might appear from different angles in space. Look at the small pictures of the continents. Can you find them on the globes?

▲ Africa bulges broadly in the north and tapers away to a rounded curve in the south. A large island — Madagascar — is to the south-east.

▲ Antarctica is not as well known as other continents. It is almost completely covered with ice and snow.

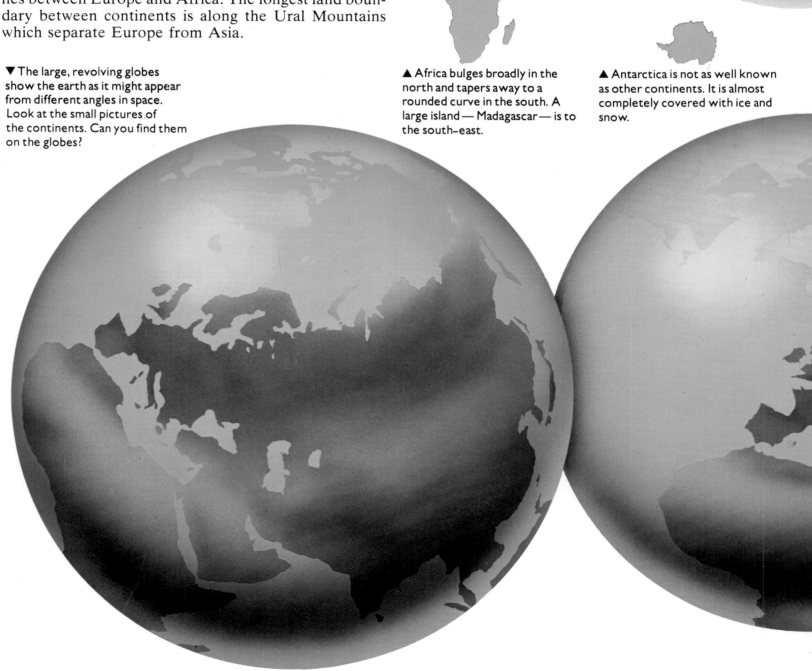

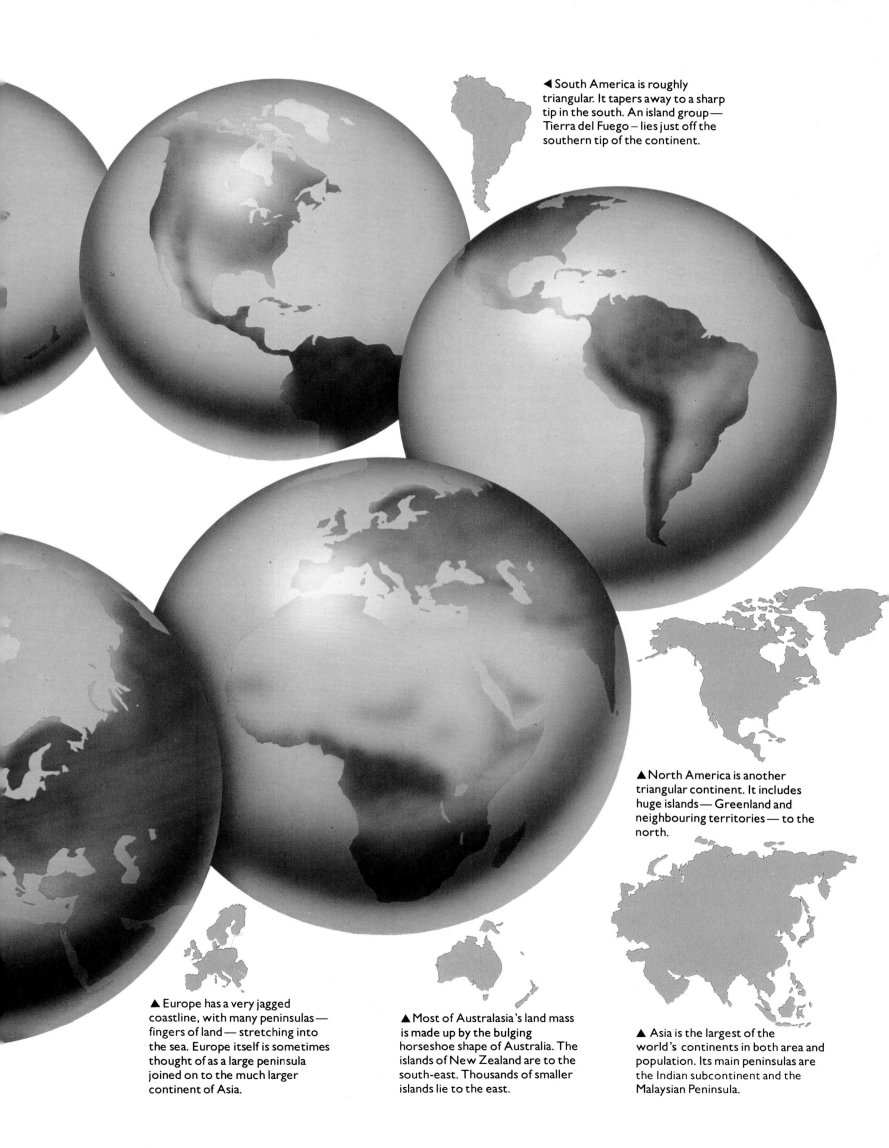

◀ South America is roughly triangular. It tapers away to a sharp tip in the south. An island group — Tierra del Fuego – lies just off the southern tip of the continent.

▲ North America is another triangular continent. It includes huge islands — Greenland and neighbouring territories — to the north.

▲ Europe has a very jagged coastline, with many peninsulas — fingers of land — stretching into the sea. Europe itself is sometimes thought of as a large peninsula joined on to the much larger continent of Asia.

▲ Most of Australasia's land mass is made up by the bulging horseshoe shape of Australia. The islands of New Zealand are to the south-east. Thousands of smaller islands lie to the east.

▲ Asia is the largest of the world's continents in both area and population. Its main peninsulas are the Indian subcontinent and the Malaysian Peninsula.

Mapping the world

The world is a sphere, like a ball, but it is slightly flattened at the North and South Poles and bulges a little at the Equator. So that countries and continents can be located accurately, a number of imaginary curved lines are drawn on a globe to divide the world into sections.

The lines are lines of latitude and longitude. The lines of latitude run around the globe parallel to the Equator. This is rather like someone cutting an apple or tomato into even slices starting at the top. The Equator is called 0° latitude and each half of the world – or hemisphere – is split into 90 slices, so the North Pole is 90° north and the South Pole 90° south.

In order to pinpoint exactly where a place is on the earth's surface another set of lines, running from north to south are needed. These are lines of longitude. These divide the world into segments like those of an orange, which are wider in the middle (the Equator) than at the top and bottom (North and South Poles).

A globe is a way of showing all the world's countries on a sphere. However, maps in books are flat. If you peel an orange, it is impossible to lay the peel out flat without cutting, stretching or tearing it. The same applies to making flat maps of the round earth. There are many ways of flattening the round shape of the earth to make maps of it. These are called map projections.

The problem with map projections is that they cannot show the earth accurately; this is only possible on a globe. For example, in Mercator's map projection the world is seen as a rectangle. It works by showing the lines of longitude as parallel rather than meeting at the Poles. This means that places near the Poles, such as Greenland, seem much larger. Many map projections show eastern Russia on the right and Alaska on the left of the map. It is also possible to show Australia at the centre.

◄ The world is round. Imagine that you are looking at it from space. You can easily recognize the shapes of the oceans and continents. However, mapping the world presents a problem to map-makers. They need to draw an accurate picture of its *round* surface on a *flat* piece of paper. Systems of projection have been invented to overcome the problem. They are not perfect, but they are important aids.

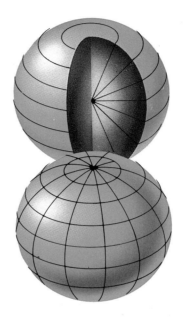

◄ One aid to map-making involves using imaginary lines called longitude and latitude. These provide a grid, making it easier to judge distances between places, and to find where one place is in relation to another.

Lines of latitude run around the earth from east to west. They are measured according to their angle from the very centre of the earth. They are parallel to the Equator which is at 0° (0 degrees). This is the line that is most often close to the sun. The North and South Poles are at 90°. These are the points that are most often far from the sun. All the other places on earth can be mapped in degrees north or south of the Equator. They are all between 0° and 90°. Lines of longitude run from the North Pole to the South Pole. They are measured in degrees east or west of Greenwich in England.

Making your own globe
To make your own globe you will need some tracing paper; a pencil; paints, crayons or felt-tip pens; thin card; scissors and paper glue.

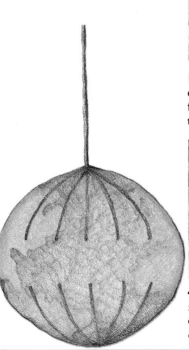

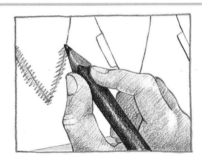

1. Place a sheet of tracing paper over the outline shown on the facing page. Now use a pencil to trace around the shape and tabs.

2. Turn the tracing paper over and scribble lightly over the outlines you have just drawn. Make sure that each line is covered.

3. Turn the tracing paper over again and place it on thin card. Draw over the outlines again. An image will appear on the card.

4. Now colour in your map, and label the countries and the oceans. When you have finished, cut around the outline.

5. Glue the tabs one by one and stick each one under the neighbouring piece of card. Wipe off any excess glue with a cloth.

6. Wait for the glue to dry. You can now hang your globe from the ceiling as a mobile, or make a stand for it with wire and a cork.

▶ Making a flat map of the world is rather like peeling an orange. If you take the peel off an orange in sections from top to bottom you can then lay it out flat even though the orange is a sphere. In the same way, map-makers may draw the shapes of the continents as if they had been peeled away from the outer crust of the earth. This is one system of projection.

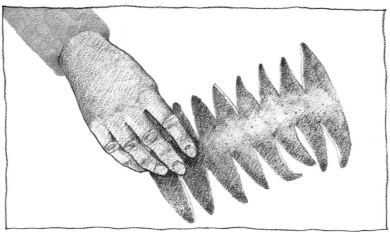

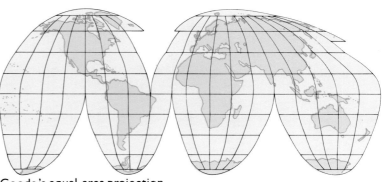

Goode's equal-area projection

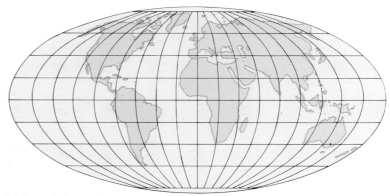

Mollweide's equal-area projection of the earth

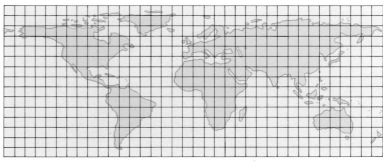

A simple cylindrical equal-space projection of the earth

▶ These maps are drawn according to three different systems of projection. The top system shows the earth's surface as if it had been cut up and laid flat like the peel of an orange. It shows the continents fairly accurately, but the oceans are all cut up. The middle system shows the earth's surface as if it were on a single curve rather than a complete sphere. Outer regions such as Australasia look narrower than they are.

The bottom map also distorts distances. Lines of longitude really meet at the poles. Here they are evenly spaced. Places near the poles — such as Greenland — look much wider than they really are. All three systems fail to show that the earth's surface is continuous. Alaska and Siberia look far apart. In fact, they are close together.

Cut along this line   Fold here   Colour   Label seas and continents

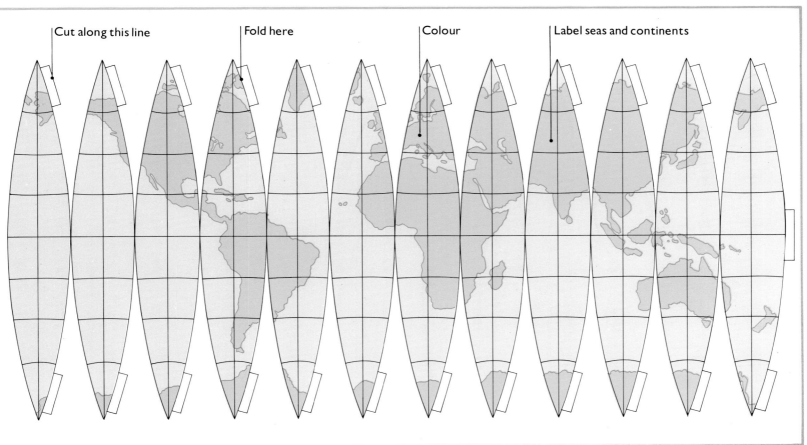

The world

There are over 100 countries in the world. The Union of Soviet Socialist Republics (USSR), usually called the Soviet Union or Russia, is the largest in area. China has the largest population. Many countries are very small, for example the islands of the Pacific Ocean. Some groups of small countries have grouped themselves together into larger units. The United Arab Emirates in the Middle East is one such group, made up of seven small states on the Arabian Gulf. Most countries have their own government. Countries which do not have an independent government are usually called colonies or dependencies. Most countries also have their own money (currency), capital town or city, and language. Some countries have more than one language.

Facts and figures about the earth
Total surface area 197,000,000 sq miles/510,000,000 sq km
Land surface 57,500,000 sq miles/149,000,000 sq km
Land as percentage of surface 29%
Water surface area 139,500,000 sq miles/361,300,000 sq km
Water as percentage of surface 71%
Circumference at Equator 24,830 miles/40,000 km
Diameter at Equator 7,926 miles/12,760 km
Highest land point (Mount Everest, Asia) 29,028 ft/8,848 m
Deepest ocean point (Marianus Trench, Pacific) 36,198 ft/11,033 m
Distance from sun 93,000,000 miles/ 150,000,000 km
Total population 3,800,000,000

Highest mountains
Everest, Asia, 29,028ft/8,848m
Godwin-Austen(K2), Asia, 28,250ft/8,611m
Kangchenjunga, Asia, 28,168ft/8,588m
Makalu, Asia, 27,805ft/8,477m
Dhaulagiri, Asia, 26,810ft/8,174m
Nanga Parbat, Asia, 26,660ft/8,128m
Annapurna, Asia, 26,504ft/8,080m
Gasherbrum, Asia, 26,470ft/8,070m
Gosainthan, Asia, 26,291ft/8,016m

Longest rivers
Nile, Africa 4,132 miles/6,912 km
Amazon, S America 3,900 miles/6,240 km
Mississippi, N America 3,860 miles/6,176 km
Irtys, Asia 3,461 miles/5,538 km
Yangtse, Asia 3,430 miles/5,488 km
Hwang Ho, Asia 2,903 miles/4,645 km
Zaire, Africa 2,900 miles/4,640 km
Amur, Asia 2,802 miles/4,483 km
Lena, Asia 2,653 miles/4,249 km
Mackenzie, N America 2,635/4,216 km

Oceans and seas
Pacific Ocean 63,855,000 sq miles/165,384,000 sq km
Atlantic Ocean 31,744,000 sq miles/82,217,000 sq km
Indian Ocean 28,371,000 sq miles/73,481,000 sq km
Arctic Ocean 5,427,000 sq miles/14,056,000 sq km
Mediterranean Sea 967,000 sq miles/2,506,000 sq km
South China Sea 895,000 sq miles/2,318,000 sq km
Bering Sea 876,000 sq miles/2,269,000 sq km
Caribbean Sea 750,000 sq miles/1,813,000 sq km
Gulf of Mexico 596,000 sq miles/1,544,000 sq km
Sea of Okhotsk 590,000 sq miles/1,528,000 sq km

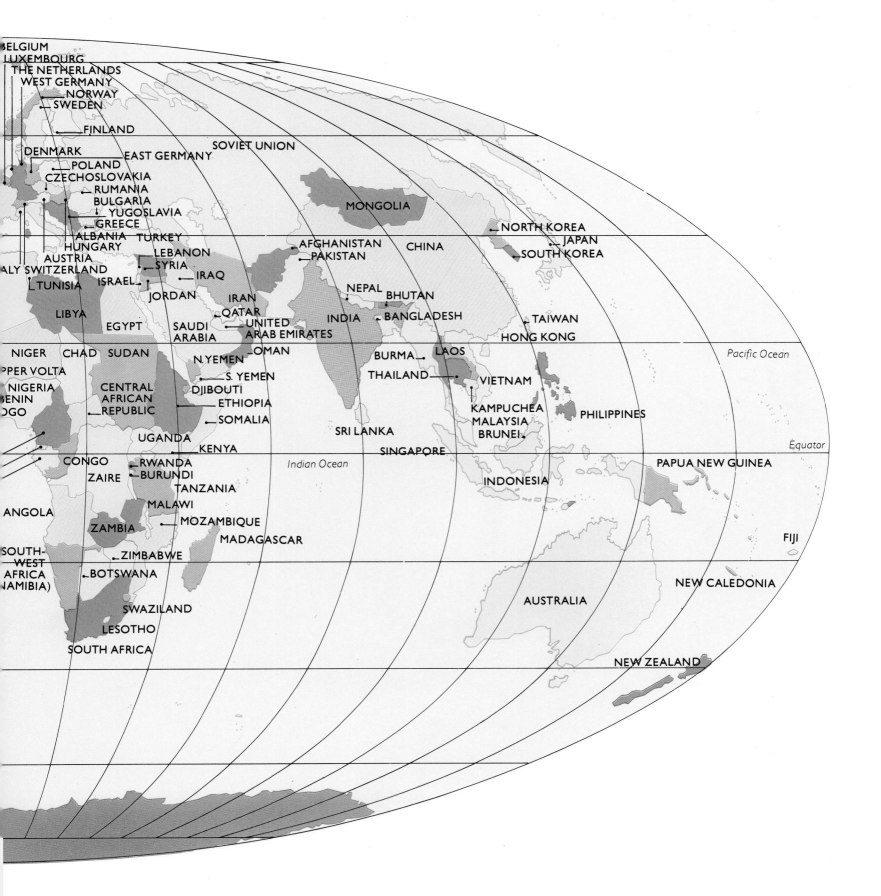

The structure of the earth

The earth is one of the nine planets in the solar system which revolve around the sun. The earth is solid and rocky and it is 93 million miles (150 million km) from the sun. The nearest body in space to the earth is the moon. It is 240,000 miles (384,000 km) from the earth.

Scientists believe that 4,500 million years ago the earth's surface was covered by molten rock. This is rock which is so hot that it melts. As the rock cooled and hardened, the heavier materials sank towards the centre of the earth, while the lighter materials stayed near the surface. The rock released steam which condensed and became the seas.

The earth is still cooling very slowly. It has three main layers – the core, the mantle and the crust. The crust is made up of several rigid but slowly moving plates on which the continents sit. Scientists believe that there was originally only one large land mass. Gradually this split up and the continents drifted to where they are today. The continents split up because at the edges of the plates new material came up from the earth's mantle and forced the plates apart. The main mountain ranges in the world are found where the plates are being pushed together.

◄ The earth revolves around the sun in an anti-clockwise direction. All the other planets except Venus move in the same way. The earth's path around the sun is known as its orbit. The earth does not orbit the sun in a perfect circle, but in an elongated one known as an ellipse. It takes a whole year for the earth to complete its orbit.

► The structure of the earth is rather like that of an apple. At the centre is the core. Next comes a second layer, like the flesh of the apple. This is known as the earth's mantle. The skin of the earth is called the crust. It is very thin compared to the inner core and mantle. The thickest parts of the crust lie beneath very high mountain ranges. It is much thinner beneath the oceans.

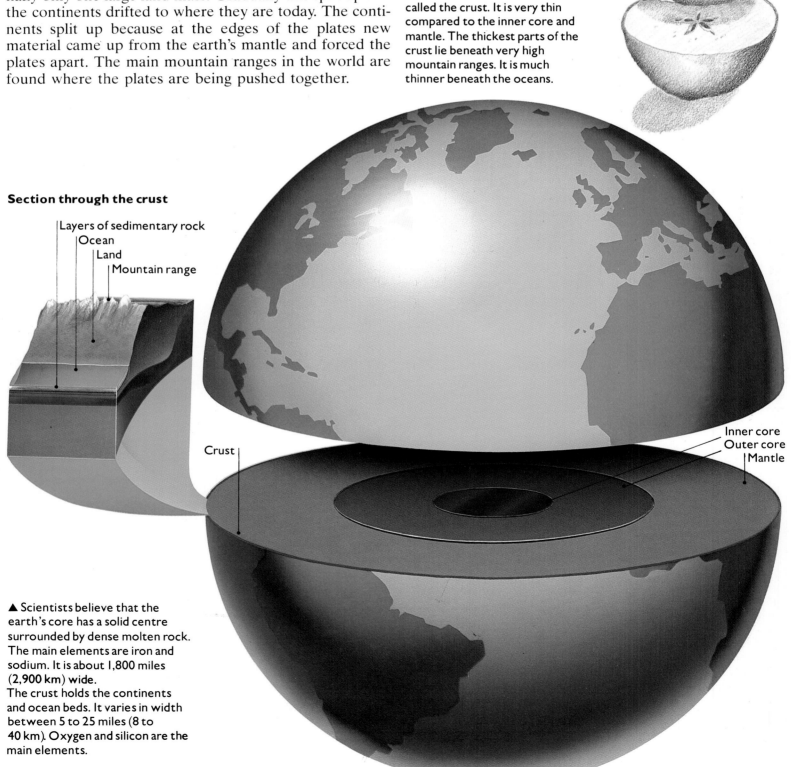

Section through the crust

Layers of sedimentary rock
Ocean
Land
Mountain range

Crust

Inner core
Outer core
Mantle

▲ Scientists believe that the earth's core has a solid centre surrounded by dense molten rock. The main elements are iron and sodium. It is about 1,800 miles (2,900 km) wide.
The crust holds the continents and ocean beds. It varies in width between 5 to 25 miles (8 to 40 km). Oxygen and silicon are the main elements.

▲ Pangaea, the earth's original land mass, began to split up about 200 million years ago.

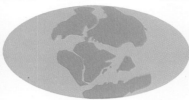

This created two basic continental regions, Laurasia and Gondwanaland.

The shapes of today's continents began to emerge about 100 million years ago.

The continents today are Asia, Africa, Australia, the Americas, Antarctica and Europe.

▲The earth's surface has grooves and ridges, like the skin of a wrinkled apple. All the little grooves on an apple's surface are like ridges on the earth, only much smaller. The earth may look as if it only has mountains on land, but in fact it has them under the sea too.

▶ If you drained the world's oceans, you could see its uneven surface more clearly. The earth's upper crust is composed of separate sections which are locked together. They are known as plates, and lie on a layer of hot, dense rock. The plates are constantly drifting, but so slowly that you do not notice their movement. Here you can see how the bulging west coast of Africa once fitted into the concave east coast of the Americas.

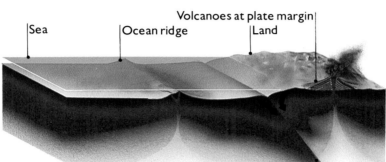

Sea | Ocean ridge | Volcanoes at plate margin | Land

Plate boundary

◀ The earth's crust is always on the move. Sometimes, land masses drift apart. This drifting causes cracks, known as faults, to appear. Sometimes, land masses push against each other, forcing rock layers upwards. These layers are then said to be folded. Many folds create mountain ranges.

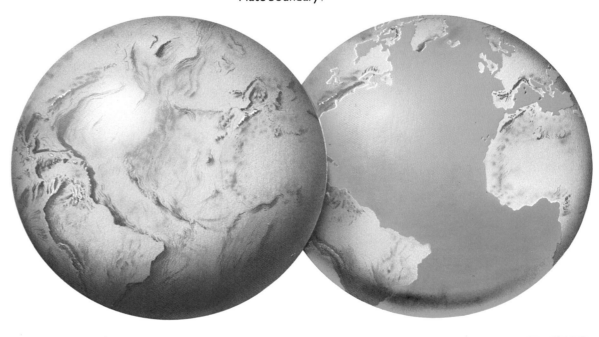

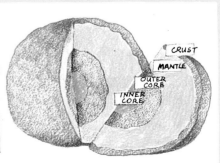

CRUST
MANTLE
OUTER CORE
INNER CORE

Make a model of the earth
1. To make a cross section of the earth, you will need four different colours of modelling clay, one for each layer. Roll a piece of clay into a ball about one inch (2.5cms) across. This represents the inner core of the earth. Now roll out a second, larger piece of clay for the second layer.

2. Place the inner core in the middle of the second sheet. This should be quite thick as it represents the outer core which is much thicker than the inner core. The outer core is also much cooler than the inner one. Try to choose colours for the layers that will show up well against each other.

3. Make sure the second sheet of modelling clay covers the inner core fully. Press the two lots of clay together with your fingers so that they stick together. Cut away any excess clay and smooth the surface so the joins do not show. Repeat this process with the third colour.

4. The fourth colour must be rolled out flat so that it is as thin as possible. This layer of clay is to be the earth's crust which is much thinner than the two cores or the mantle — the third layer. To see the cross section, cut through the clay with a knife or a piece of wire held taut.

Earthquakes and volcanoes

Earthquakes and volcanic eruptions often happen at the edges of the plates in the earth's crust. When one plate moves against another, a series of violent jerks and shudders occur. This is an earthquake.

Like the waves which spread out from the centre when you throw a stone into a pond, the vibrations of an earthquake travel out from a centre called the focus. The surface of the earth above the focus is the epicentre. If an earthquake is very strong it can start landslides and floods.

Volcanoes are openings in the earth's crust out of which molten rock (called lava), rocks, ashes, dust and gases come from the inside of the earth. The lava, rocks and ashes sometimes form a mountain shaped like a cone. Sometimes the lava comes up through long cracks and flows over large areas to make a flat area called a plateau. Many volcanoes do not erupt for long periods. These are called dormant volcanoes. In volcanic regions there are also many geysers which produce steam and hot water.

Earthquakes and volcanic eruptions occur mainly in certain areas of the earth. These areas are often at the edges of the plates on the earth's crust. For example, the largest belt is called the 'Fiery Girdle' and goes around the shores of the Pacific Ocean. A second belt follows the ridge in the middle of the Atlantic. A third belt runs from the Mediterranean to the Himalayas.

◄ The earth seems solid. But below its surface lie seething masses of hot gases and molten rock. These are known as magma. This is very hot and exists at great pressure. Magma which has reached the surface is called lava.

◄ As the earth's plates drift, cracks may appear in the surface of the crust. Magma may force its way up at high pressure. As it reaches the surface, a volcano is born.

◄ Molten lava moves to the surface. It may rise slowly and seep out to form a lake of lava. It may also force its way up at great pressure and erupt in a series of explosions.

◄ As layers of lava and ash cool, they harden. In some volcanic areas, eruptions often occur in the same place. The layers of ash and lava build up over the years and form a mountainous cone.

▲ Guatemala in Central America has a range of volcanoes along its Pacific coast. Some of these, such as Tacaná and Agua, are still active.

► The shapes of volcanoes vary. Mauna Loa in Hawaii has a low cone. The lava seeps out from the pipe at the centre.

▲ This shows the shape of Mount Pelée – a volcano on the island of Martinique in the West Indies. When this volcano erupted violently in 1902, magma forced its way out through vents in the side rather than out through the top.

► This diagram shows the structure of a volcano. Lava rises through the central pipe. After many eruptions, the pipe may get blocked. Vents appear at the sides. They sometimes form separate peaks as the lava hardens. Some lava never reaches the surface. It may form a slanting channel which hardens beneath the surface. This is called a dyke. Laccoliths are lava lakes which may harden underground in the same way. Volcanoes which are no longer active are called dormant.

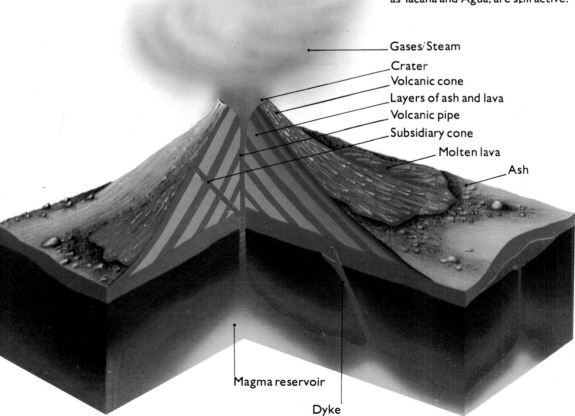

Gases/Steam
Crater
Volcanic cone
Layers of ash and lava
Volcanic pipe
Subsidiary cone
Molten lava
Ash
Magma reservoir
Dyke

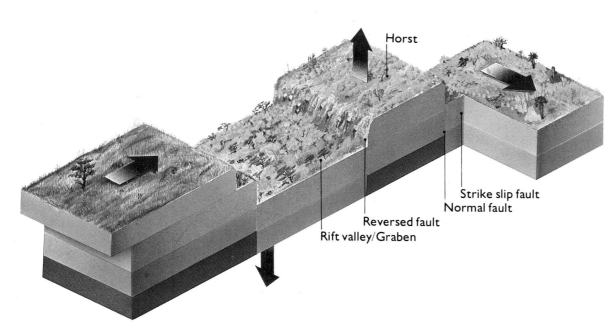

Horst

Strike slip fault
Normal fault
Reversed fault
Rift valley/Graben

▼ As land masses shift, the rock tends to fold. A downfold is called a syncline. An upfold is an anticline. Underground reservoirs of gas and oil may collect between layers of rock in an anticline. Before people drill for oil, they study rock folds carefully.

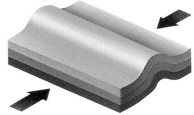

▼ As the rock folds, layers of earth fall away from its peaks. The bare rock is exposed. Wind and weather erode the surface leaving pits and crags.

▲ As land moves and shifts it may bend and crack. These cracks in the earth's crust are faults. There are several different types of fault. A thrust fault happens when one section of land breaks away and slides over another next to it.

If a wedge of rock sinks between two neighbouring masses it is called a graben or rift valley. These valleys form when two parallel faults occur. They have steep sides and flat floors.
If it is forced upwards between its

neighbours it is known as a horst. When a mass of rock slides sideways along a fault, the fault is called a strike slip.
These changes occur over millions of years. They cannot often be seen as clearly as on the diagram.

Direction of plate movement

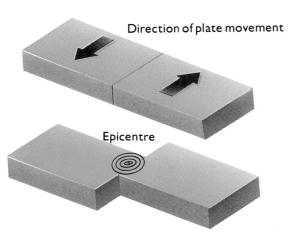

Epicentre

▲ When two plates slide side by side along a fault, danger threatens. The grinding masses lock together and pressure builds up. It may be released in the sudden shudder of an earthquake.

▲ The origin of the earthquake lies underground at the focus. Shock waves travel out from the epicentre above this. The Richter Scale is used to measure the strength of the waves.

Make a fold mountain
This demonstrates how mountains are formed.
1. You need lots of modelling clay in at least four different colours. First roll each colour into a ball so the clay is soft and easy to work with.

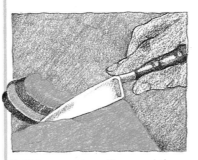

2. Each ball of clay represents a layer of rocks in the earth's crust. Take each ball and roll it out flat with a rolling pin. An empty bottle will do if you have not got one. Roll each ball so it is about $\frac{1}{2}$ inch (1.25cm) all over.

Volcanic zone

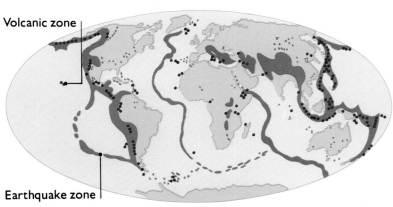

Earthquake zone

▲ The most violent areas of earthquakes and volcanic activity are the edges of the earth's

plates. Tokyo and San Francisco lie on them. Both have experienced disastrous earthquakes.

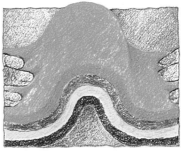

3. When you have flattened the clay, place the layers one on top of another like strata. Press them together quite firmly so they stick together but do not squash them too much. Tidy up the edge by trimming the clay with a knife.

4. Take hold of each end of the clay and gently push the two ends towards each other. This is like two plates in the earth's crust pushing together. With more pressure from your hands, a ridge like a mountain will form in the middle of the clay.

Rocks and minerals

Three kinds of rock make up the crust of the earth. These are called igneous rocks, sedimentary rocks and metamorphic rocks. Igneous rocks are formed when hot, molten material, which has come up from the earth's interior, hardens. There are two types of igneous rock – volcanic and intrusive. Volcanic rocks have cooled and hardened on the surface. Basalt is a common volcanic rock. The second type – intrusive rock – forms when molten rock does not reach the earth's surface and hardens underground. Granite is an important intrusive igneous rock.

Most of the earth's surface is now made up of sedimentary rocks. But at one time all rocks were igneous rocks. Gradually water, wind and ice wore away the rocks on the surface. Over a long period of time the materials which had been worn away – they are called sediments – collected in the oceans. This collection took many million years and is still going on. As the sediments pressed together they formed new kinds of rock.

Metamorphic rocks are the third type of rock in the earth's crust. 'Metamorphic' means that the rocks have been changed – by heat, pressure or by having their chemical structure altered. For example, heat can change limestone into marble and pressure changes shale to slate.

A rock is a collection of particles of various minerals. For example, the rock granite is composed of the minerals felspar, quartz and mica. There are over 2,000 different minerals, but most rocks consist of about 12 minerals. Gold, silver and uranium are metallic minerals.

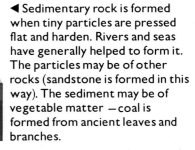

◀ Igneous rocks form when magma hardens, either above or below ground. Intrusive igneous rocks such as granite often contain crystals. Granite contains quartz, felspar and sometimes mica. The crystals give granite its distinctive mottled appearance.

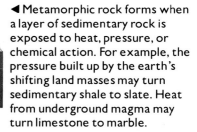

◀ Sedimentary rock is formed when tiny particles are pressed flat and harden. Rivers and seas have generally helped to form it. The particles may be of other rocks (sandstone is formed in this way). The sediment may be of vegetable matter —coal is formed from ancient leaves and branches.

◀ Metamorphic rock forms when a layer of sedimentary rock is exposed to heat, pressure, or chemical action. For example, the pressure built up by the earth's shifting land masses may turn sedimentary shale to slate. Heat from underground magma may turn limestone to marble.

▼ This diagram shows how different types of rock have been formed. The processes have often taken millions of years.
Oolitic limestone is a sedimentary rock formed by the action of deep water on tiny clusters of calcium carbonate.
A conglomerate is a mixture of sedimentary rocks. They may vary greatly in size.
Slate is a metamorphic rock. It forms when sedimentary shale is under pressure and heated by magma.
Basalt is an igneous rock. It forms fairly quickly as magma cools and hardens above the ground.
Granite is an intrusive igneous rock. It hardens slowly below the surface.

▲The Devil's Tower National Monument is a huge mass of igneous rock columns. It is 865 feet (284 metres) high.

▲Ice expanding in cracks made these limestone boulders break away from cliffs. They are in a desert in New Mexico.

▲Slate is a metamorphic rock which is quarried in many countries. It is often made into tiles and used for roofing.

Limestone   Conglomerate of sedimentary rock   Slate   Basalt   Granite

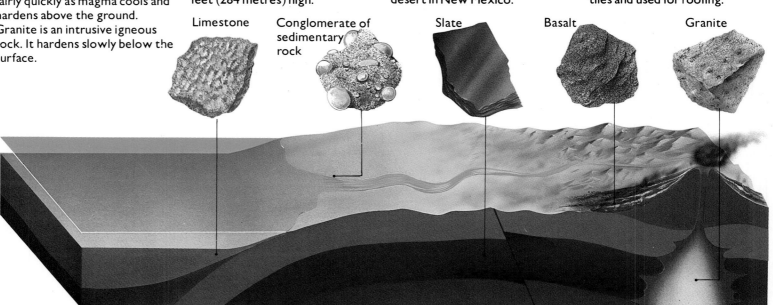

▶ Millions of years ago, the earth's ancient forests decayed. They were gradually covered with layers of sediment. The sediment turned to rock. The rotten vegetation was pressed flat. It gradually hardened and turned to coal. The layers of coal are called seams. To reach them, people have dug shafts underground. Miners hack at the coal face. Winding gear is needed to take them up and down. Pumps and fans keep fresh air circulating while they work. Machines are often used in mining today.

▶ Oil was formed when millions of tiny sea creatures and plants died and decomposed. Layers of rock gradually covered them. The decayed remains turned to liquid oil and natural gas. These substances seeped into soft, porous rocks and collected in gaps between soft and hard layers. An oil company's first task is to find these underground reservoirs by drilling in likely areas. Then they need pumping equipment to control the flow of oil to the surface. Pipelines then take the oil to refineries.

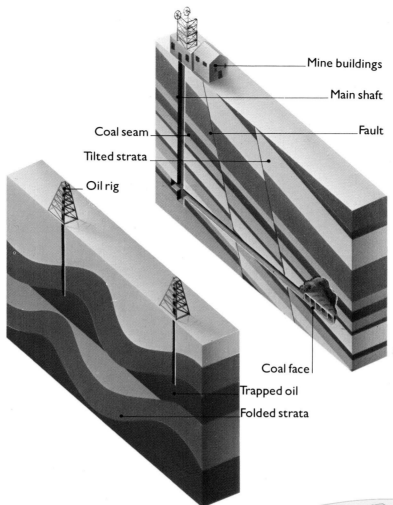

Mine buildings
Main shaft
Fault
Coal seam
Tilted strata
Oil rig
Coal face
Trapped oil
Folded strata

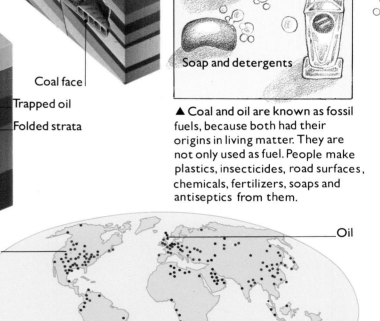

Fertilizer
Plastic
Medicine
Soap and detergents

▲ Coal and oil are known as fossil fuels, because both had their origins in living matter. They are not only used as fuel. People make plastics, insecticides, road surfaces, chemicals, fertilizers, soaps and antiseptics from them.

▶ Coal and oil are perhaps the most important natural sources of energy. Modern society depends heavily on them. This map shows the main centres of production. The stocks will not last forever. Today, people are urgently exploring alternative sources of energy. Nuclear power is one. Harnessing solar energy, wind and waves are others.

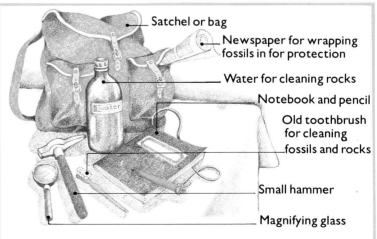

Coal
Oil

▲ Most rocks contain some metallic minerals. They are called ores, and can often be seen as a thin vein where the mineral has seeped into a crevice.
The metal is generally extracted in a heat process known as smelting. Oxygen is taken from the ore to purify the metal. Here, copper has been extracted from its ore in a furnace.

▲ These men are working at a diamond mine. This mineral is made of carbon. It is the hardest natural substance in the world and it can cut glass.

◀ Precious metals include gold and silver. Gold ore may be mined, or extracted from river beds in the form of gold dust or nuggets. Gold is a soft metal which is very easy to work.

Satchel or bag
Newspaper for wrapping fossils in for protection
Water for cleaning rocks
Notebook and pencil
Old toothbrush for cleaning fossils and rocks
Small hammer
Magnifying glass

How to find fossils
Fossils are the remains or imprints of prehistoric animals and plants. They are not easy to find but if you have got lots of time to spare they are fun to look for and collect.

Chalk cliffs and disused slate quarries are usually good places for finding fossils but you should always make sure it is safe for you to go there. You will find all the things in the picture very useful.

How the landscape is formed

The earth's scenery is formed by processes called weathering and erosion which begin as soon as the land forms. Weathering and erosion mean that the land is worn away by changes in temperature or by wind, water or ice.

In cold areas such as mountain tops, rainwater collects in the cracks in rocks. When it freezes the water expands and makes the rock split apart. In hot deserts, the surfaces of rocks expand during the day and contract at night when the temperature falls. This change gradually weakens the rock and makes the outer layers peel off. Tree roots and burrowing animals also make rocks split apart.

Water can alter the minerals in some rocks. For example, water dissolves chalk and limestone rocks to make features such as limestone caves.

A river is one of the main agents of erosion. As a river flows downhill, it gathers more and more material such as stones and sediment and deposits it in the lowland areas. This is how river deltas are formed. A glacier, which is a river of ice, is like a harsh file which scrapes away more of the earth's surface than a river. Much of the earth's surface was shaped by glaciers in the past, and the same process continues in cold mountain regions and around the poles.

The wind is another important shaper of the land. For example, in the deserts, the wind blows sand away and deposits it to make dunes. The sea can both wear land away and build it up. Bays, cliffs and caves result from the sea wearing away the land. Beaches and sand bars are examples of how the sea builds up the land. The action of the wind often builds sand up into ridges called dunes.

The sole and heel of an old boot are a simple example of erosion. When they have been walked on for a long time they become worn away.

▶ If you dry out an onion, the layers of skin will blister, crack and peel away. Some rocks are composed of layers of sediment. They react like the skin of an onion to changes in temperature. The layers expand and contract. They blister and crack. This is called mechanical weathering and it takes many years.

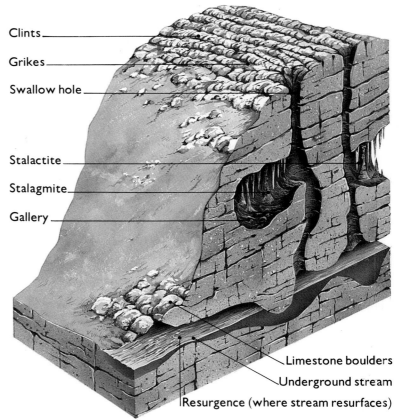

▶ Scree can be found in the Grand Canyon, Arizona, USA. Scree is the name given to lots of pieces of rock that have broken away from larger boulders. Weathering by wind and rain causes the scree to form.

◀ When rain falls on mountains it collects in pools and lakes. It also seeps into cracks in the rock itself. In cold weather, the water freezes and forms ice.

◀ Water expands as it freezes. The ice presses against the surface of the rock. Pressure builds up. New cracks appear in the rock and pieces begin to crumble away.

◀ The rock falls and tumbles down the mountainside. It often collects at the base in the form of scree. The mountain begins to look craggy. This is mechanical erosion.

▼ Chemical erosion often occurs in limestone regions. The rock contains chemicals which react with other chemicals in water to produce a weak solution of carbonic acid. This dissolves limestone. It seeps into surface cracks and these are enlarged to form ridges and grooves called clints and grikes. The acid also makes vertical and horizontal shafts – joints and bedding planes. Caves with stalactites and stalagmites are found in limestone areas.

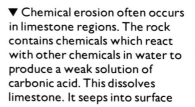

Clints

Grikes

Swallow hole

Stalactite

Stalagmite

Gallery

Limestone boulders

Underground stream

Resurgence (where stream resurfaces)

▼ When a river flows down a mountainside it passes through three stages: youth, maturity and old age. In youth it flows swiftly down steep slopes. It carves out a deep V-shaped valley. In maturity it flows more slowly. It begins to swerve, and forms a broader valley. In old age it winds very slowly over flat land to the sea. It brings down much sediment which collects as mudflats.

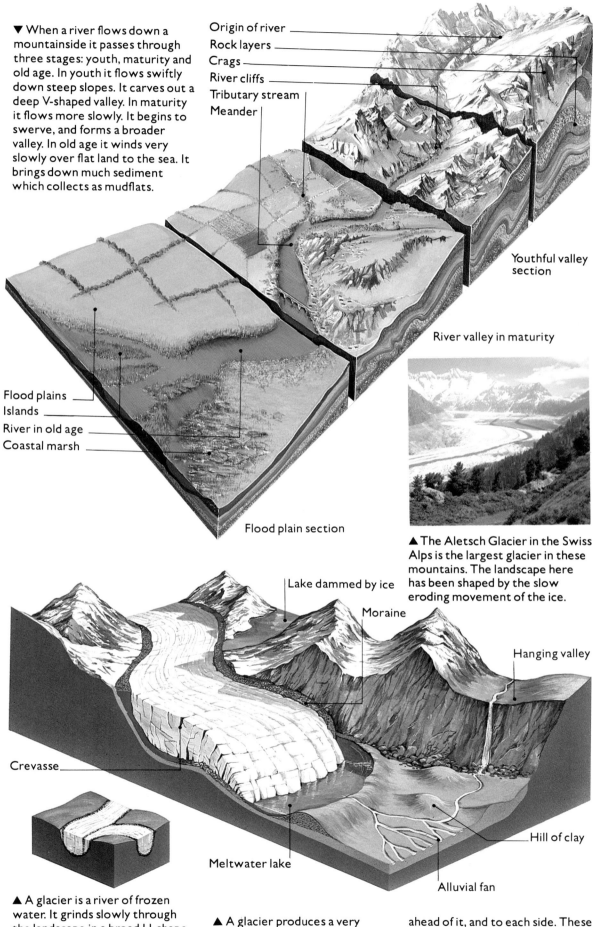

Origin of river
Rock layers
Crags
River cliffs
Tributary stream
Meander

Youthful valley section

River valley in maturity

Flood plains
Islands
River in old age
Coastal marsh

Flood plain section

▲ The Aletsch Glacier in the Swiss Alps is the largest glacier in these mountains. The landscape here has been shaped by the slow eroding movement of the ice.

▼ The wind is often the main eroding force in hot, dry countries. The dry atmosphere makes plants wither. Little is left to hold the earth together. It dries and turns to dust. The wind gathers up the dust and sweeps it around the landscape. It scours at the surrounding rocks. They begin to erode. The shifting, dusty soil makes it even harder for plants to flourish. However, in some places cacti and coarse grasses grow well.

▲ In desert lands, the wind collects sand. This cuts into the surrounding rocks. In some deserts, the swirling wind has carved startling rock towers out of the landscape.

▲ The sea acts as a powerful eroding force around the world's coastlines. The continual crashing of the waves breaks down the rocks. Sand and pebbles strike the cliffs with great force. Water forces its way into cracks. As it rushes out again it sucks out the fragments that have broken away. This process forms caves. Some rocks dissolve slowly in seawater. Chalk dissolves even in calm seas. The chalk is eroded at the base of a cliff. After a while, the rocks above fall down. The process forms steep, white cliffs like those of Flamborough Head in north-east England (above). The white cliffs of Dover are another good example of chalk cliffs. Chalk is easily dissolved, but it takes many years for other types of rock, such as granite, to be eroded.

Lake dammed by ice
Moraine
Hanging valley
Crevasse
Hill of clay
Meltwater lake
Alluvial fan

▲ A glacier is a river of frozen water. It grinds slowly through the landscape in a broad U-shape. When the glacier melts, it leaves distinctive, U-shaped valleys.

▲ A glacier produces a very special sort of landscape. The glacier itself is pitted with deep cracks called crevasses. The ice walls sheer away the neighbouring valleys. They become hanging valleys which often end in waterfalls. The glacier pushes mud and boulders ahead of it, and to each side. These deposits are called moraines. Ice melts and trickles down to form a meltwater lake. Then water often seeps out of the lake to produce an alluvial fan of streams. An alluvial fan is a fertile area of deposited mud and sand which is fan-shaped. Crops grow well in this soil.

The seasons

The earth orbits the sun which is at the centre of the solar system. This process takes one year. At the same time, the earth spins on its axis once every 24 hours. The earth's spinning produces light and darkness – day and night.

The revolution of the earth around the sun and the angle at which the earth is tilted causes the seasons. These are spring, summer, autumn and winter. When the North Pole is tilted towards the sun, the northern hemisphere has its summer and the southern hemisphere has its winter. It is summer in the southern hemisphere when the South Pole is tilted to the sun.

Time is measured by the earth's rotation and is linked to lines of longitude. It is always the same time at all the places which are along a line of longitude. For example, if it is noon in Greenwich, England, then it is also noon in France, Ghana and all the countries through which the 0° line of longitude passes. This line is called the Prime Meridian. Time throughout the world is calculated from this line.

There are 24 time zones in the world each with their own time. Travellers going east must put their watches on an hour for every time zone boundary they cross. Travellers going west must put their watches back.

The date changes near the 180th meridian. This lies almost completely in the Pacific Ocean and not many people cross it. It is known as the International Date Line.

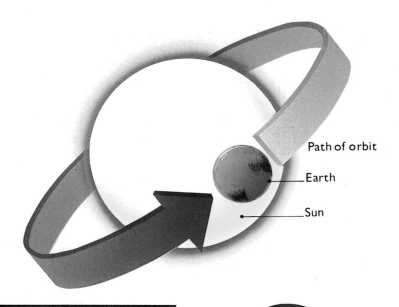

▼The earth revolves around the sun once every 365¼ days. This makes a full year. To make things simpler for ourselves, we count 365 days in a normal year. Every fourth year we add a day. This is a leap year. There are 366 days in a leap year. While the earth revolves around the sun it is also spinning on its axis. So two things are going on at the same time: the earth revolving around the sun produces the year; and the earth spinning on its axis produces day and night. The sun looks as if it is moving, but it is still all the time.

Path of orbit

Earth

Sun

▲The earth is like a great ball. It spins on its axis. The axis is like an imaginary rod passing through the middle of the ball. The angle of the axis always stays the same.

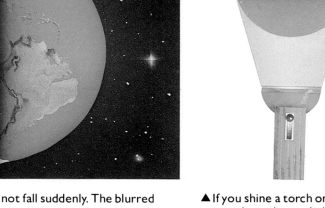

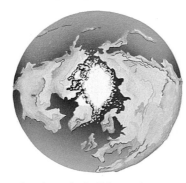

▲ Look at the ball from above. The point at which the rod emerges is called the pole of the axis. In our world, the North Pole is at one end of the axis. The South Pole is at the other end. Of course, the axis itself is invisible. The poles are regions of ice and snow where temperatures are very low so that few people live there and vegetation is scarce.

▲ As the earth spins on its axis, only half of its surface is in sunlight at any one time. The rest is in darkness. The sunlight gives us our daytime. The darkness gives us our night. The darkness does not fall suddenly. The blurred areas between darkness and light are the twilight zones of dawn and dusk. Dawn begins when the first light shows and dusk begins when the sun starts to set.

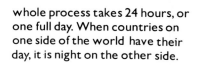

▲ If you shine a torch on a ball you can see how the sun lights up the world. The light can only reach half of the surface at one time. The rest of the surface of the ball remains in shadow.

▲ The world does not stand upright on its axis. It is tilted. As the world spins on its axis, different regions are lit up by the sunlight. One by one, the countries of the world pass through the same cycle: dawn, daylight, dusk and night. The whole process takes 24 hours, or one full day. When countries on one side of the world have their day, it is night on the other side.

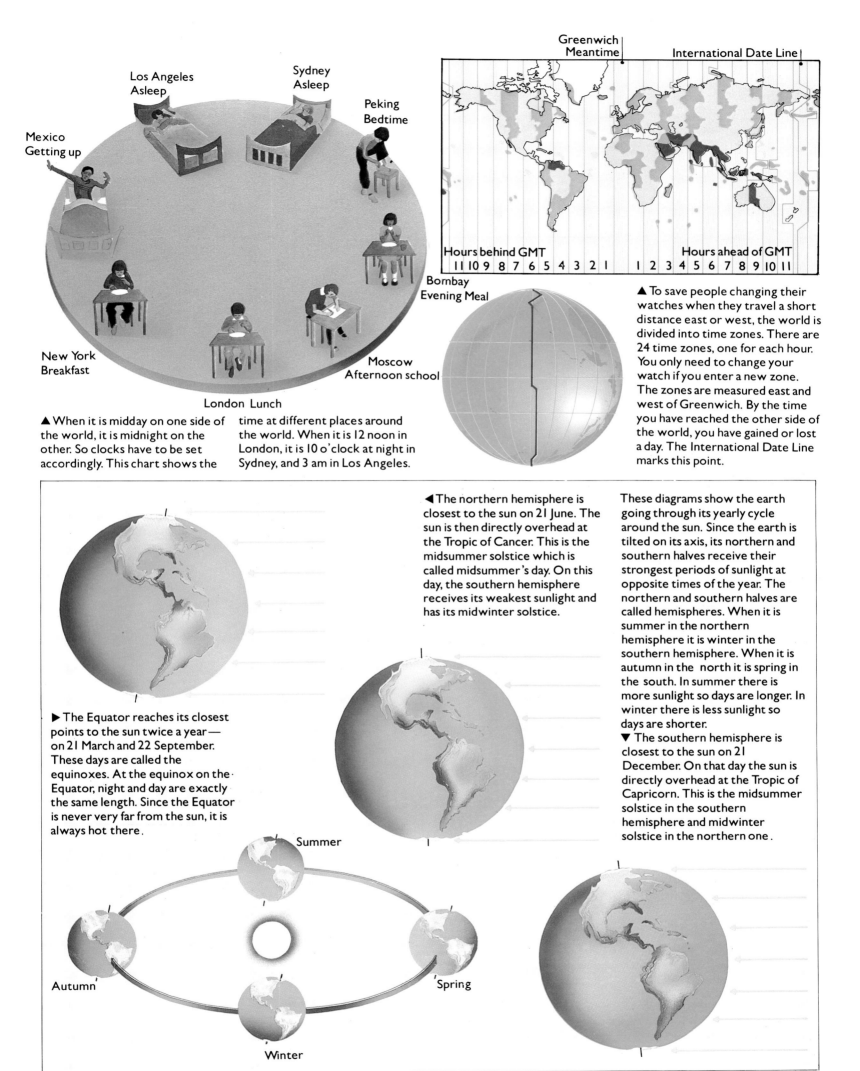

Greenwich Meantime

International Date Line

Hours behind GMT
11 10 9 8 7 6 5 4 3 2 1

Hours ahead of GMT
1 2 3 4 5 6 7 8 9 10 11

Los Angeles Asleep

Sydney Asleep

Peking Bedtime

Mexico Getting up

Bombay Evening Meal

New York Breakfast

Moscow Afternoon school

London Lunch

▲ When it is midday on one side of the world, it is midnight on the other. So clocks have to be set accordingly. This chart shows the time at different places around the world. When it is 12 noon in London, it is 10 o'clock at night in Sydney, and 3 am in Los Angeles.

▲ To save people changing their watches when they travel a short distance east or west, the world is divided into time zones. There are 24 time zones, one for each hour. You only need to change your watch if you enter a new zone. The zones are measured east and west of Greenwich. By the time you have reached the other side of the world, you have gained or lost a day. The International Date Line marks this point.

▶ The Equator reaches its closest points to the sun twice a year— on 21 March and 22 September. These days are called the equinoxes. At the equinox on the Equator, night and day are exactly the same length. Since the Equator is never very far from the sun, it is always hot there.

◀ The northern hemisphere is closest to the sun on 21 June. The sun is then directly overhead at the Tropic of Cancer. This is the midsummer solstice which is called midsummer's day. On this day, the southern hemisphere receives its weakest sunlight and has its midwinter solstice.

These diagrams show the earth going through its yearly cycle around the sun. Since the earth is tilted on its axis, its northern and southern halves receive their strongest periods of sunlight at opposite times of the year. The northern and southern halves are called hemispheres. When it is summer in the northern hemisphere it is winter in the southern hemisphere. When it is autumn in the north it is spring in the south. In summer there is more sunlight so days are longer. In winter there is less sunlight so days are shorter.

▼ The southern hemisphere is closest to the sun on 21 December. On that day the sun is directly overhead at the Tropic of Capricorn. This is the midsummer solstice in the southern hemisphere and midwinter solstice in the northern one.

Summer

Autumn

Spring

Winter

Weather and climate

The surface of the earth is wrapped in an envelope of gases which is called the atmosphere. The main gases are nitrogen and oxygen. The lowest layer of the atmosphere is the troposphere. The troposphere consists of many masses of air which are always moving. Air masses determine the world's weather. A front develops where two different types of air mass meet. For example, a cold front is where a mass of cold air moves into a warm air area. A warm front is where warm air pushes into a cold air area.

Weather means the day-to-day conditions of the troposphere – temperature, air pressure, wind, clouds and humidity. Humidity is the amount of water vapour which the air contains. Climate is like a yearly average or summary of weather conditions. The three main types of climate are tropical, temperate and polar. A tropical climate is very hot and is found around the Equator. Temperate climates are less hot and are found north and south of the tropics. Polar climates are the coldest and are found in the far north and south. The nearness of a place to the sea affects its climate. The sea stores warmth from the sun. This means that the climate of places near the sea have fairly even temperatures. Areas far away from the sea are hotter in summer and colder in winter. This type of climate is called continental.

Height above the sea – or altitude – also affects climate. For every 1,000 feet (300 metres) above sea level the temperature falls by about 7°F (3°C). This means that mountains like Mount Kilimanjaro in Africa have snow on their peaks even though they are very near the Equator.

▶ Clouds form when air becomes saturated with water vapour. Tiny droplets of moisture condense. They hang in the air as clouds. You can see how clouds form when you breathe out on a cold winter's day. Your breath is warm and moist. It condenses as it reaches the cold air outside.

◀ Seen from space, the earth looks like this. Some areas are covered by cloud, making dull weather. Others are free of clouds and the weather is sunny.
As the earth's air masses move, the weather changes. Clouds hide the sun from some areas, and the sky is clear in others. This process is going on all the time. Weather forecasting depends on studying cloud movements.

▲ Nome in Alaska is close to the Arctic Circle. Temperatures stay below freezing point for most of the year. They only reach 50° F/10°C in midsummer.

▲ Moscow is in a temperate zone. It is also in the middle of a great continent, so temperatures vary. It is bitterly cold in winter and very hot in summer.

Key
- Cold climates
- Cool temperate climates
- Dry climates
- Warm temperate climates
- Tropical climates

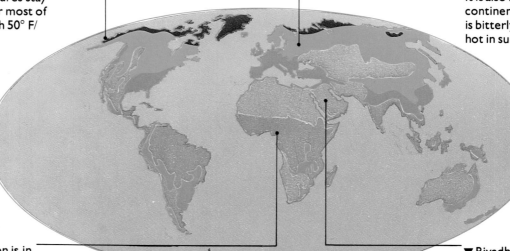

▼ Debundja in Cameroon is in the tropics. Temperatures are hot and the climate is humid. A slight drop in temperature in autumn brings a very rainy season.

▼ Riyadh in Saudi Arabia is in a tropical zone. It is always hot, and daily temperatures never fall below 68°F/20°C. It is in a desert region with hardly any rainfall.

▶ Scientists divide the world into three main climatic regions. To the north and south are the cold regions within the Arctic and Antarctic Circles. The tropics are the hot regions north and south of the Equator. Their outer boundaries are marked by the Tropic of Cancer in the north, and the Tropic of Capricorn in the south. Between these hot and cold regions lie the temperate regions where climates vary greatly.

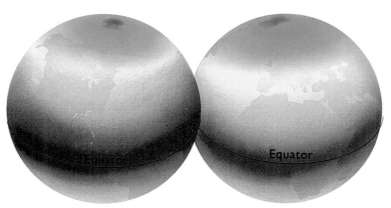

▼ Many things influence climate, and height above sea level is one of them. The air grows colder the higher up you go. A mountain may have many different climates. Mount Kenya is in the tropics. As you would expect, the climate is tropical around the base. However, higher up, it becomes temperate. Higher still it grows colder and trees will not grow. At the top, the peak is covered with snow all the year round — even in midsummer.

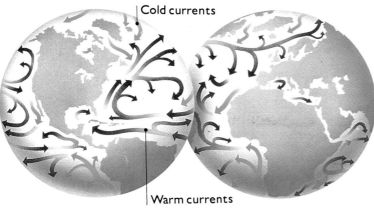

Cold currents

Warm currents

▲ The oceans affect the world's climate. The sea stores the sun's heat, and keeps coastal temperatures more stable than inland. The oceans also have other effects. Warm currents, such as the Gulf Stream, bring extra warmth to the coastal regions in their path. Cold currents bring cooler weather to coastal regions.

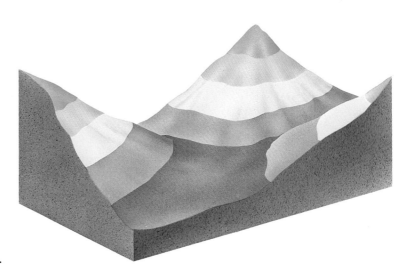

Rainfall and humidity

Rain falls when the moisture in a cloud cools and condenses. The drops of moisture grow too big to remain in the air and fall as rain.
These projects show how to measure the rainfall in your area, and how to measure the level of humidity (the amount of moisture in the air).

Making a rain gauge

You will need a glass jar, a larger straight-sided tin and a plastic funnel. The funnel should fit as tightly as possible into the rim of the tin. It should not overlap at the top. If it is a bit too small, pack foam rubber around the rim for a good, tight fit.
Fill the tin with water to a depth of 20 millimetres.
Now pour the water into the jar. Glue a strip of paper to the side of the jar, and mark off the water level. Now divide the distance from this mark to the base of the jar into 20 equal parts. Each part will now represent one millimetre of rain when it falls.
Empty out the water and put the jar, with the funnel, into the tin. Place your rain gauge in the open and write down the level of rainfall every day.

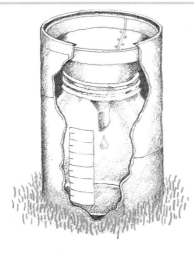

Making a hygrometer

A hygrometer is an instrument for measuring humidity. You need two identical household thermometers with the degrees in Centigrade.
Fix one thermometer to a piece of board. This is the dry bulb thermometer.
The other thermometer needs a wet bulb. Fix a hollow bootlace around the bulb. Fit the thermometer to the board, with the end of the lace dangling into a jar of water. Water will travel up the lace and around the bulb.
In dry weather, the water around the bulb will evaporate, and there will be a large difference between the readings on your two thermometers.
In wet weather, less water will evaporate giving a higher reading. To find the level of humidity, find the dry bulb reading in the column running across the top of the table (below). Subtract the wet bulb reading to find the difference. Find the difference in the column running down the side of the table. Now run down from the top column and across from the side column and find the point at which they meet. This tells you the humidity.
For example, if your dry bulb reading is between 18° and 19°, and the wet bulb reading is 5° lower, the humidity is 61%.

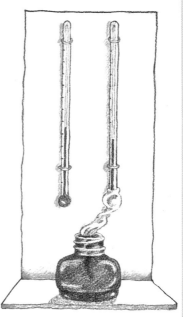

Difference between wet and dry bulb in degrees C	Dry bulb temperatures				
	15-16°	16-17°	17-18°	18-19°	19-20°
1	88%	90%	91%	92%	92%
1.5	83%	85%	86%	87%	88%
2	77%	81%	82%	83%	84%
2.5	74%	77%	78%	79%	80%
3	67%	72%	74%	75%	77%
3.5	64%	68%	70%	71%	73%
4	60%	63%	66%	68%	70%
4.5	55%	60%	62%	64%	66%
5	50%	55%	58%	61%	63%
5.5	47%	52%	55%	57%	60%
6	45%	47%	51%	53%	57%
6.5	40%	44%	47%	50%	53%
7	37%	41%	44%	48%	50%
7.5	34%	37%	40%	44%	48%

The world's vegetation

There are several different plant zones on the earth which are similar to the climate zones. This is because climate has a great effect on which plants can grow in different areas. Temperature, rain and soil are important. Without soil, the earth's surface would have no plants. Soil is very small pieces of rocks and minerals mixed with decayed plants and animals. These decayed materials are called humus. Soils with a lot of humus in them are rich and fertile so that plants and crops grow well in them.

In areas near the Equator, heavy rain washes minerals and humus out of the soil. This means the soil is not good for farming but thick forests grow there because of the heat and heavy rain. Further away from the Equator where it only rains in one half of the year the vegetation is mainly grassland with some trees. This type of region is called savanna and it is found in many parts of Africa.

Areas with temperate climates have great varieties of vegetation. The plants include deciduous forests and, in the north, coniferous forests. A deciduous tree loses its leaves in winter while a coniferous tree is evergreen. This means that it has leaves all the year round.

Between the icy regions around the North Pole and the coniferous forests is an area called the tundra. No trees grow on the tundra but there is some thin vegetation. There is no tundra area around the South Pole.

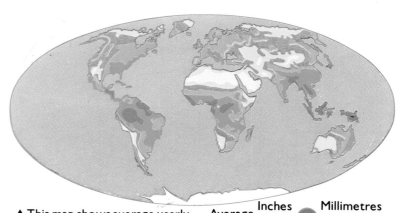

▲ This map shows average yearly rainfall. The amount of rainfall greatly affects plant life. Trees need plenty of moisture. Few grow in the dry tropical Sahara. However, trees grow tall in wet tropical rainforests. Deciduous trees need moderate rainfall.

Average yearly rainfall	Inches	Millimetres
	Over 196.8	Over 5000
	78.7	2000
	39.3	1000
	19.6	500
	11.8	300
	Under 3.9	Under 100

▲ Coniferous trees bear seeds in cones. Examples include pine, spruce and fir. Their leaves are thin. Most conifers keep them all year. They can survive in cold climates which would kill a deciduous tree. Conifers grow quickly, and new forests are often planted for timber.

▲ Deciduous trees shed their leaves in winter. Deciduous forests grow in temperate climates where rain falls fairly evenly throughout the year. The trees include chestnut, beech, oak, maple, ash and lime. Willows are deciduous and grow very well on damp waterside banks.

▼ Grasslands are regions where the rainy season is fairly short. While the rain falls, vegetation flourishes. However, the long dry season tends to kill off the larger plants. Few trees survive, but the roots of sturdy grasses are not harmed. Grasslands include the prairies and pampas of America and the African savanna.

▲ Tropical forests are always hot and wet. The vegetation grows and flowers all year round. The trees tend to grow tall, with broad leaves at the top. Their long stems are often entwined by creepers growing up towards the sunlight. Fungi often grow on the cool and shaded forest floor. Many exotic birds and animals live here.

Key

 Mediterranean forest and scrub

Savanna

Tropical rain forest

Monsoon forest

Dry tropical scrub

Desert

Scrub, steppe and semi-desert

Deciduous and broadleaf forest

Coniferous forest

Tundra and ice

▲No vegetation can grow in the true polar regions. The climate is much too cold. This is Port Lockroy in the Antarctic.

▲ This is the Alaskan tundra in autumn. The climate is too cold for trees to grow, but grasses and other plants may survive.

▲ Mount Ararat in Turkey rises from a high steppe. A few trees may take root and survive the dry summer and cold winter.

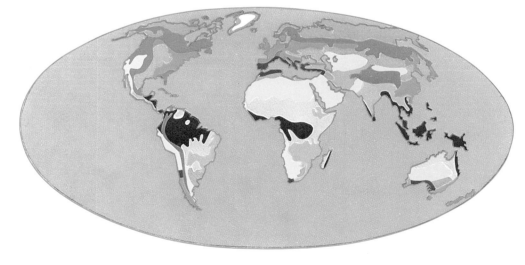

▲ Tropical scrublands are hot, dry regions where there is just enough rain to support desert vegetation such as coarse grasses and cacti.

▲ Temperate forests grow on the north coast of Algeria. Further south lies the Sahara where there are few trees and no forests.

▲ The North American prairies are grasslands. Few trees grow here, but the fertile soil is good for grazing cattle and growing corn.

▲ Certain regions of the Sahara are true deserts. They are hot and dry, and absolutely nothing can take root in the shifting sands.

The world's crops

Many raw materials and kinds of food come from the earth's plants. Since earliest times, people have gathered nuts, berries and plants for food, used bark and tree roots for dyes and medicine, and fibres and leaves for making houses and cloth.

Wood is the most important plant product. People have used it for building, and for making tools, toys and paper. Forests cover almost two thirds of the surface of the earth. There are two main types of forest – the coniferous forests in the far north and south, and the deciduous forests of the temperate and tropical lands.

The wood from the coniferous forests in northern Europe and Asia is used for making paper and furniture. The woods from the tropical forests, which are called hardwoods, include mahogany, ebony and teak.

Grass also has many uses. Some people still wear grass skirts and grass is used to make the walls and roofs of houses in many parts of the world. Bamboo is a woody kind of tropical grass. Its stems are used for building, making furniture, tools and the fibres are used in making some kinds of paper and in weaving.

Rubber is another major product obtained from trees. Rubber trees grow naturally in the forests of South America. The great plantations of south-east Asia developed from plants taken from the Amazon basin.

▼ Wood is valuable both as a fuel and a building material. It can be carved and shaped to make beams, beds or boats. Wood is also crushed to pulp and pressed to make paper and cardboard.

▼ Rubber is made from the sap of rubber trees. This is a special type of sap called latex. It is stretchable, solid and waterproof. It is valuable for many goods including tyres, waterproof fabrics and rubber bands.

▼ Wheat is a cereal plant whose seeds grow as edible grain. It was one of the first crops which people learnt to sow and harvest.
The grains are crushed to make flour. Flour is the basic material in bread.

▲ Cotton grows as a low shrub in hot climates throughout the world. Since ancient times, people have twisted and woven the fibre to make thread, fabrics, and many kinds of clothing.

◄ Sugar is a substance containing a mixture of carbon, hydrogen and oxygen – sugary foods are called carbohydrates. Sugar is present in many plants, especially sugar cane and sugar beet, a root vegetable.

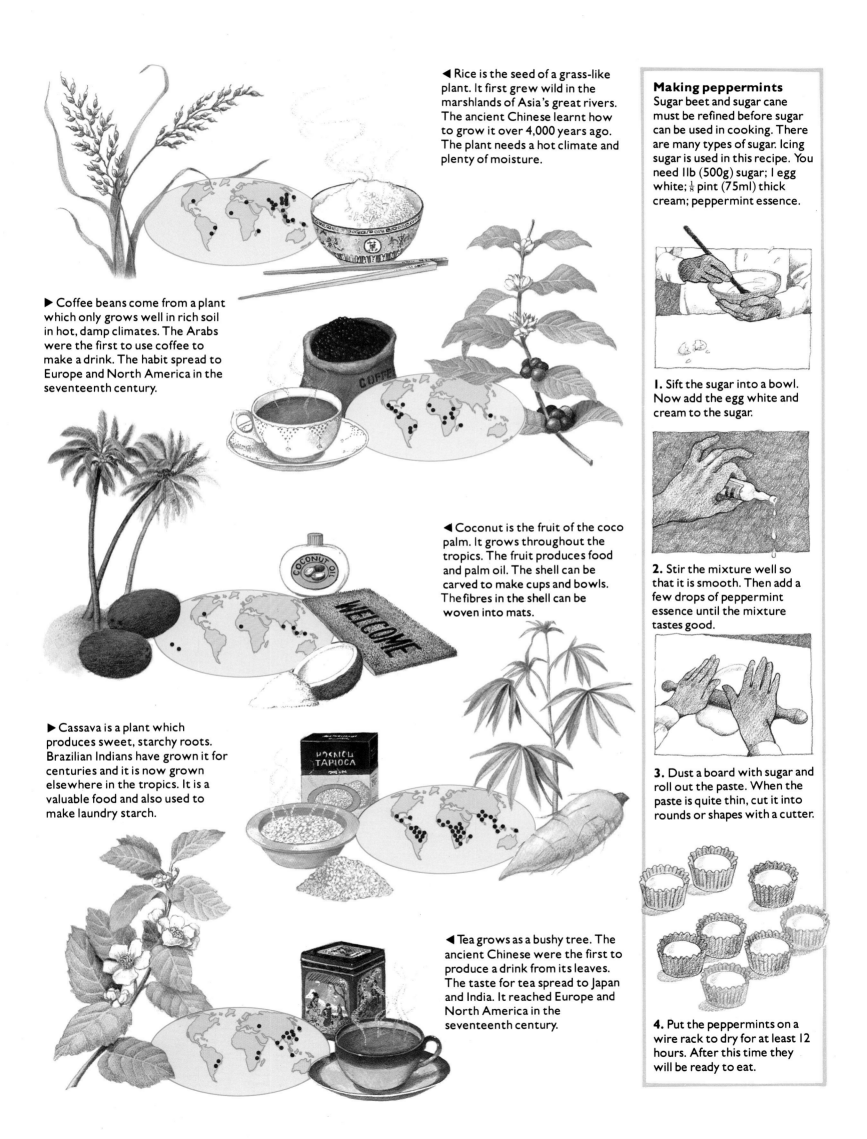

◄ Rice is the seed of a grass-like plant. It first grew wild in the marshlands of Asia's great rivers. The ancient Chinese learnt how to grow it over 4,000 years ago. The plant needs a hot climate and plenty of moisture.

► Coffee beans come from a plant which only grows well in rich soil in hot, damp climates. The Arabs were the first to use coffee to make a drink. The habit spread to Europe and North America in the seventeenth century.

◄ Coconut is the fruit of the coco palm. It grows throughout the tropics. The fruit produces food and palm oil. The shell can be carved to make cups and bowls. The fibres in the shell can be woven into mats.

► Cassava is a plant which produces sweet, starchy roots. Brazilian Indians have grown it for centuries and it is now grown elsewhere in the tropics. It is a valuable food and also used to make laundry starch.

◄ Tea grows as a bushy tree. The ancient Chinese were the first to produce a drink from its leaves. The taste for tea spread to Japan and India. It reached Europe and North America in the seventeenth century.

Making peppermints
Sugar beet and sugar cane must be refined before sugar can be used in cooking. There are many types of sugar. Icing sugar is used in this recipe. You need 1lb (500g) sugar; 1 egg white; $\frac{1}{8}$ pint (75ml) thick cream; peppermint essence.

1. Sift the sugar into a bowl. Now add the egg white and cream to the sugar.

2. Stir the mixture well so that it is smooth. Then add a few drops of peppermint essence until the mixture tastes good.

3. Dust a board with sugar and roll out the paste. When the paste is quite thin, cut it into rounds or shapes with a cutter.

4. Put the peppermints on a wire rack to dry for at least 12 hours. After this time they will be ready to eat.

The seas and oceans

There are five oceans in the world – the Pacific, which is the largest, the Atlantic, the Indian, the Arctic and the Antarctic. They cover almost three quarters of the earth's surface. Land, particularly peninsulas and islands, divides the oceans into seas. The islands of the West Indies, for example, separate the Caribbean Sea from the Sargasso Sea in the North Atlantic Ocean.

The ocean floor is made up of shelves, slopes and deeps. The continental shelf is the shallow part of the oceans around the continents. The ocean floor gradually slopes away from the continental shelf to the ocean deeps. The deeps off the coast of Japan reach down to over 34,000 feet (10,300 metres). There are also huge mountain ranges, such as the Mid-Atlantic Ridge, on the ocean floor. These mountains were formed in the same way as mountains on land but they are hidden under water.

The oceans and seas are always moving because of waves, currents and tides. Waves are made by winds blowing across the surface of the water. Ocean currents can be either cold or warm and they have an important effect on climate. Tides are regular rises and falls of the sea. They happen when the gravity of the moon attracts and pulls the sea water slightly towards it. Tides vary in different parts of the world but they always happen twice in every 24 hours 50 minutes. This is the time it takes for the moon to orbit the earth.

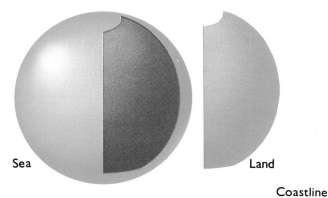

Pacific Ocean

Sea

Land

◄ Geographers tend to look at the continents when they study the earth. However, the oceans cover much more of the earth's surface than the continents do. If you look at the globe from the Pacific side, you can hardly see any land at all. The seas cover about 71 per cent of the earth's surface. The ocean bed goes down much deeper below sea level than the mountains rise above it.

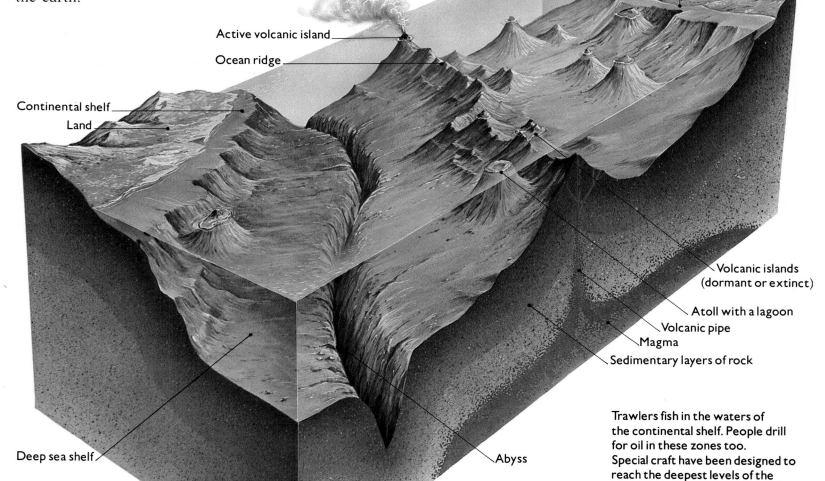

Coastline

Sea level

Active volcanic island

Ocean ridge

Continental shelf

Land

Volcanic islands (dormant or extinct)

Atoll with a lagoon

Volcanic pipe

Magma

Sedimentary layers of rock

Deep sea shelf

Abyss

▲ This picture shows a section of the ocean bed. It is divided into four main zones – the continental shelf, the continental slope, the deep sea shelf, and the abyss. These zones do not slope down evenly to the middle of the oceans. The ocean bed contains ridges, trenches, and some great mountain ranges below sea level.

Trawlers fish in the waters of the continental shelf. People drill for oil in these zones too. Special craft have been designed to reach the deepest levels of the abyss. In some places, the peaks of underwater ranges form reefs and islands. The skeletons of tiny sea creatures form coral after many years. This may build up around the crater of a volcanic island. As the island sinks, the coral forms a shallow lagoon called an atoll.

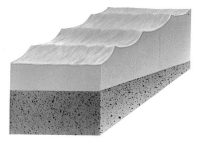

◀ The oceans move with the tides. The waves on the surface are caused by winds. On calm days far out at sea, the shape of the waves tends to be fairly regular and they are evenly spaced. The highest points are called the crests. The lowest points are called the troughs.

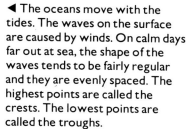

◀ As the waves approach a large mass of land, the ocean bed tends to shelve less steeply. There is not enough water ahead of a wave to complete the shape of the crest. The front of the crest begins to fall away sharply. The crest may almost overlap the trough ahead.

◀ When the wave reaches the coast, water surges up the beach. Since it cannot keep travelling onward, it falls back and meets the next wave as it advances. It slides back under the advancing crest. Nothing now supports the weight of the wave's crest and so it breaks.

▲ Surfing is a popular sport, especially in countries with long ocean beaches where high waves build up far from the shoreline.

The surfer tries to catch a wave before the crest breaks. The forward-moving face of the wave travels inshore at high speed.

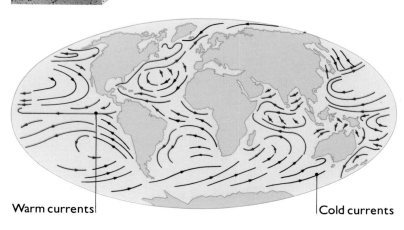

Warm currents | Cold currents

▲ Ocean currents are major movements of water in the oceans. They may be warm or cold — the Gulf Stream is warm. It keeps European harbours ice-free in winter.

◀ **Tides**

The moon exercises a strong gravitational pull on the oceans. The sun's influence is less great because it is so much further away. So-called spring tides are the highest tides. They occur at new and full moon. At these times, the sun, moon and earth are in a direct line. The sun and moon's gravitational pulls act together pulling the oceans most strongly.

The lowest tides are called neap tides. These occur at the moon's first and third quarters — times when exactly a quarter, or three quarters of the moon can be seen at night. At these times the sun and moon are at right angles to the earth. They are out of phase, so they do not exercise such a direct gravitational pull on the oceans and the tides are low.

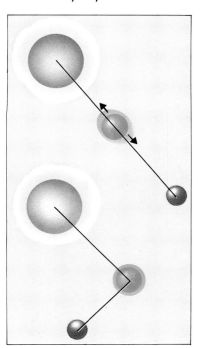

Floating in salt water
Have you noticed that it is easier to float in the sea than in a swimming pool? This is because sea water is salty. The more salt there is in water the more things float in it. To prove this, take a drinking straw and plug one end with modelling clay.

Now fill a glass jar with water and float the straw in it.

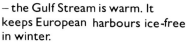

With a pen mark off the water level on the straw so that you can see how much it floats in ordinary water.
To see how much more the straw floats in salt water, add two tablespoonfuls of salt to the jar. Stir it in well and then put in the straw. You will see how much more it floats.

Travel and communications

There are three main kinds of transport – land, water and air. All these are vital for carrying people, food, raw materials and goods from one place to another. Countries in North America and Western Europe have advanced transport systems. The world's poorer countries do not have such good communications and they often rely on primitive methods for transport.

The earliest way of carrying things about was on the backs of people or animals. Horses, camels, elephants, yaks, llamas, donkeys and mules are useful animals either for carrying goods and people or for working in the fields and pulling carts. One of the best ways to travel across snow and ice in the Arctic regions is on a dog-sledge.

Railways were invented in the nineteenth century in Britain and they soon spread to the rest of the world. A fairly cheap way of transporting heavy goods is by rail, but today many people and industries use motorways and roads instead.

Another important way of moving products and materials is by sea, rivers and canals. The type of boat used on a canal is called a barge. Container ships are easy to load and unload as all the goods are pre-packed in crates. The fastest form of transport is by air. There are now airports all over the world and people who want to travel quickly go by aeroplane. Travelling by air is becoming much more popular, especially with holidaymakers.

◄ Cars zoom round the 'octopus', a clover-leaf highway in Caracas. Motor cars were developed by inventors in Europe and the United States in the late nineteenth century. They have transformed our way of life since then. However, rising fuel costs may mean that many people will give up owning a car.

▼ Trains are still a vital form of overland transport. The first steam train service ran between Stockton and Darlington in England. It opened in 1825. Modern trains often run on electricity. New, high-speed passenger services run between major cities.

▼ People still perform many important carrying tasks in poor countries. Goods may be put on the head so that the whole of the body takes their weight. Horses and donkeys are the oldest beasts of burden used by man. They were probably used first by the ancient Egyptians over 6,000 years ago.

◄ There are very few cars in China. Most people use bicycles to get about. They can also be adapted for carrying light cargoes.

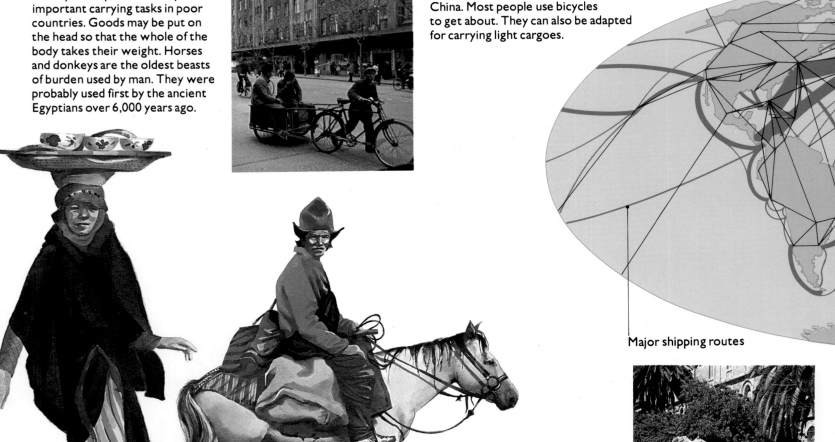

Major shipping routes

► Camels are animals well suited to desert travel. They can go without water for many days, and their broad hooves do not sink into the sand. There are two main types. The dromedary has one hump. The Bactrian camel has two.

◄Aircraft offer the fastest form of transport. However, they are not as suitable as ships or trains for carrying heavy cargoes.
Two Americans called Wilbur and Orville Wright made the first true aircraft powered by motor, in 1903. Modern aircraft, like the one shown here are powered by jets.

► Aircraft have replaced ships as the main way for passengers to cross the oceans. However, ships like this container vessel can carry much bulkier cargoes.
Sailing ships have been used since ancient times. The first steamship was built in 1783. Diesel engines came later. Nuclear energy now powers some modern ships.

▼ Large trucks have many advantages over trains for carrying goods overland. They are not faster, but they are more adaptable. The goods do not have to be unloaded and reloaded at a station. 'Big rigs' like this can carry container goods straight to a dock for loading onto a ship. However, these large trucks can cause problems such as air pollution to the environment.

Major air routes

This map shows the main sea lanes and aircraft routes around the world.

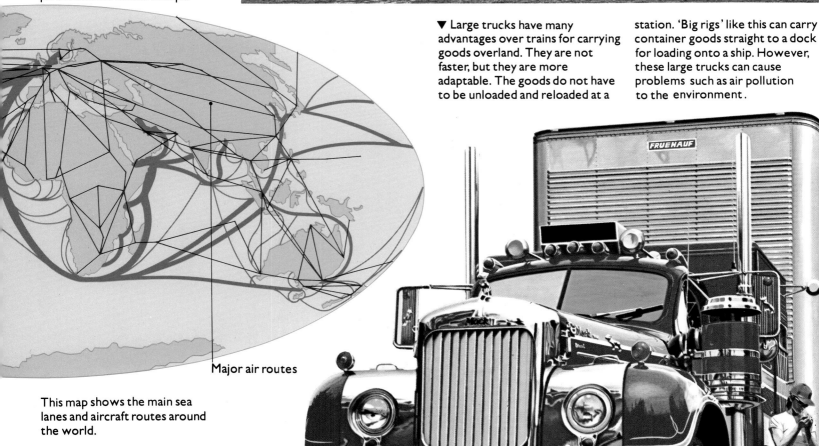

The shrinking globe

Today, the world often seems smaller than it is because people can speed from one continent to another in just a few hours. In fact, the time it takes to travel from place to place has become more important than actual distances.

In the middle of the nineteenth century, sailing boats took one to three months to cross the Atlantic Ocean. Steam ships later completed the same journey in about 10 days. The fastest way to cross the Atlantic now is by supersonic passenger jet. Concorde, for example, takes only 3½ hours to fly from New York to London. This is half the time taken by other aircraft.

The aeroplane has also speeded up postal services throughout the world. Letters can arrive in another country within a few days of being posted. It is also possible to communicate directly with people without travelling. The international telephone system links almost all parts of the world, and teleprinters and computers enable people to send messages over great distances. This is useful for anyone who has business dealings abroad. Another reason the world seems quite small is that television pictures, by using satellites, can show events as they actually happen on the other side of the world.

504 hours 1860

Clipper

Steamer

DC-4

Concorde

◄ When the clipper sailing ship was designed in the nineteenth century, it was the fastest type of transport in the world. However, it was later replaced by the steamer, which was driven by steam turbines and not by sail. The DC-4 used to be the fastest passenger plane in the world, but the supersonic Concorde is the fastest today.

288 hours 1906

24 hours 1963

3½ hours Today

◄ These globes are all at the same angle showing the Atlantic Ocean and how long the journey from London to New York has taken over the years. They vary in size because the less time it takes to go from one place to another, the smaller the world seems to be. In the 1800s the only way of crossing the Atlantic Ocean was by ship. The clipper sailing ship was the fastest kind, but even this took over three weeks to make the journey. One of the major uses of the clipper was to carry tea from Asia to England. The introduction of the steamer as a means of transport meant that travelling time was nearly halved in the early part of this century. Most steam ships were designed to carry passengers and mail. The invention of aeroplanes meant that it took even less time for people to cross the Atlantic. Today it can take only 3½ hours.

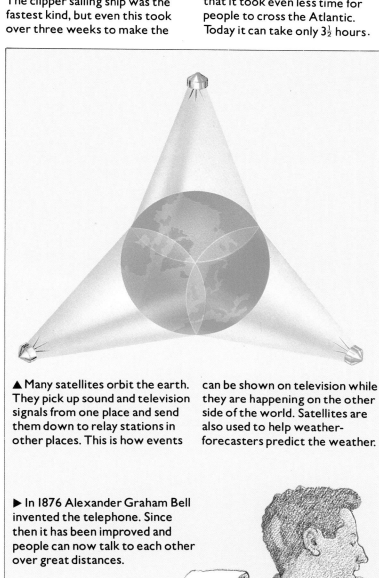

▲ Many satellites orbit the earth. They pick up sound and television signals from one place and send them down to relay stations in other places. This is how events can be shown on television while they are happening on the other side of the world. Satellites are also used to help weather-forecasters predict the weather.

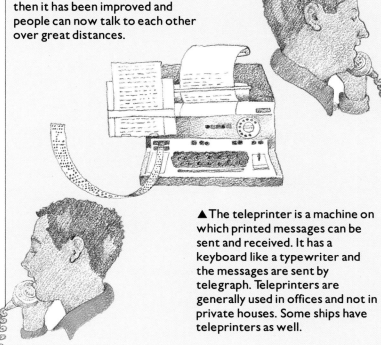

► In 1876 Alexander Graham Bell invented the telephone. Since then it has been improved and people can now talk to each other over great distances.

▲ The teleprinter is a machine on which printed messages can be sent and received. It has a keyboard like a typewriter and the messages are sent by telegraph. Teleprinters are generally used in offices and not in private houses. Some ships have teleprinters as well.

COUNTRIES OF THE WORLD

The key explains what the symbols on the maps of the different countries mean. They show where the main farming and industrial areas are, and where the main crops and mineral resources can be found. The symbols are in four colours — blue for animals and animal farming, green for plants and vegetation, red for minerals and mining, and purple for industry and tourism. The maps also show the main mountains, rivers, towns, roads and railways.

The facts and figures panel gives the most important information about the country — its population, area, language, capital and currency. You can easily compare the facts about different countries.

- ● Towns with over 1,000,000 people

- ● Towns with under 1,000,000 people

- ▲ Mountains

- ⌒ Railways

- ⌒ Major roads

- Wheat

- Corn/Maize

- Rice

- Cereal crops — oats, barley, rye etc

- Citrus fruits

- Grapes, mainly for making wine

Sugar cane

Bananas

Potatoes

Palm oil

Coconuts from which copra is made

Cacao from which chocolate and cocoa are made

Fruit which is not citrus fruit

Vegetables

Cotton

Olives, especially for making olive oil

Timber grown for wood products

Rubber

Jute

Flowers

Tobacco

Crops which cannot be eaten, like sisal

Tea

Coffee

Groundnuts

Spices

Industrial areas

Shipbuilding

Cities and areas which attract many tourists

Major ports

Cattle ranching for meat and hides

Dairy farming for milk, cheese and butter

Sheep rearing for wool and meat

Goat rearing, particularly for milk

Fishing

Pig farming for pork and bacon

Arctic animals such as reindeer

Rearing of other animals, such as llamas in South America

Subsistence farming — growing food to live on rather than sell

Oil fields

Coal mining

Natural gas

Other energy – this usually means hydro-electric power which is energy produced by using masses of water

Iron deposits

Steel industry

Gold mining

Copper mining

Bauxite mining

Diamond mining

Silver mining

Uranium mining – this mineral is needed for nuclear power

Mining other minerals — today over 2,000 minerals are mined

Facts and Figures

This is the national flag

Flag

Language Japanese

A word of greeting in the country's language

The area is the size of the country

Area 145,809 sq miles (377,643 sq km)

Each rectangle represents 2,000,000 square kilometres

This shows the total population of the country. Each person represents 3,000,000 people in real life — so half a person equals 1,500,000 people

An example of the money used in the country

Population 115,920,000

Yen

Tokyo

Currency

Capital

This shows where abouts the capital is

Looking at Europe

Europe is the world's second smallest continent. It covers an area of 3,850,000 square miles (9,972,000 sq km). This is about one million square miles larger than Australia.

Despite its small area, Europe is very densely populated. Its population of 660 million is 47 times larger than Australia's of 14 million.

Europe is surrounded by seas to the north, west and south. The only land boundary is with Asia in the east. The coastline of Europe is very irregular because deep seas and inlets divide the land into peninsulas and islands. In the south, Spain and Portugal form one peninsula and Italy another. In the north, the Scandinavian countries also form peninsulas.

There are many great rivers in Europe. These include the Rhine which flows into the North Sea and the Danube which runs into the Black Sea. The five main mountain ranges are the Pyrenees, Alps, Apennines, Carpathians and the mountains of Scandinavia. The nearness to the sea greatly modifies Europe's climate, especially in the west where the warm Gulf Stream makes the climate milder.

In Europe there are many countries and most have their own language. More than 70 languages are spoken in Europe. Some of Europe's boundaries are political, others follow mountain ranges and river valleys.

▼The most densely populated area of Europe is an arc sweeping down from northern Britain to southern Italy. It includes north-eastern France, Belgium, Holland, Denmark, West and East Germany, Poland, Czechoslovakia and Hungary. Much of this is made up of lowland industrial and farming regions, broken up by hills and mountain ranges: the Alps, Apennines and Carpathians.

Spain, Portugal, Greece and the Balkan countries are less densely populated. Here, many centres of population are around the coasts, away from the mountainous terrain inland.
In the north, Iceland, Norway, Finland and Sweden are much more thinly populated. Together, they make up almost a third of Europe's land mass. However, much of the land is mountain,

forest or tundra. Most Swedes, Finns and Norwegians live on the coasts.
West Germany has a population of over 61 million people. This makes it the most populated country in Europe. Next come Italy (57 million), the United Kingdom (56 million), and France (53 million). There are nine cities in Europe with populations of over 2 million people. London is the largest.

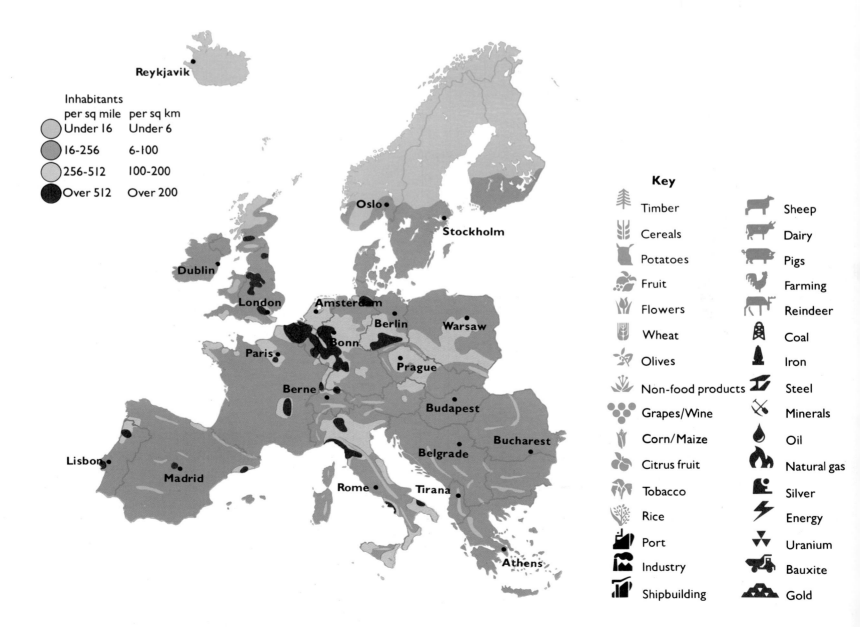

Inhabitants

per sq mile	per sq km
Under 16	Under 6
16-256	6-100
256-512	100-200
Over 512	Over 200

Key

Timber		Sheep	
Cereals		Dairy	
Potatoes		Pigs	
Fruit		Farming	
Flowers		Reindeer	
Wheat		Coal	
Olives		Iron	
Non-food products		Steel	
Grapes/Wine		Minerals	
Corn/Maize		Oil	
Citrus fruit		Natural gas	
Tobacco		Silver	
Rice		Energy	
Port		Uranium	
Industry		Bauxite	
Shipbuilding		Gold	

▼ Europe is heavily industrialized. However, agriculture is still important, especially in the south. The forests of Scandinavia provide much timber, and fishing is important on the Atlantic coast. Oil and natural gas have been found beneath the North Sea, and coal is still vital to Europe's industries. Europe's great seaports have always been thriving centers of world trade. Inland, goods are carried by many roads, railways, rivers and canals.

Reykjavik
ICELAND

FAEROE
ISLANDS

Norwegian Sea

HAMMERFEST

SWEDEN

FINLAND

Gulf of Bothnia

NORWAY

Oslo

Helsinki

Stockholm

SHETLAND
ISLANDS

ORKNEY
ISLANDS

HEBRIDES

UNITED KINGDOM

Glasgow   Edinburgh

Belfast

North Sea

DENMARK

GOTLAND

Baltic Sea

Copenhagen

Gdansk

Dublin

Atlantic Ocean

IRELAND Liverpool

Cork

Manchester

Birmingham

Cardiff

R Thames

HOLLAND
Amsterdam

Hamburg   EAST
GERMANY

Berlin

R Vistula

Warsaw

London

Antwerp

Essen

Leipzig

POLAND

SOVIET UNION

English Channel

CHANNEL ISLANDS

Brussels

Bonn

R Oder

Le Havre

BELGIUM

Brest

Frankfurt

WEST
GERMANY

Prague

Krakow

R Seine

Paris

R Meuse

R Rhine

Stuttgart

CZECHOSLOVAKIA

Carpathian Mountains

FRANCE

R Danube

Nantes

Basle Berne

Munich

Vienna

Budapest

Bay of Biscay

R Loire

SWITZERLAND

Vaduz

AUSTRIA

Innsbruck

HUNGARY

Geneva

Alps

Bordeaux

*Massif
Central*

Lyon

Trieste

Zagreb

R Sava

RUMANIA

R Rhône

Turin

Milan

Venice

SPAIN

Bilbao

R Garonne

Pyrenees

R Po

Belgrade

R Danube

Bucharest

Madrid

Marseille

Nice

Florence

YUGOSLAVIA

BULGARIA

Varna

R Douro

Lisbon

PORTUGAL

R Tagus

R Ebro

Barcelona

CORSICA

Rome

ITALY

Adriatic Sea

Sofia

Balkans

ALBANIA

Tirana

Thessaloniki

R Guadalquivir

BALEARIC
ISLANDS

SARDINIA

Naples

Apennines

Tyrrhenian Sea

CORFU

GREECE

Aegean Sea

Strait of Gibraltar

Palermo   SICILY

Ionian Sea

Athens

Mediterranean Sea

Iraklion

CRETE

Scale

0   500 miles

0   500 km

British Isles

The British Isles are two large islands – Great Britain and Ireland – and many smaller islands. They are the most westerly part of Europe except Iceland. Great Britain consists of three countries – England, Scotland and Wales. Ireland is divided into the Republic of Ireland (or Eire) and Northern Ireland. Great Britain and Northern Ireland together are called the United Kingdom.

The northern part of Great Britain, is more mountainous than the southern part. The main mountain ranges are the Grampians in Scotland, the Pennines in England, and the Cambrian Mountains in Wales.

England is the most densely populated country and has many important industrial areas. London is the capital and is the centre of the road and railway system. It is one of the world's most important industrial and commercial cities.

Scotland is divided into highland and lowland areas. The scenery is often spectacular in the highland area which includes many islands around the coast. In the south are the two main cities – Edinburgh, the capital, and Glasgow, the industrial centre. Oil from the North Sea is an important new industry.

Wales is the smallest country. It is mountainous and most of the population live in the industrial southern area. Cardiff is the capital.

Ireland is often called the 'Emerald Isle' because of its green fields. It is shaped like a bowl with a rim of mountains around the coast and a low-lying central plain. Dublin is the capital of Eire and Belfast of Northern Ireland. The Shannon is the longest river in the British Isles. It is 224 miles (358 km) long. The largest lake in the British Isles – Lough Neagh – is in Northern Ireland. Eire is mainly a farming country but industry and tourism are becoming more important. It exports meat and dairy products.

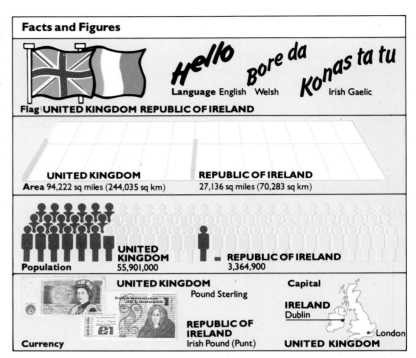

Facts and Figures

Flag	UNITED KINGDOM	REPUBLIC OF IRELAND

Language English Welsh Irish Gaelic
Hello Bore da Konas ta tu

Area	UNITED KINGDOM	REPUBLIC OF IRELAND
	94,222 sq miles (244,035 sq km)	27,136 sq miles (70,283 sq km)

Population	UNITED KINGDOM 55,901,000	REPUBLIC OF IRELAND 3,364,900

Currency	UNITED KINGDOM Pound Sterling REPUBLIC OF IRELAND Irish Pound (Punt)	Capital IRELAND Dublin London UNITED KINGDOM

▼ Oil was found under the North Sea bed in 1970. Oil production is now very important to Britain's economy.

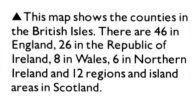

▲ This map shows the counties in the British Isles. There are 46 in England, 26 in the Republic of Ireland, 8 in Wales, 6 in Northern Ireland and 12 regions and island areas in Scotland.

◀ A Scottish piper plays the bagpipes. Bagpipes were also used in other countries but became most popular in Scotland, Northumberland and Ireland, where they are still played today.

▶ Castle Stewart stands in the Firth of Lorne — the mouth of the Lorne river — on Scotland's west coast. It is near the resort of Oban.

▲ Whisky is distilled in Scotland. Malt and barley are two main ingredients in this important Scottish product. After distilling, the whisky matures in casks.

◀ This cottage with its thatched roof and whitewashed walls is typical of the west coast of Ireland. Many of the people who live here are farmers. They often divide up their fields with stone walls.

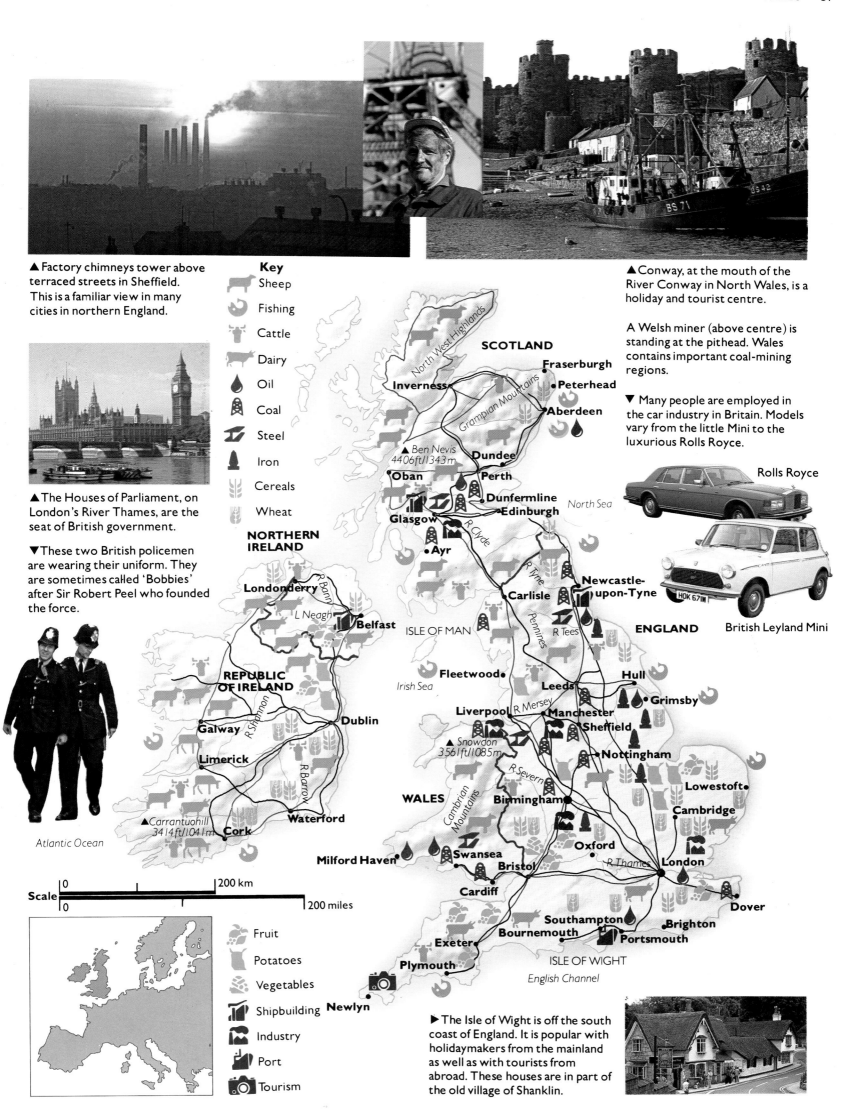

▲ Factory chimneys tower above terraced streets in Sheffield. This is a familiar view in many cities in northern England.

▲ The Houses of Parliament, on London's River Thames, are the seat of British government.

▼These two British policemen are wearing their uniform. They are sometimes called 'Bobbies' after Sir Robert Peel who founded the force.

▲Conway, at the mouth of the River Conway in North Wales, is a holiday and tourist centre.

A Welsh miner (above centre) is standing at the pithead. Wales contains important coal-mining regions.

▼ Many people are employed in the car industry in Britain. Models vary from the little Mini to the luxurious Rolls Royce.

Rolls Royce

British Leyland Mini

Key

Sheep
Fishing
Cattle
Dairy
Oil
Coal
Steel
Iron
Cereals
Wheat

Fruit
Potatoes
Vegetables
Shipbuilding
Industry
Port
Tourism

SCOTLAND

North West Highlands

Fraserburgh
Peterhead
Inverness
Grampian Mountains
Aberdeen

▲ Ben Nevis 4406ft/1343m
Dundee
Oban
Perth
Dunfermline
North Sea
Glasgow
Edinburgh
R Clyde

• Ayr

NORTHERN IRELAND

Londonderry
R Bann
L Neagh
Belfast

ISLE OF MAN

R Tyne
Newcastle-upon-Tyne
Carlisle
Pennines
R Tees
ENGLAND

REPUBLIC OF IRELAND

Irish Sea
Fleetwood

R Shannon
Galway
Dublin
Leeds
Hull
Grimsby

Limerick
Liverpool
R Mersey
Manchester
Sheffield

▲ Snowdon 3561ft/1085m
Nottingham

Atlantic Ocean
▲Carrantuohill 3414ft/1041m
Cork
Waterford
R Barrow

WALES
Cambrian Mountains
R Severn
Birmingham
Lowestoft
Cambridge

Oxford
R Thames
London

Milford Haven
Swansea
Bristol

Cardiff

Exeter
Bournemouth
Southampton
Portsmouth
Brighton
Dover

Plymouth
ISLE OF WIGHT
English Channel

Newlyn

Scale
0 ————— 200 km
0 ————— 200 miles

▶ The Isle of Wight is off the south coast of England. It is popular with holidaymakers from the mainland as well as with tourists from abroad. These houses are in part of the old village of Shanklin.

France

France is the second largest country in Europe after the Soviet Union. Three of France's boundaries are with seas – the English Channel in the north-west, the Bay of Biscay in the west and the Mediterranean Sea in the south. France also has boundaries with Belgium, Luxembourg, West Germany, Switzerland, Italy and Spain. The boundaries with Switzerland and Italy follow the Jura and the Alps. The boundary with Spain follows the Pyrenees.

Mont Blanc in south-east France is the highest mountain in France and in the whole of Europe. It is 15,771 feet (4,807 metres) high. The country's largest upland area is the Massif Central. France has four large rivers – the Seine, the Loire, the Garonne and the Rhône. The main ports in France are Le Havre on the Atlantic and Marseille on the Mediterranean. Paris is the capital of France and is a big centre of communications for France and Europe. In Paris there are many main railway terminals and three international airports.

One quarter of all French people make their living from farming. France produces fruit and cheese as well as one third of all the world's wine. France is also an important industrial country. Industry is found mainly in the north and east where there are coal and iron deposits. Lille is a big industrial city. France exports motor vehicles, chemicals, machinery and textiles.

Facts and Figures

Flag

Bonjour

Language French

Area 210,040 sq miles (544,000 sq km)

Population 53,383,000

French Franc

Currency

Paris

Capital

▲ The Eiffel Tower in Paris attracts many tourists. It is made of iron and stands 948 feet (400 metres) high. There is a radio station and a television aerial at the top.

◀ Antibes is a popular resort on the Riviera, a region along the Mediterranean coast. It is also a port and centre of a flower growing area.

▶ This chateau is in the Loire valley. It was built in the fifteenth century and is separated from the land by a moat. Moats were built around most chateaux for protection.

▲ Mont Blanc is in the Alps on the border between France and Italy. It is the highest mountain in Europe. There is a seven mile (11.3kms) tunnel under the mountain linking France and Italy.

▶ France is famous all over the world for its food and chefs. Most chefs must go through years of training at one of the many cooking schools before they are allowed to work in the top restaurants.

▼ The French enjoy eating as much as they enjoy cooking. There are many outdoor cafés in Paris where people spend hours sitting, talking and eating.

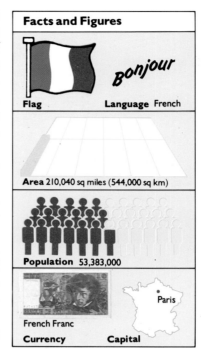

▲ One of France's most popular exports is wine. Many different types of wine are produced. Here workers are treading on the grapes to turn them into wine.

◀ Bread is eaten with almost every meal in France. There are many types of bread. Here a baker is carrying out the long loaves known as baguettes.

► The city of Nantes lies on the Loire river and has been a trading port since Roman times. Many products are produced here and sent all over the world.

◄ The Dordogne river joins the Garonne river north of Bordeaux to form the Gironde. The valley is popular as a tourist attraction and there are many vineyards here.

► The Michelin tyre man is recognized the world over. Tyres are an important French product and they are known for their high quality.

▲ This French racing car is a Renault. The French make many cars both for racing and for ordinary use.

◄ This Citroën is known as the 'Deux Chevaux' because it has a two horsepower engine.

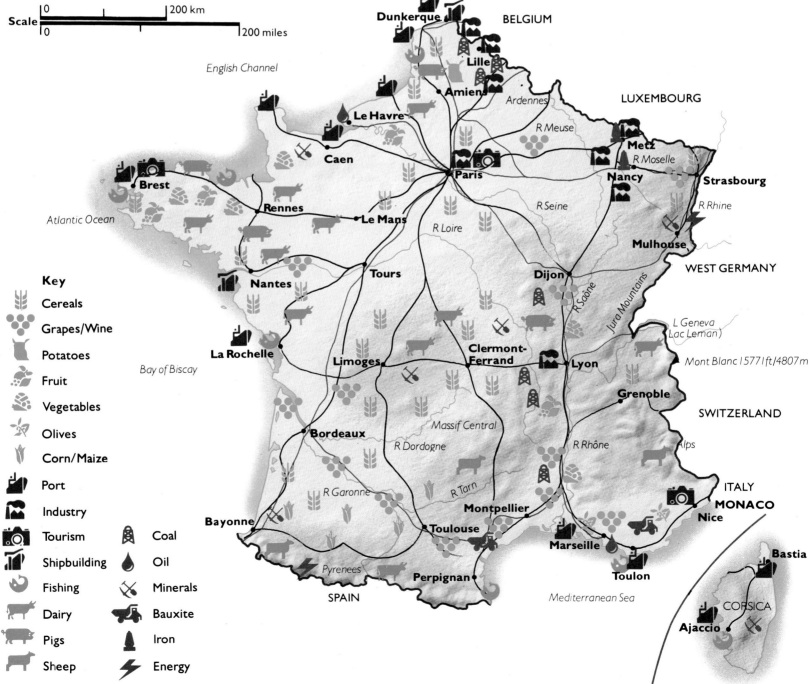

Scale
0 — 200 km
0 — 200 miles

Key

Cereals		Coal	
Grapes/Wine		Oil	
Potatoes		Minerals	
Fruit		Bauxite	
Vegetables		Iron	
Olives		Energy	
Corn/Maize			
Port			
Industry			
Tourism	Coal		
Shipbuilding	Oil		
Fishing	Minerals		
Dairy	Bauxite		
Pigs	Iron		
Sheep	Energy		

English Channel

Atlantic Ocean

Bay of Biscay

BELGIUM

LUXEMBOURG

WEST GERMANY

SWITZERLAND

ITALY

SPAIN

Mediterranean Sea

Dunkerque
Lille
Amiens
Ardennes
Le Havre
R Meuse
Metz
R Moselle
Caen
Paris
Nancy
Strasbourg
Brest
R Rhine
Rennes
R Seine
Le Mans
Mulhouse
R Loire
Tours
Dijon
Nantes
R Saône
Jura Mountains
L Geneva (Lac Leman)
Mont Blanc 15771ft/4807m
La Rochelle
Clermont-Ferrand
Lyon
Limoges
Grenoble
Massif Central
Bordeaux
R Dordogne
R Rhône
Alps
R Garonne
R Tarn
Montpellier
MONACO
Nice
Bayonne
Toulouse
Marseille
Bastia
Pyrenees
Toulon
Perpignan
CORSICA
Ajaccio

The Low Countries

The Netherlands, Belgium and Luxembourg are often grouped together as the Low Countries. This is because they lie in a lowland region near the North Sea.

The Netherlands is also known as Holland and the people who live there are called the Dutch. The Netherlands is a flat land with many canals and windmills. Much of it lies below sea level. The Dutch have built dykes to keep back the sea. They have also built dams to prevent flooding by the rivers Rhine and Maas. The Dutch grow flowers, vegetables and fruits and make cheeses like Edam and Gouda. They also produce radios, textiles and electronic goods. Rotterdam is the major industrial port in the Netherlands, and Amsterdam is the capital. The government of the Netherlands works from The Hague.

Belgium is south of the Netherlands. The River Meuse divides the country into two main areas. In the south-east is a wooded upland area called the Ardennes. To the north and west is good farmland where arable crops are grown. Dairy farming is also important in this area. French and Flemish are the two Belgian languages. In the capital city, Brussels, people speak both these. The River Schelde flows through the port of Antwerp in the north. Ostend is a car ferry port.

Although they are small countries, the Netherlands and Belgium have the most dense population in Europe. The Grand Duchy of Luxembourg lies to the south-east of Belgium. This is a very small country which has an important steel industry and rich farmlands.

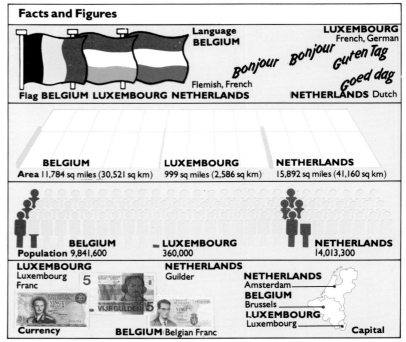

Facts and Figures

Language **BELGIUM** Flemish, French	**Flag** BELGIUM LUXEMBOURG NETHERLANDS	**LUXEMBOURG** French, German *Bonjour Bonjour Guten Tag* *Goed dag* **NETHERLANDS** Dutch
BELGIUM **Area** 11,784 sq miles (30,521 sq km)	**LUXEMBOURG** 999 sq miles (2,586 sq km)	**NETHERLANDS** 15,892 sq miles (41,160 sq km)
BELGIUM **Population** 9,841,600	**LUXEMBOURG** 360,000	**NETHERLANDS** 14,013,300
LUXEMBOURG Luxembourg Franc **Currency**	**NETHERLANDS** Guilder BELGIUM Belgian Franc	**NETHERLANDS** Amsterdam **BELGIUM** Brussels **LUXEMBOURG** Luxembourg **Capital**

▶ Delft, in South Holland, is a very old city. It is famous for china, tiles and pottery.

◀ Visitors to the capital of Holland may take a boat trip on one of its many canals. Amsterdam is built on a network of canals and there are more than 1,000 bridges. There are two universities and the city is also a centre of science.

▼ Nearly one half of the land in Holland is below sea level. There are huge engineering projects to keep the sea out. Ijsselmeer Dyke (formerly the Zuiderzee) was built in 1932. Gradually the land behind the dyke is being reclaimed.

▲ Haarlem is the centre of the bulb-growing industry. Holland earns 485 million guilders a year from exports of bulbs.

Making a windmill
Cut out a piece of card in the shape shown. Place an unsharpened pencil on the back and tape it down. Draw and cut out the arms of the windmill on another bit of card.

Using a paper fastener, secure the arms to the big piece of card. Put a small piece in between the two so the arms will move freely in the wind.

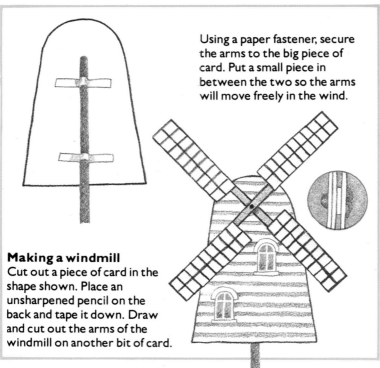

▲ Dairy farming is very important in Holland. Windmills were once used to pump up water from the low-lying polders to stop them from flooding.

◀ The best-known Dutch cheeses are Gouda and Edam.

◄ The headquarters of the Common Market are in Brussels, the capital of Belgium. Brussels is a very old city on the Senne river in central Belgium. It is also an important industrial centre. It produces electronic equipment, machine tools, rubber and lace.

◄ The Ardennes, in south-east Belgium, rise to 2,300 feet (700 metres). Two main rivers, the Meuse and the Sambre, flow through the woods and valleys.

▼ Ostend is the largest holiday resort on the Belgian coast. It is also a fishing port. It is connected with Bruges and Ghent by canals. A ferry port is here too.

►The waterways of Bruges give it the name 'Venice of the North.' It is said to be the best preserved medieval city in Europe. There are winding cobbled streets and gabled houses. Bruges is famous for lace.

▼ Antwerp, on the River Schelde, is the major port of Belgium.

THE NETHERLANDS

North Sea

Leeuwarden
Groningen
Ijsselmeer

Ijmuiden
Haarlem
Amsterdam
R Ijssel
Hengelo
Den Haag
(The Hague)
R Lek
Utrecht
Arnhem
Rotterdam
R Waal
Nijmegen
Breda
Eindhoven

Ostende
(Ostend)
Brugge (Bruges)
Gent
(Ghent)
Antwerpen
(Antwerp)
R Schelde
R Maas

WEST GERMANY

Bruxelles
(Brussels)
Liège
Namur
R Meuse
Mons
Charleroi
BELGIUM

FRANCE

LUXEMBOURG

Luxembourg
Esch-sur-Alzette

Key

🌾 Wheat
🌼 Flowers
🥬 Vegetables
🍒 Fruit
🌾 Cereals
🏭 Industry
📷 Tourism
🏭 Port
🐄 Dairy
🐖 Pigs
🐄 Cattle
🐓 Farming
⛏ Coal
🔩 Steel
🔺 Iron
🔥 Natural gas
⬛ Oil

Scale
0 ———————— 200 km
0 ———————— 200 miles

West Germany

West Germany extends from the North Sea and Baltic in the north to the Alps in the South. It has borders with nine countries – Denmark in the north, the Netherlands, Belgium, Luxembourg and France in the west, East Germany and Czechoslovakia in the east and Switzerland and Austria in the south.

In the north is the North German Plain. This flat, lowland area is used for growing wheat, rye, potatoes and sugar beet. The central area includes the Harz and Sauerland mountains, the Rhine valley and the Ruhr area. This area is densely populated.

The upland plain of Bavaria has rich farmlands. To the south of Munich are the Alps which form the border with Austria.

The Rhine is the largest river in West Germany and the most important river in Europe. It rises near St Gotthard in Switzerland and flows for 800 miles (1,280 kms) to the North Sea. Many important German cities stand on the Rhine. These include Bonn, Düsseldorf, Mainz and Cologne. The Rhine valley is famous for its beautiful scenery and castles. Many wines come from the Rhine valley and they are also made on some of the Rhine's tributaries especially the Moselle.

West Germany is the greatest industrial country in Europe. The main industrial area is around the River Ruhr. The main towns include Dortmund, Duisburg and Essen. Frankfurt is the financial centre of the country. The two main ports are Bremen and Hamburg on the North Sea. West Germany also has an important canal system. The country's non-industrial products include many kinds of beer.

West Germany is a federal republic. 'Federal' means that the country is divided into different states. Each of the 10 states has its own capital and government. The capital of the whole country is Bonn.

Facts and Figures

Flag

Language German

Area 96,004 sq miles (248,651 sq km)

Population 61,321,700

Deutsche Mark
Currency

Bonn
Capital

▼ After 1945 Germany was split into East and West Germany. Another name for West Germany is the Federal Republic of Germany. The country has 10 federal states, each with its own government.

▲ The south Rhineland, which contains the Eifel and Hunsruck Mountains, is mainly agricultural. Cereals are grown in the Hunsruck Highlands and there are also famous vineyards here.

◄ The Germans drink more beer than any other nationality. There are many hand-made beer mugs, all of different designs. The Munich Beer Festival is famous throughout the world. Many people go to it each year.

▲ The Bavarian Alps in the southeast are on the border with Austria. Berchtesgaden is a popular holiday resort. There is good skiing nearby.

► This stretch of the River Rhine is particularly famous for its castles and vineyards. The fine wines which are made here are exported to countries all over the world.

▲ Mannheim is a major Rhine port and industrial town. The Rhine carries more traffic than any other waterway. It is navigable by ocean-going vessels as far as Mannheim.

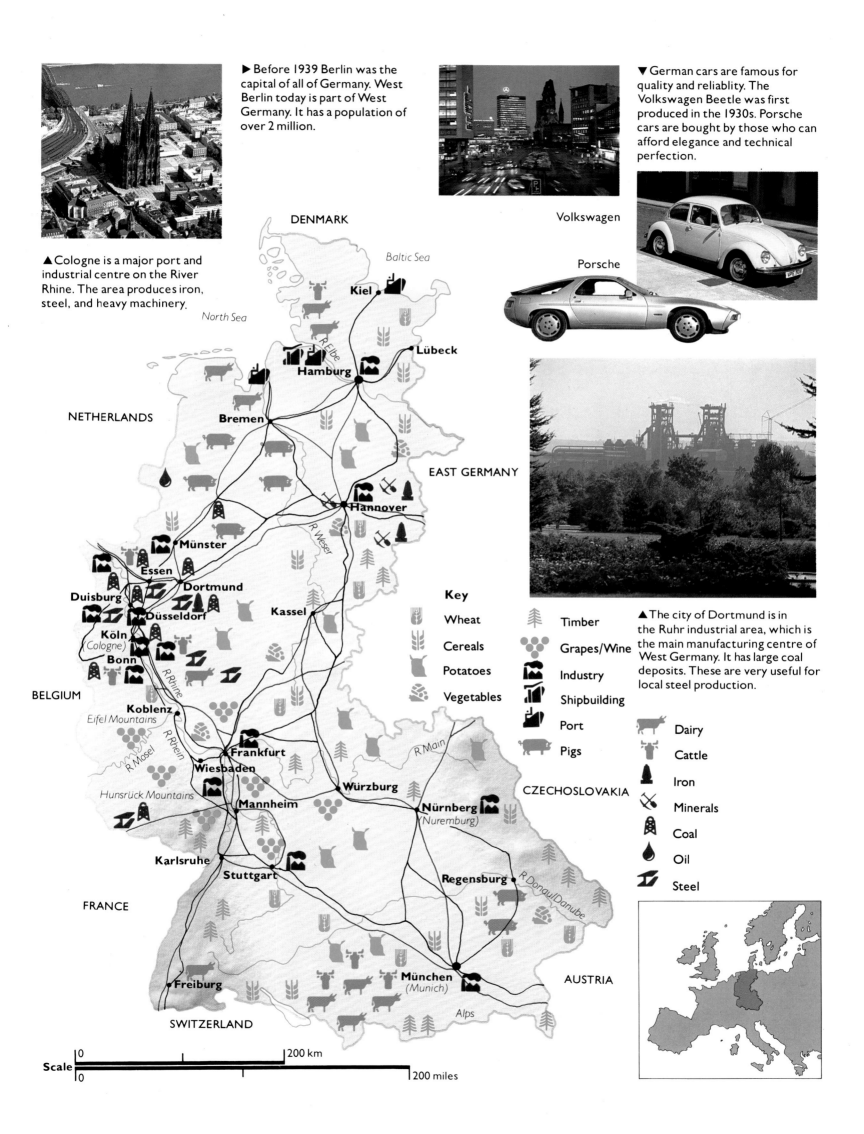

► Before 1939 Berlin was the capital of all of Germany. West Berlin today is part of West Germany. It has a population of over 2 million.

▼ German cars are famous for quality and reliablity. The Volkswagen Beetle was first produced in the 1930s. Porsche cars are bought by those who can afford elegance and technical perfection.

Volkswagen

Porsche

▲ Cologne is a major port and industrial centre on the River Rhine. The area produces iron, steel, and heavy machinery.

DENMARK

Baltic Sea

Kiel

North Sea

Lübeck

NETHERLANDS

R Elbe

Hamburg

Bremen

EAST GERMANY

Hannover

R Weser

Münster

Essen

Dortmund

Duisburg

Düsseldorf

Köln
(Cologne)

Bonn

Kassel

BELGIUM

Eifel Mountains

Koblenz

R Rhine

R Rhein

R Mosel

Hunsrück Mountains

Frankfurt

Wiesbaden

Mannheim

Würzburg

R Main

CZECHOSLOVAKIA

Nürnberg
(Nuremburg)

Karlsruhe

Stuttgart

Regensburg

R Donau/Danube

FRANCE

Freiburg

München
(Munich)

AUSTRIA

Alps

SWITZERLAND

Key

Wheat	
Cereals	
Potatoes	
Vegetables	

Timber	
Grapes/Wine	
Industry	
Shipbuilding	
Port	
Pigs	

Dairy

Cattle

Iron

Minerals

Coal

Oil

Steel

▲ The city of Dortmund is in the Ruhr industrial area, which is the main manufacturing centre of West Germany. It has large coal deposits. These are very useful for local steel production.

Scale

0   200 km

0   200 miles

Scandinavia, Finland and Iceland

Northern Europe is made up of Finland, Iceland and Norway, Sweden and Denmark. These last three countries are sometimes called Scandinavia. The Arctic Circle passes through the northern parts of Norway, Sweden and Finland and it just touches the northern coasts of Iceland. North Cape in Norway is the most northerly point of Europe.

Norway is a long, narrow country with many mountains, glaciers and fjords. A fjord is a narrow inlet on the coast with steep sides like cliffs. Because of its fjords, Norway has the most jagged coastline in the world. It also has over 150,000 small rocky islands called skerries. Most Norwegians live in the south-east near Oslo, the capital. Fishing is a major industry and all the large cities in Norway are seaports.

Sweden lies to the east of Norway. This is another long country and it stretches for over 1,000 miles (1,600 kms) from north to south. Like Norway, Sweden has many forests. Its main industries are timber, paper, iron ore and steel. Stockholm, the capital, Gothenburg and Malmo are the largest cities in Sweden.

Denmark is a flat country to the south-west of Sweden. It is separated from Sweden by a narrow strip of water called The Sound. Denmark is made up of many islands and the Jutland peninsula. The capital, Copenhagen, is on the largest island, Zealand. Fishing, shipping and tourism are all important in Denmark. Danish farm products such as bacon, butter and cheese are known throughout the world.

Finland is to the east of Sweden across the Gulf of Bothnia. Southern Finland is made up of thousands of tiny islands and a great number of lakes. Timber is the most important industry here. The capital is Helsinki. The northern part of Finland, Norway and Sweden is called Lapland. The people who live here are called the Lapps and they herd reindeer.

Iceland is the most western country in Europe. It is an island with many volcanoes, geysers and glaciers. Fishing is the main industry and the capital is Reykjavik.

▲ There are about 30,000 Lapps in northern Scandinavia. Lapps follow their herds and use the reindeer for both food and transport.

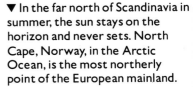

▼ In the far north of Scandinavia in summer, the sun stays on the horizon and never sets. North Cape, Norway, in the Arctic Ocean, is the most northerly point of the European mainland.

▼ Geirangerfjord on the west coast of Norway is a typical fjord. It winds along for many miles with high mountains and cascading waterfalls on either side. Boats sail from a village at the head of the fjord around the coast.

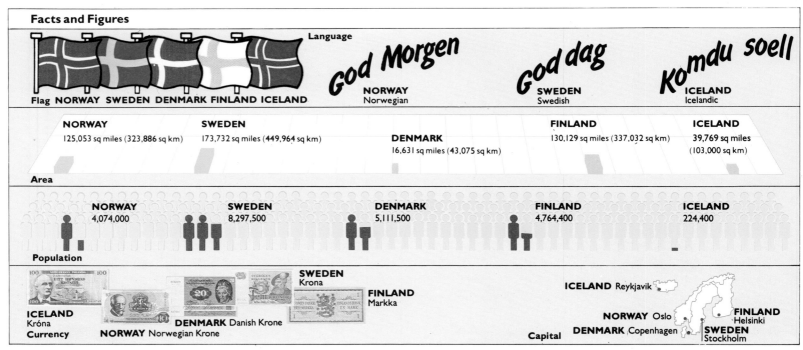

Facts and Figures

Flag NORWAY SWEDEN DENMARK FINLAND ICELAND	**Language** *God Morgen* **NORWAY** Norwegian	*God dag* **SWEDEN** Swedish	*Komdu soell* **ICELAND** Icelandic	

NORWAY	SWEDEN		FINLAND	ICELAND
125,053 sq miles (323,886 sq km)	173,732 sq miles (449,964 sq km)	**DENMARK** 16,631 sq miles (43,075 sq km)	130,129 sq miles (337,032 sq km)	39,769 sq miles (103,000 sq km)

Area

NORWAY	SWEDEN	DENMARK	FINLAND	ICELAND
4,074,000	8,297,500	5,111,500	4,764,400	224,400

Population

ICELAND Króna	SWEDEN Krona	ICELAND Reykjavik
	FINLAND Markka	
ICELAND Króna		NORWAY Oslo FINLAND Helsinki
Currency DENMARK Danish Krone NORWAY Norwegian Krone		**Capital** DENMARK Copenhagen SWEDEN Stockholm

▼ Iceland is an island just south of the Arctic Circle. At Lake Myvatn in the north of the island, there are many geysers and hot springs caused by volcanic activity. The Icelanders use the hot water from the springs as a cheap form of heating both private houses and public buildings .

◄ Timber is one of Sweden's main exports. Trees are felled using modern equipment. The logs are floated downstream to the timber plant where they are turned into wood products for export. Matches, paper and pine furniture are just some of these.

▶ Pork is Denmark's biggest export. It produces more than half the Danish farmers' income. Over 10 million pigs go to bacon factories each year.

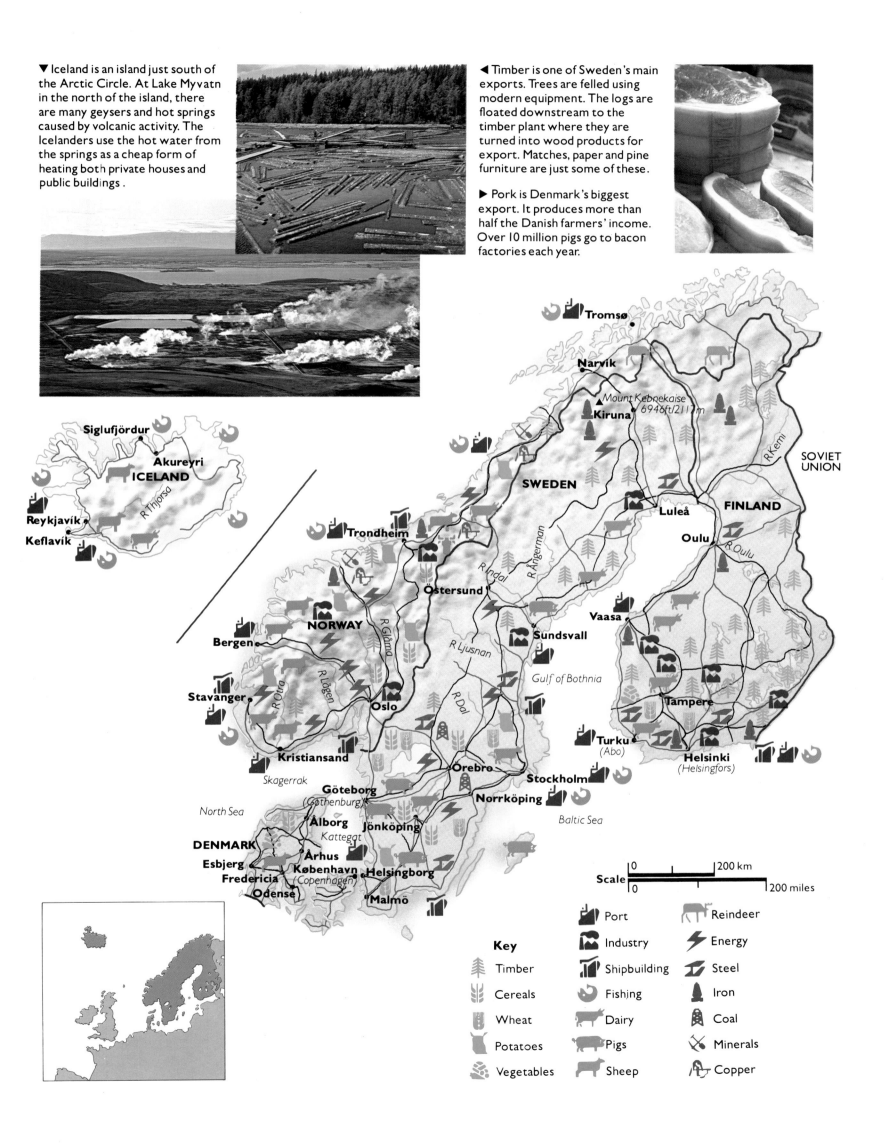

Scale

| 0 | | 200 km |
| 0 | | 200 miles |

Key

🌲 Timber	🏭 Port
🌾 Cereals	🏭 Industry
🌾 Wheat	🚢 Shipbuilding
Potatoes	🐟 Fishing
Vegetables	🐄 Dairy
	🐖 Pigs
	🐑 Sheep
🦌 Reindeer	
⚡ Energy	
Steel	
Iron	
Coal	
Minerals	
Copper	

The Alpine Countries

Much of Switzerland and Austria are in the Alps. They are the most mountainous countries in Europe. Many visitors go to see the beautiful scenery with its mountain peaks, deep valleys and lakes. Switzerland and Austria are good countries for mountain climbing and skiing. One of the most famous mountains in Switzerland is the Matterhorn. It is 14,690 feet (4,478 metres) high.

Important roads and railway lines run through the Alps. The Simplon Tunnel and Simplon Pass link Switzerland and Italy and the Brenner Pass runs through Austria to Italy. The longest road tunnel in the world is the Alberg Tunnel in Austria. It is almost 9 miles (14 km) long.

The capital of Switzerland is Berne. The regions of Switzerland are called cantons. In Switzerland most people speak German, but French and Italian are also important languages. Basle is Switzerland's only port. It stands on the River Rhine where the borders of Switzerland, France and Germany meet. Barges come up the river to Basle. The largest city is Zürich which is the business and industrial centre. The Swiss produce cheese, chocolate, clocks, watches and toys.

In Austria people speak German. Austria produces brown coal, iron ore, oil, timber and paper. Graz and Linz are industrial cities. Salzburg and Innsbruck are tourist centres. Vienna is the capital of Austria. It is called the crossroads of Europe because many roads and railways meet there.

The small country of Liechtenstein lies between Austria and Switzerland. It is only 15 miles (24 km) long and 5 miles (8 km) wide. The population is 24,000 and the capital is Vaduz.

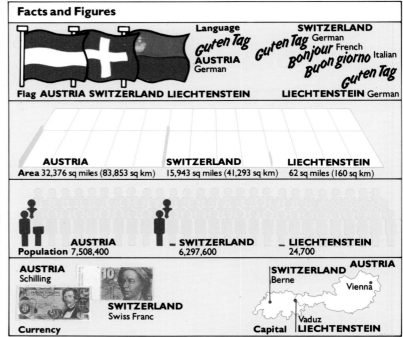

Facts and Figures

	Language
Flag AUSTRIA SWITZERLAND LIECHTENSTEIN	**SWITZERLAND** German / French / Italian *Guten Tag / Bonjour / Buon giorno* **AUSTRIA** German *Guten Tag* **LIECHTENSTEIN** German *Guten Tag*

AUSTRIA	SWITZERLAND	LIECHTENSTEIN
Area 32,376 sq miles (83,853 sq km)	15,943 sq miles (41,293 sq km)	62 sq miles (160 sq km)

AUSTRIA	SWITZERLAND	LIECHTENSTEIN
Population 7,508,400	6,297,600	24,700

AUSTRIA Schilling	**SWITZERLAND** Swiss Franc	**SWITZERLAND** Berne / **AUSTRIA** Vienna
Currency		**Capital** Vaduz LIECHTENSTEIN

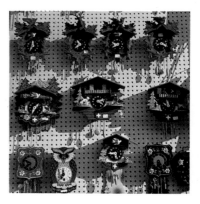

◄Cuckoo clocks are on display in this Swiss tourist shop. They are shaped like chalets (wooden Alpine cottages).

▼The summit of the Matterhorn rises above the surrounding peaks. In 1865, an English mountaineer called Edward Whymper became the first to reach the summit. Four of his seven-man party fell to their deaths on the way down but this has not deterred others.

◄A farmer brings his cattle to market in Switzerland. Dairy produce is used to make cheeses and chocolates. Alpine cattle wear bells around their necks in case they should get lost in the mountains' wooded slopes and valleys.

▶Women wrap sweets in a Swiss chocolate factory. The Swiss make chocolate of the finest quality, and their brand names are famous throughout the world.

◄Swiss Emmental cheese comes from the valley of the Emme river. Here, Emmental is stored in a cheese cellar.

◄Cheeses are named according to region. Emmental and Gruyère contain distinctive 'holes' formed by air bubbles.

▶Holidaymakers ski in the Swiss Alps. The mountains have good, snow-covered slopes. They are above cloud level, so the skies are often blue, even in the winter. The Alps are ideal for winter sports and attract many tourists.

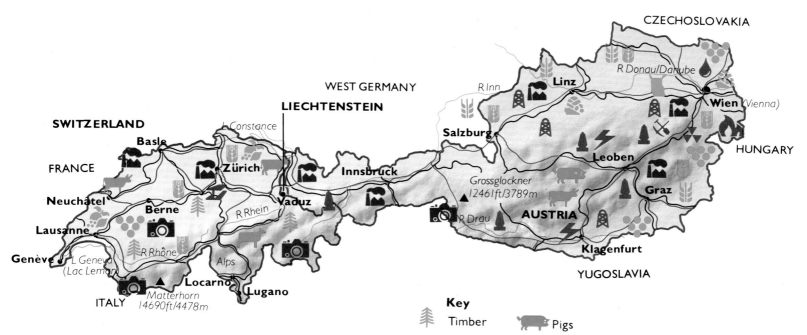

CZECHOSLOVAKIA

WEST GERMANY

LIECHTENSTEIN

SWITZERLAND

Basle

FRANCE

Zürich

Neuchâtel

Berne

Lausanne

Genève
(Lac Leman)
L Geneva

ITALY
Matterhorn
14690ft/4478m

Locarno

Lugano

L Constance

Vaduz

Innsbruck

R Rhein

R Rhône

Alps

Salzburg

R Inn

Linz

R Donau/Danube

Wien (Vienna)

Leoben

Grossglockner
12461ft/3789m

R Drau

AUSTRIA

Graz

Klagenfurt

YUGOSLAVIA

HUNGARY

Key

🌲 Timber

🌾 Wheat

🍇 Fruit

🍇 Grapes/Wine

🌾 Cereals

🥔 Potatoes

🥬 Vegetables

🏭 Industry

📷 Tourism

🐄 Dairy

🐖 Pigs

🐑 Sheep

Coal

Iron

Steel

Oil

Natural gas

Minerals

Uranium

Energy

Scale
0 ———— 200 km
0 ———— 200 miles

◀ A man works a cash dispenser outside a Swiss bank. Switzerland is peaceful and prosperous. People feel safe banking their money there. As a result, it is a world banking centre.

▶ Barges are docked in Basle's harbour. The city is an important inland port and centre for trade and industry. The surrounding region is good farming country.

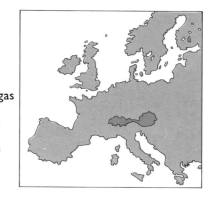

▼ The State Opera House in Vienna is one of the city's famous historic buildings.
Austria's capital has attracted artists and musicians for many years. The composers Brahms and Mahler worked here. Johann Strauss made the city famous with his series of Viennese waltzes which are still popular today.

Making a cheese fondue
This is a very popular Swiss meal. Rub garlic around a ceramic dish and put it over a spirit burner with a low flame. Now mix 1lb (500g) grated Gruyère cheese and two glasses of wine in the dish. Stir it all gently until it melts. This makes enough fondue for four people. Eat it by dipping chunks of bread on long forks into the cheese.

Italy

Italy is a long and narrow peninsula that juts into the Mediterranean Sea. In the north it has borders with France, Switzerland, Austria and Yugoslavia. Italy is shaped rather like a large riding boot. In the south-west the Strait of Messina, which is only 2 miles (3.2 km) wide, separates the island of Sicily from the mainland. Although it is like a triangle in shape, Sicily is sometimes described as a 'football' about to be kicked by the Italian 'boot'. Sicily is the largest island in the Mediterranean.

In the north of Italy are the Alps and south of these mountains is the Po river valley. This is a very large lowland with rich soil. Almost half the population of Italy live in the Po valley. South of the valley, the Apennine Mountains stretch down Italy from north to south. Southern Italy has a number of volcanoes and suffers from earthquakes. Mount Etna is a volcano in Sicily which is 10,958 feet (3,340 metres) high. Another famous Italian volcano is Mount Vesuvius near Naples which is 4,000 feet (1,219 metres) high.

Most of the Italian industry and farming is done in the north of the country. Rice, tomatoes, sugar beet and wheat (which is used for making pasta) are all grown in the Po valley. The dairy industry is also important and the Italians make many cheeses including Gorgonzola. Turin is the centre of Italy's motor-car industry and Milan is the country's main business centre.

Tourism is an important Italian industry. Tourists visit the many historic cities such as Venice, Florence and the capital, Rome.

Facts and Figures

Flag	Language Italian
Area 116,318 sq miles (301,263 sq km)	
Population 56,828,500	
Currency Lira	Capital Rome

▲ Italy is divided into 20 regions which are divided into another 94 provinces. San Marino and Vatican City are independent small states.

▲ Saint Mark's church in Venice was built in the ninth century as a shrine for the bones of Saint Mark.

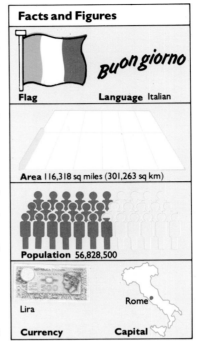

▼ Cars are a major export for Italy, and also a major source of employment for many people. The Fiat company is one of the oldest car manufacturers in Italy.

◀ The city of Venice is built on a marshland beside the Adriatic Sea. Many waterways and canals run through the city and are used for transportation instead of roads. A gondola is a boat which is used on the canals to carry people and goods from place to place.

Cooking spaghetti

Spaghetti is very popular in Italy. To cook it first bring salted cold water to the boil. To keep the spaghetti from breaking, don't drop it in all at once, but lower it slowly into the boiling water. Eating spaghetti can be messy unless you eat it the way the Italians do. Grab a bunch of spaghetti with a fork and then roll it around the fork, using a spoon as a support. With some luck, the spaghetti will stay on the fork until it reaches your mouth!

▲ The bakery shops of Milan are often filled with these special cakes with names written on them.

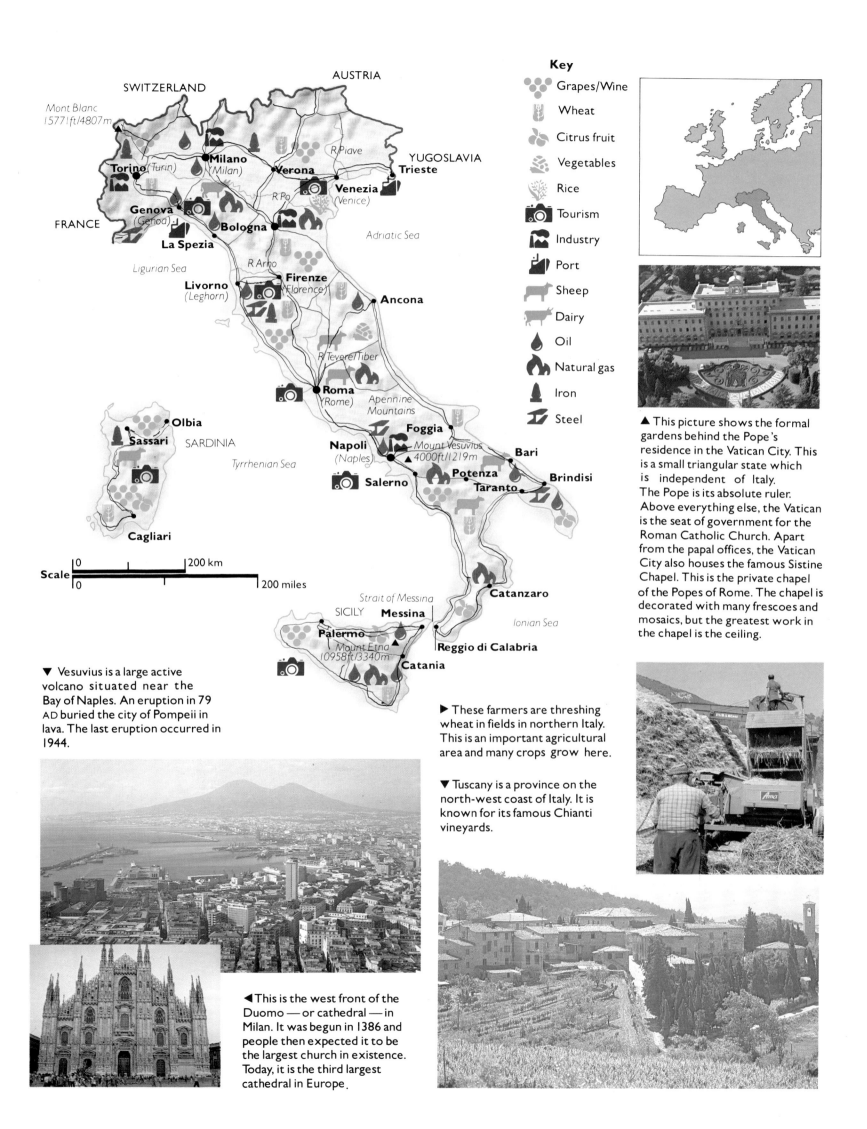

Key

- Grapes/Wine
- Wheat
- Citrus fruit
- Vegetables
- Rice
- Tourism
- Industry
- Port
- Sheep
- Dairy
- Oil
- Natural gas
- Iron
- Steel

SWITZERLAND

AUSTRIA

Mont Blanc 15771ft/4807m

Torino (Turin)

Milano (Milan)

Verona

R.Piave

YUGOSLAVIA

Trieste

Venezia (Venice)

R.Po

FRANCE

Genova (Genoa)

Bologna

La Spezia

Adriatic Sea

Ligurian Sea

R.Arno

Firenze (Florence)

Livorno (Leghorn)

Ancona

R.Tevere/Tiber

Roma (Rome)

Apennine Mountains

Olbia

Sassari

SARDINIA

Tyrrhenian Sea

Foggia

Napoli (Naples)

Mount Vesuvius 4000ft/1219m

Bari

Potenza

Brindisi

Salerno

Taranto

Cagliari

Scale 0 — 200 km

0 — 200 miles

Catanzaro

Strait of Messina

SICILY

Messina

Ionian Sea

Palermo

Mount Etna 10958ft/3340m

Reggio di Calabria

Catania

▲ This picture shows the formal gardens behind the Pope's residence in the Vatican City. This is a small triangular state which is independent of Italy. The Pope is its absolute ruler. Above everything else, the Vatican is the seat of government for the Roman Catholic Church. Apart from the papal offices, the Vatican City also houses the famous Sistine Chapel. This is the private chapel of the Popes of Rome. The chapel is decorated with many frescoes and mosaics, but the greatest work in the chapel is the ceiling.

▼ Vesuvius is a large active volcano situated near the Bay of Naples. An eruption in 79 AD buried the city of Pompeii in lava. The last eruption occurred in 1944.

▶ These farmers are threshing wheat in fields in northern Italy. This is an important agricultural area and many crops grow here.

▼ Tuscany is a province on the north-west coast of Italy. It is known for its famous Chianti vineyards.

◀ This is the west front of the Duomo — or cathedral — in Milan. It was begun in 1386 and people then expected it to be the largest church in existence. Today, it is the third largest cathedral in Europe.

Spain and Portugal

The south-western peninsula of Europe is called the Iberian Peninsula. The main countries here are Spain and Portugal, but there are also the small areas of Gibraltar in the south and Andorra in the eastern Pyrenees.

The Pyrenees form the border with France in the north-east. This mountain range makes communications difficult and many of the passes are snow-bound in winter. The peninsula is also bounded by the Atlantic in the north and west and the Mediterranean in the south and east. Punta Marroqui, the most southerly point of Europe, is only 6 miles (10 km) from the coast of Africa.

Spain is the third largest country in Europe. In its centre is a dry upland area called the Meseta. This reaches an average height of 2,000 feet (610 metres) and is very hot in summer and cold in winter. The highest mountain in Spain is in the Sierra Nevada and is 11,421 feet (3,480 metres) high.

Spain is an agricultural country. It produces wine, sherry, oranges and other fruit. The country has always been split into regions which each have their own capitals. Barcelona, the second largest city, is the capital of Catalonia. The capital of the Basque region in the north is Bilbao. Many of the regions also have their own language or dialect. For example, Catalan is spoken in Catalonia and Basque in the Basque region.

Madrid is the largest city in Spain and its capital. It is in the centre of the country and is also the centre of all the main roads and railways.

Portugal borders on the Atlantic in the west. Shipping and tourism have always been important. Portugal, like Spain, is also agricultural. Its products include cork and wine. Port, a type of strong wine, is produced around the city of Porto which is the second largest city in Portugal. Lisbon is the largest city and the country's capital. The southern region is called the Algarve. It is an important tourist area.

Facts and Figures

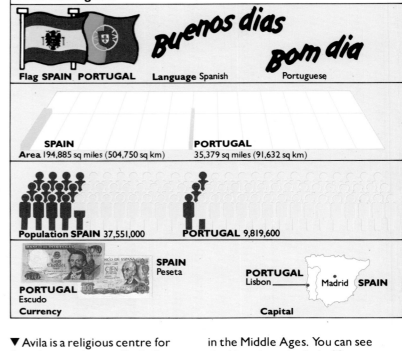

| Flag SPAIN PORTUGAL | Language Spanish | Portuguese |

Buenos dias **Bom dia**

| SPAIN | PORTUGAL |
| Area 194,885 sq miles (504,750 sq km) | 35,379 sq miles (91,632 sq km) |

Population SPAIN 37,551,000   PORTUGAL 9,819,600

SPAIN Peseta	PORTUGAL Lisbon — Madrid SPAIN
PORTUGAL Escudo	
Currency	Capital

▼ Avila is a religious centre for Spain's many devout Catholics. The city's fortified walls were built in the Middle Ages. You can see the historic cathedral of San Salvador in the background.

► The Sierra Nevada is a mountain range near Spain's Mediterranean coast. There are olive groves on its southern slopes.

▼ Dancers perform the flamenco. This Spanish dance involves clapping and stamping of feet.

► Benidorm is a popular tourist resort on Spain's Mediterranean Costa Blanca (the White Coast). The towering modern hotels take holidaymakers from all over Europe.

◄ Citrus fruits such as lemons and oranges grow in groves in southern Spain. They need plenty of sunshine and well-drained soil.

▼ Cork comes from the bark of cork trees like this one in Portugal. Cork is waterproof. Air trapped inside allows it to float.

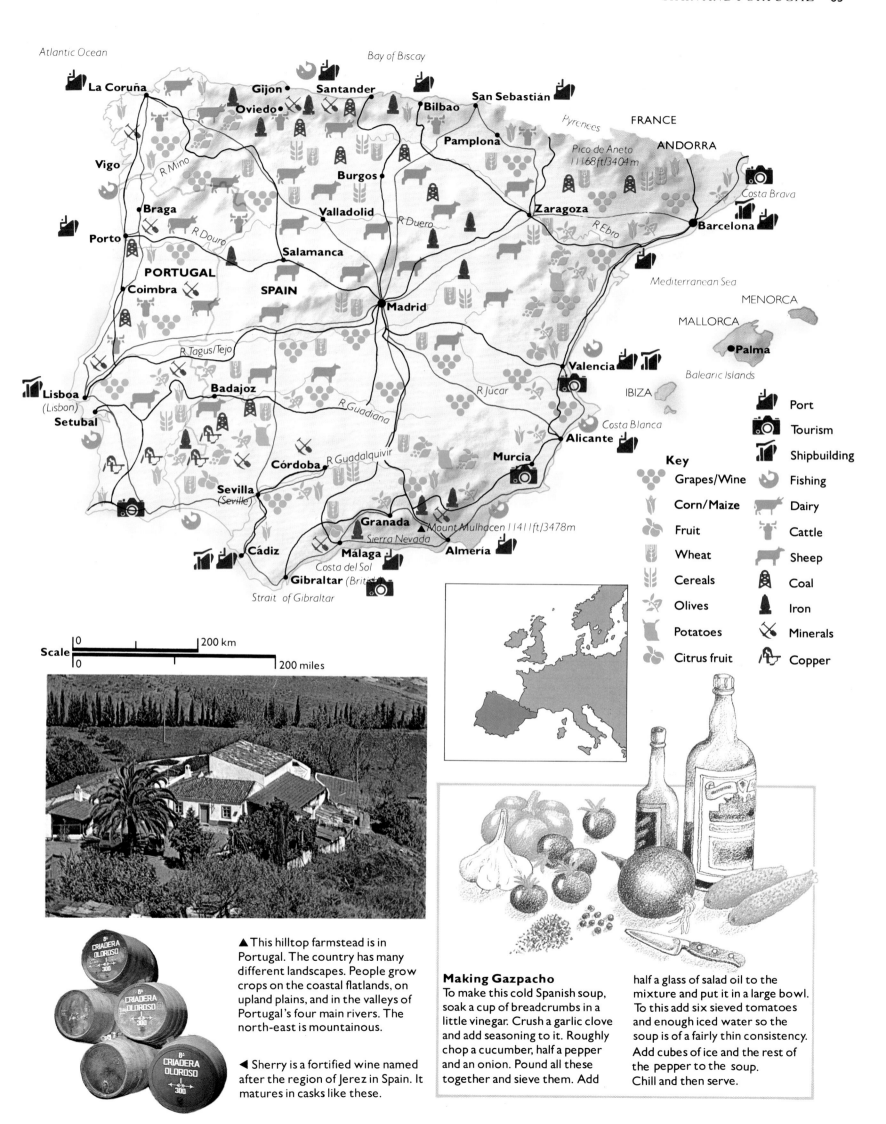

Atlantic Ocean

Bay of Biscay

La Coruña

Gijon • • Santander

Oviedo •

Bilbao

San Sebastián

Pyrenees FRANCE

Vigo

R Miño

Pamplona

ANDORRA

Pico de Aneto 11168ft/3404 m

Burgos

Braga

Valladolid

R Duero

Zaragoza

R Ebro

Costa Brava

Porto

R Douro

Barcelona

Salamanca

PORTUGAL

Coimbra

SPAIN

Madrid

Mediterranean Sea

MENORCA

MALLORCA

Palma

R Tagus/Tejo

Balearic Islands

Lisboa
(Lisbon)

Badajoz

Valencia

Setubal

R Guadiana

IBIZA

R Jucar

Costa Blanca

Alicante

Córdoba

R Guadalquivir

Murcia

Sevilla
(Seville)

Granada

▲ *Mount Mulhacen 11411ft/3478m*

Sierra Nevada

Cádiz

Málaga

Almería

Costa del Sol

Gibraltar (Brit...

Strait of Gibraltar

Key		
🍇 Grapes/Wine		🏭 Port
🌽 Corn/Maize		📷 Tourism
🍒 Fruit		🚢 Shipbuilding
🌾 Wheat		🐟 Fishing
🌾 Cereals		🐄 Dairy
🌿 Olives		🐂 Cattle
🥔 Potatoes		🐑 Sheep
🍊 Citrus fruit		⛏ Coal
		⚒ Iron
		✕ Minerals
		Copper

Scale

0 ————— 200 km

0 ————— 200 miles

▲ This hilltop farmstead is in Portugal. The country has many different landscapes. People grow crops on the coastal flatlands, on upland plains, and in the valleys of Portugal's four main rivers. The north-east is mountainous.

◀ Sherry is a fortified wine named after the region of Jerez in Spain. It matures in casks like these.

CRIADERA OLOROSO 300

Making Gazpacho

To make this cold Spanish soup, soak a cup of breadcrumbs in a little vinegar. Crush a garlic clove and add seasoning to it. Roughly chop a cucumber, half a pepper and an onion. Pound all these together and sieve them. Add half a glass of salad oil to the mixture and put it in a large bowl. To this add six sieved tomatoes and enough iced water so the soup is of a fairly thin consistency. Add cubes of ice and the rest of the pepper to the soup. Chill and then serve.

Eastern Europe

Poland, East Germany, Czechoslovakia and Hungary are all in the east of Europe. The largest of these countries is Poland. In the north of Poland is a low plain. This rises to a plateau in the south where the Carthusian and Sudeten mountains form a border with Czechoslovakia. The main crop grown in Poland is rye. Potatoes, sugar beet, vegetables, milk and cheese are also produced. Poland has many coal and metal mines and large chemical and textile industries. The capital of Poland is Warsaw which stands on the River Vistula.

The Oder and Neisse rivers separate Poland from East Germany. This is another low-lying country. The land is higher in the south-east where the border with Czechoslovakia follows the Ore Mountains. In the west and south-west there is a boundary between East and West Germany. Most of East Germany's industries, which are based on chemicals and steel, are in the south. Some industrial goods are also made in the city of Dresden in the south-east. Leipzig is East Germany's largest city after Berlin, the capital.

Czechoslovakia is a long country of mountains, basins and valleys. It takes its name from the Czechs and the Slovaks who are the people who live there. Czechoslovakia is mainly a farming country but it also has many minerals such as coal, iron and copper. The timber, glass and porcelain industries are important as well. Prague, the capital, stands on the Vltava river. The country's other main centres are Brno, its second largest city, Bratislava the old capital of Slovakia, and Ostrava, an important industrial town. Pilsen is famous as it is the place where lager beer was first brewed.

Hungary is a lowland country and, like Czechoslovakia, away from the sea. Its main rivers are the Danube and the Tisza. The lowlands produce good crops of grain, sugar beet, vegetables, tobacco and fruits. Hungary is a farming country but it also has a mining industry. The capital is Budapest, which is really two cities linked by a number of bridges. Buda, on the west bank of the Danube, is the old fortress town, and Pest, on the other bank, is the newer city.

▼The spires of St Vitus' Cathedral tower above the Hradcany Palace in Prague. The historic city is famous for its architecture, but Prague is also a bustling modern capital with over one million inhabitants. The bridge links the old city with the industrial centre over the Vltava river.

▶A world clock stands in East Berlin's Alexanderplatz. It shows the time in the main places in the world. Berlin is the capital of the German Democratic Republic – or East Germany.

▼The mountainous borderlands of Czechoslovakia are sparsely populated. The church plays an important part in the daily life of the village people.

Facts and Figures

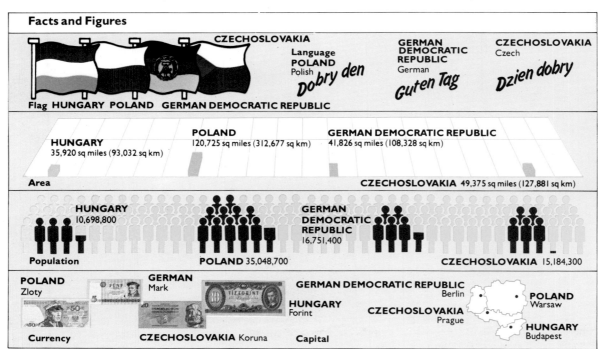

	CZECHOSLOVAKIA	GERMAN DEMOCRATIC REPUBLIC	CZECHOSLOVAKIA
	Language POLAND Polish *Dobry den*	German *Guten Tag*	Czech *Dzien dobry*

Flag **HUNGARY POLAND GERMAN DEMOCRATIC REPUBLIC**

HUNGARY 35,920 sq miles (93,032 sq km)	POLAND 120,725 sq miles (312,677 sq km)	GERMAN DEMOCRATIC REPUBLIC 41,826 sq miles (108,328 sq km)

Area   CZECHOSLOVAKIA 49,375 sq miles (127,881 sq km)

HUNGARY 10,698,800   GERMAN DEMOCRATIC REPUBLIC 16,751,400

Population   POLAND 35,048,700   CZECHOSLOVAKIA 15,184,300

POLAND Zloty	GERMAN Mark	GERMAN DEMOCRATIC REPUBLIC Berlin	POLAND Warsaw
		HUNGARY Forint CZECHOSLOVAKIA Prague	HUNGARY Budapest

Currency   CZECHOSLOVAKIA Koruna   **Capital**

▲Farm workers operate a threshing machine in Poland. Rye and wheat are the country's main cereal crops. Poland lies on a low plain between the much larger country of the Soviet Union and East Germany. It is mainly an agricultural country but there is shipbuilding at Gdansk and coal mining in the south.

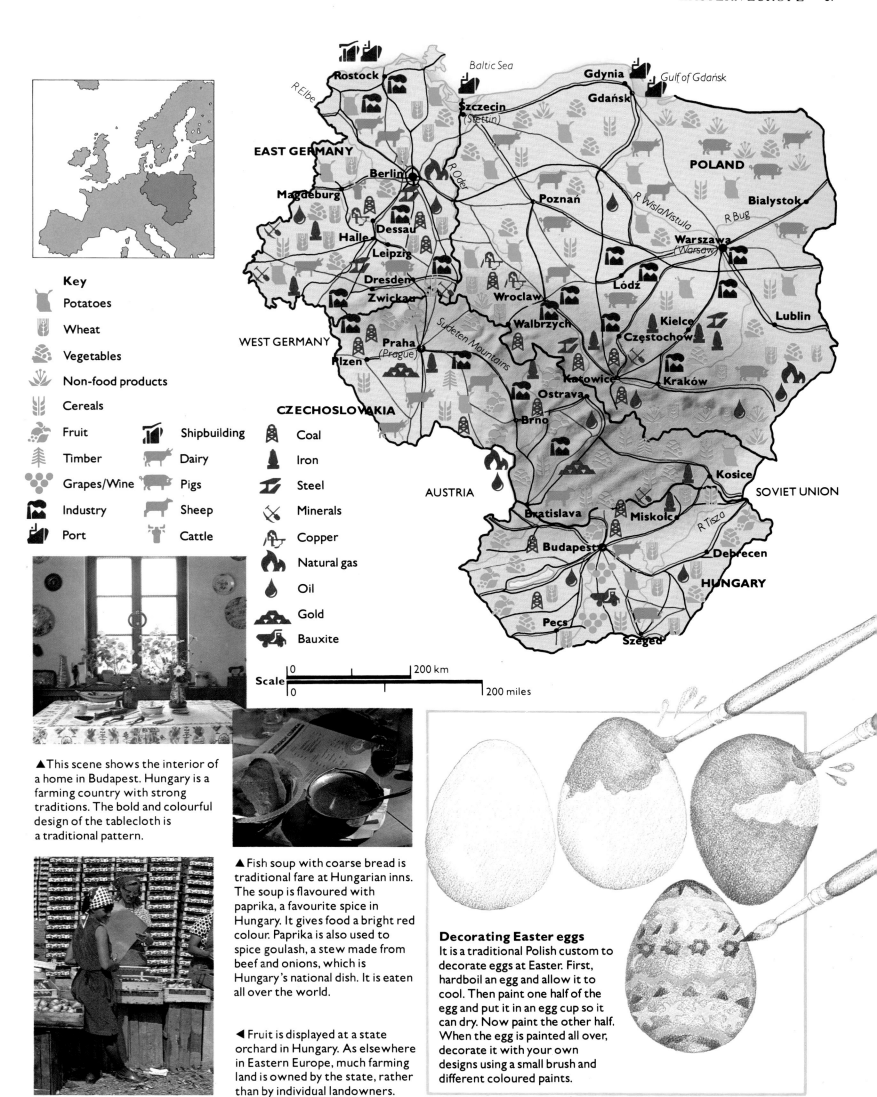

Key

Potatoes
Wheat
Vegetables
Non-food products
Cereals
Fruit
Timber
Grapes/Wine
Industry
Port

Shipbuilding
Dairy
Pigs
Sheep
Cattle

Coal
Iron
Steel
Minerals
Copper
Natural gas
Oil
Gold
Bauxite

Scale 0 ___ 200 km
0 ___ 200 miles

EAST GERMANY
WEST GERMANY
CZECHOSLOVAKIA
AUSTRIA
POLAND
HUNGARY
SOVIET UNION

Baltic Sea
Gulf of Gdańsk
Rostock
Szczecin (Stettin)
Gdynia
Gdańsk
Berlin
Magdeburg
Poznań
Bialystok
Halle
Dessau
Leipzig
Warszawa (Warsaw)
Dresden
Łódź
Zwickau
Wrocław
Lublin
Praha (Prague)
Wałbrzych
Kielce
Plzen
Częstochow
Katowice
Kraków
Ostrava
Brno
Kosice
Bratislava
Miskolc
Budapest
Debrecen
Pecs
Szeged
R Elbe
R Oder
R Wisla/Nistula
R Bug
Sudeten Mountains
R Tisza

▲This scene shows the interior of a home in Budapest. Hungary is a farming country with strong traditions. The bold and colourful design of the tablecloth is a traditional pattern.

▲Fish soup with coarse bread is traditional fare at Hungarian inns. The soup is flavoured with paprika, a favourite spice in Hungary. It gives food a bright red colour. Paprika is also used to spice goulash, a stew made from beef and onions, which is Hungary's national dish. It is eaten all over the world.

◀ Fruit is displayed at a state orchard in Hungary. As elsewhere in Eastern Europe, much farming land is owned by the state, rather than by individual landowners.

Decorating Easter eggs
It is a traditional Polish custom to decorate eggs at Easter. First, hardboil an egg and allow it to cool. Then paint one half of the egg and put it in an egg cup so it can dry. Now paint the other half. When the egg is painted all over, decorate it with your own designs using a small brush and different coloured paints.

The Balkans

The Balkans is a name for the countries of Rumania, Bulgaria, Yugoslavia, Greece, Albania and the European part of Turkey. The area is very mountainous. The word 'Balkan' comes from the Turkish for mountain and the area is named after the Balkan Mountains which cross Bulgaria from east to west. Other Balkan mountain ranges are the Rhodope in Bulgaria, the Pindus in Greece, the Dinaric Alps in Yugoslavia and the Carpathian and Transylvanian Alps in Rumania.

The Danube is the area's major river and many of the Balkan cities stand on the Danube or its tributaries. Belgrade, the capital of Yugoslavia, is on the Danube and the capital of Bulgaria, Sofia, is close to one of its many tributaries, the Iskâr. Bucharest, the capital of Rumania, is situated in the Wallachia Plain which is partly formed by the Danube valley.

Many of the mountains are made of limestone. In Greece the mountains continue into the Aegean Sea as lines of islands which are like stepping stones across the sea to Turkey. Crete is the largest of the many Greek islands and the fourth largest in the Mediterranean.

Athens is the capital of Greece. Its port on the Aegean is called Piraeus. Shipping and tourism are major industries. Currants and tobacco are important Greek crops. Greece also produces wine. One of the most famous types of Greek wine is called retsina.

Yugoslavia means 'south Slavia' and is a union of the southern Slavic peoples – the Serbs, Croats, Slovenes and Macedonians. It is the largest of the Balkan countries and is mainly agricultural. However, in the last 30 years industry has developed a lot. Many of Yugoslavia's cities have grown in size. The main cities are Belgrade, the capital, Zagreb, and Ljubljana.

Both Rumania and Bulgaria have coasts on the Black Sea. They grow maize, wheat and tobacco. Albania is the smallest and poorest Balkan country. Its capital is Tirana.

Throughout the Balkans the main types of livestock are sheep, goats and poultry. The donkey is still a very important means of transport for both people and all types of farm products and crops.

◄The Rhodope Mountains in the south of Bulgaria form the border with Greece. Woodworking and the wool and textile industries are the main occupations. Here a local folk music group are playing the bagpipes.

►A shepherd brings his flock through the Rugovska Kusora gorge in Yugoslavia. These mountains form the border between Yugoslavia and Albania. They are the highest part of the Dinaric Alps. There are caves, canyons, gorges and lakes throughout the mountains here.

▲ Sheep farming is important in Rumania. Women wash raw wool in a stream before using it to make clothes.

◄Rumania's main crops are wheat, maize, sugar beet, barley, sunflower seeds and tobacco. Much wine is also produced.

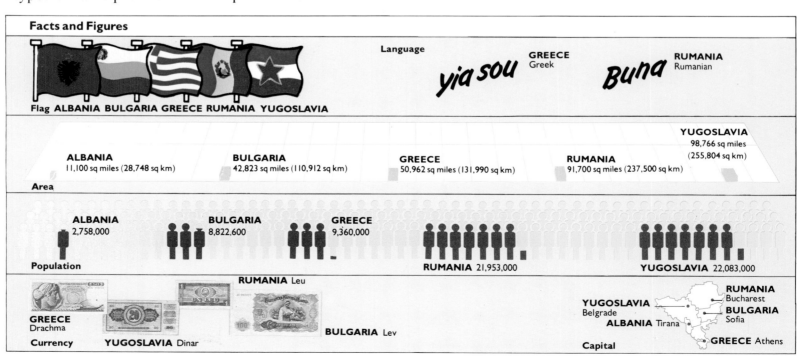

Facts and Figures

Language

yia sou GREECE Greek

Buna RUMANIA Rumanian

Flag ALBANIA BULGARIA GREECE RUMANIA YUGOSLAVIA

Area

ALBANIA 11,100 sq miles (28,748 sq km)	BULGARIA 42,823 sq miles (110,912 sq km)	GREECE 50,962 sq miles (131,990 sq km)	RUMANIA 91,700 sq miles (237,500 sq km)	YUGOSLAVIA 98,766 sq miles (255,804 sq km)

Population

ALBANIA 2,758,000 BULGARIA 8,822,600 GREECE 9,360,000 RUMANIA 21,953,000 YUGOSLAVIA 22,083,000

Currency

GREECE Drachma YUGOSLAVIA Dinar RUMANIA Leu BULGARIA Lev

Capital

YUGOSLAVIA Belgrade ALBANIA Tirana RUMANIA Bucharest BULGARIA Sofia GREECE Athens

▲ Greece has many olive groves and is the third largest producer in the world of olive oil. It produces over 150,000 metric tons each year and exports most of it.

▶ Sikinos is an island in the Aegean Sea. The steep hillsides are farmed in steps. Only one quarter of Greek land is fertile.

▶ The Acropolis is a rocky hill in the centre of Athens, Greece. It is the site of the ancient part of Athens. Today, Athens is a modern industrial city with a population of over 2.5 million. It is the capital of Greece.

▲ This busy street is in the town of Berat, in central Albania. It is a mountainous country with only 2.5 million people, but it has the fastest growing population in Europe.

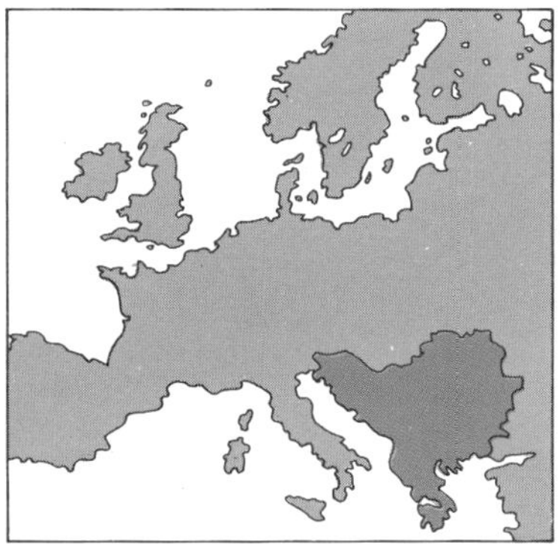

AUSTRIA
HUNGARY
SOVIET UNION
RUMANIA
YUGOSLAVIA
BULGARIA
ALBANIA
GREECE
TURKEY
Ljubljana
Zagreb
Rijeka
Oradea
Cluj
Braşov
Ploieşti
Bucureşti
(Bucharest)
Constanţa
Craiova
Ruse
Varna
Burgas
Beograd
(Belgrade)
Sarajevo
Split
Dubrovnik
Skopje
Nis
Sofija
(Sofia)
Plovdiv
Tiranë
Thessaloniki
Mount Olympos 9570ft/2917m
Tríkkala
Pátrai
Athinai
(Athens)
Piraievs
(Piraeus)
Mitilini
Iráklion
R Siret
R Mures
R Donau/Danube
R Sava
Transylvanian Alps
Dinaric Alps
R Iskar
R Marica
Rhodope Mountains
R Vardar
R Struma
Adriatic Sea
KERKYRA/CORFU
Ionian Sea
LESVOS/LESBOS
Aegean Sea
DODECANESE
CYCLADES
Mediterranean Sea
RODHOS/RHODES
KRITI/CRETE

◀ Dubrovnik is an important Yugoslavian port and tourist resort. It is a beautiful city with many medieval buildings.

◀ Tobacco is grown in southern Yugoslavia. The tobacco leaves are hung out to dry after being harvested.

Key

Corn/Maize	Olives	Port	Minerals
Cotton	Fruit	Cattle	Oil
Potatoes	Tobacco	Sheep	Iron
Vegetables	Citrus fruit	Pigs	Bauxite
Wheat	Grapes/Wine	Dairy	Copper
Timber	Industry	Goats	Coal
Rice	Tourism	Fishing	Gold
			Natural gas

Scale 0 — 200 km; 0 — 200 miles

Looking at Asia

Asia is the largest continent in the world. The whole of the smallest continent, Australia, would fit into Asia six times. More people live in Asia than in any other continent. Over 2,000 million people live there. Most of them live in China, India, Malaysia, Indonesia and Japan. Very few people live in Mongolia, Siberia and the deserts of south-west Asia. The continent stretches from the Arctic Ocean in the north to the Indian Ocean in the south and from the Ural Mountains in the west to the Pacific Ocean in the east.

In the south of Asia there are several large peninsulas. A peninsula is like a finger of land which juts out into the sea. Malaya is a long narrow peninsula and India a larger, wider one. In central Asia there are the high mountains of the Himalayas. Mount Everest in the Himalayas is the highest mountain in the world. It is 29,028 feet (8,848 metres) high and stands on the borders between Nepal and Tibet, which is part of China.

North of the Himalayas are large upland areas called plateaus. Many of these are deserts like the Gobi Desert in Mongolia. Further north still are the steppes of Siberia. These are huge flat areas with few trees. Asia also includes important island groups such as Japan, the Philippines and Indonesia.

The longest river in Asia is the Yangtse Kiang. It flows for 3,200 miles (5,120 km) from the centre of China to the Pacific Ocean.

▶ It is easiest to think of Asia as five separate subcontinents— south-west Asia, the Soviet Union, China, the Indian subcontinent and south-east Asia.

There are immense differences in climate and landscape from the tropical Pacific islands to Arctic Siberia; from the sands of Arabia to industrial Japan.

Communications have always been limited by the great natural barriers.

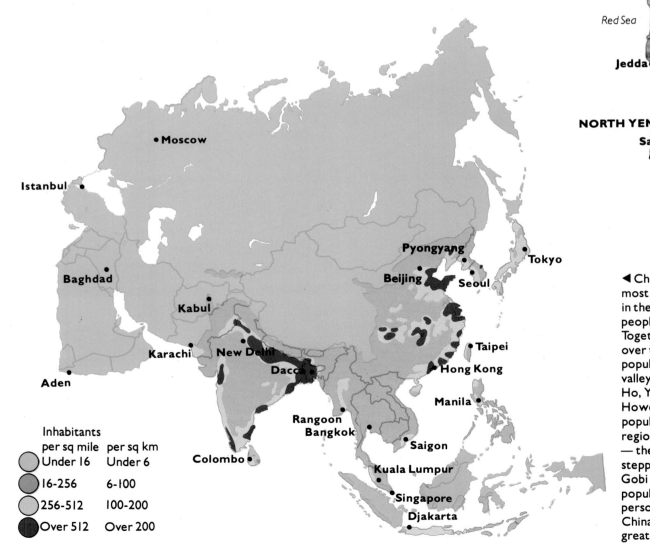

Inhabitants
per sq mile / per sq km
Under 16 / Under 6
16-256 / 6-100
256-512 / 100-200
Over 512 / Over 200

◀ China and India are the two most heavily populated countries in the world. China has 960 million people and India 638 million. Together, their people make up over three quarters of Asia's total population. Many live in the fertile valleys of the great rivers Huang Ho, Yangtse Kiang and Ganges. However, much of Asia is sparsely populated, and there are vast regions which are almost deserted — the Himalaya Mountains, the steppes of Siberia, the Arabian and Gobi Deserts. Mongolia's population averages less than one person per square mile/kilometre. China's average is 100 times greater than this.

Key

Rice
Citrus fruit
Fruit
Tea
Wheat
Corn/Maize
Groundnuts
Cereals
Coffee
Bananas
Cotton
Sugar cane
Industry
Cattle
Fishing
Sheep
Pigs
Oil
Minerals
Iron
Coal
Natural gas
Gold
Bauxite

Arctic Ocean

East Siberian Sea

Laptev Sea

Bering Sea

Kara Sea

Gulf of Ob

UNION OF SOVIET SOCIALIST REPUBLICS

R Lower Tunguska

R Lena

Sea of Okhotsk

Gorky

Perm'

Svedlovsk

R Ob

Ural Mountains

R Yenisey

R Angara

Omsk

R Irtys

Aral Sea

Tashkent

Ulan Bator

MONGOLIA

Gobi Desert

Vladivostok

JAPAN

Sea of Japan

Mukden

NORTH KOREA

Pyongyang

Beijing

Tientsin

Seoul

SOUTH KOREA

Tokyo

Osaka

Hiroshima

Yellow Sea

AFGHANISTAN

Kabul

Islamabad

Lahore

PAKISTAN

Karachi

CHINA

R Hwang Ho

Chengtu

Chungking

Nanking

Shanghai

East China Sea

Himalayas

NEPAL

Katmandu

New Delhi

Lucknow

Varanasi

SIKKIM

BHUTAN

R Ganges

BANGLADESH

Dacca

Calcutta

Chittagong

R Irrawaddy

Mandalay

BURMA

LAOS

Vientiane

Hanoi

Taipei

TAIWAN

Canton

Hong Kong

Macau

R Yangtse

R Mekong

Bombay

INDIA

Hyderabad

R Krishna

Bangalore

Madras

Western Ghats

Bay of Bengal

Rangoon

THAILAND

Bangkok

KAMPUCHEA

Phnom Penh

Ho Chi Minh City

Gulf of Siam

VIETNAM

South China Sea

Manila

PHILIPPINES

Pacific Ocean

SRI LANKA

Colombo

Indian Ocean

Penang

Strait of Malacca

Kuala Lumpur

SINGAPORE

BORNEO

MALAYSIA

BRUNEI

Java Sea

INDONESIA

Djakarta

Timor Sea

Scale

0

1000 miles

0

1000 km

Soviet Union

The Union of Soviet Socialist Republics is the largest country in the world. It covers one eighth of the world's total land surface. It has a large population; only China and India have more inhabitants. The country is often called Russia, but Russia is in fact only one of the 15 republics which make up the Union of Soviet Socialist Republics or Soviet Union. An important part of the Soviet Union is in Europe, but most of the country is in northern Asia.

In Europe, the Soviet Union has borders with Norway, Finland, Poland, Czechoslovakia, Hungary and Rumania. In Asia it borders on Turkey, Iran, Afghanistan, China and Mongolia. The country extends west from Poland to the Pacific Ocean where Vladivostock is a major port.

Much of the Soviet Union has a very cold climate, especially in Siberia which is in the north and east. Siberia is three times larger than Europe. In the south the Soviet Union has a hot climate where it borders on the deserts of central Asia.

The Soviet Union is an industrial country, but farming, mining and forestry are also important. Wheat and sugar beet are two main crops. Oil, timber and iron ore are among the country's chief resources.

Most of the country's population lives in a triangular area linking the cities of Leningrad, Odessa and Sverdlovsk. Moscow is in the middle of this area.

Facts and Figures

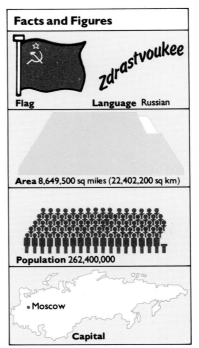

Flag

Language Russian

Zdrastvoukee

Area 8,649,500 sq miles (22,402,200 sq km)

Population 262,400,000

● Moscow

Capital

▲ The Soviet Union is made up of 15 separate socialist republics. Russia is the largest republic. Armenia is the smallest.

▶ St Basil's Cathedral stands in Red Square, Moscow. The Kremlin, the Soviet seat of government, is nearby. Moscow has nearly 8 million people and is one of the biggest cities in the world.

▶ Lake Baikal in Siberia is frozen from November to May. Cars can cross the ice, which is 2.5 feet (70 cm) thick. It is about 5,000 feet (1,524 metres) deep, so it is the deepest freshwater lake in the world.

▼ Children from a village near the lake build a snow fortress.

Key

Timber	
Wheat	Port
Cereals	Industry
Potatoes	Reindeer
Rice	Sheep
Fruit	Cattle
Cotton	Dairy
Vegetables	Fishing

Arctic Ocean

FINLAND

NOVA ZEMLYA

Kara Sea

Baltic Sea

Tallinn

Leningrad

Archangel'sk

Gora Narodnaja 6214ft/1894m ▲

POLAND

Minsk

Kijev (Kiev)

Moskva (Moscow)

Gor'kij (Gorky)

Ural Mountains

R.Ob'

RUMANIA

R.Dnepr

R.Volga

Kujbysev

Sverdlovsk

R.Irtys

Odessa

Rostov-na-Donu

Volgograd (Stalingrad)

Omsk

Novosibirsk

Black Sea

Mount Elbrus 18481ft/5663m ● Astrachen'

Caucasus

Caspian Sea

Aral Sea

TURKEY

Baku

IRAN

Taskent

Alma-Ata

CHINA

AFGHANISTAN

Scale | 0 | 200 km | 0 | 200 miles

▲ These are traditional wooden dolls from Russia. They are painted in bright colours to show Russian national costume. Each one is hollow, so that a smaller one will fit inside.

▶ Sport is an important part of life in the Soviet Union. Children may specialize in sports from an early age, and gymnastics are especially popular. Yelena Davydova is an Olympic gold medallist. She is seen here performing at the 1980 Olympics which were held in Moscow.

АБВГДЕЖЗИКЛП

МНОПРСТ УФХЦЧ

ШЪЫ Э ЮЯ

You can see from the alphabet written out above that Russian letters are very different to your own. However, the date on the stamp – issued to celebrate a space mission – shows that the same numbers are used in the Soviet Union as in your country.

▶The Soviet Union exports iron, steel and machinery. This factory is producing tractors for the Russian market.

▼ Kiev, the capital of the Ukraine, is an important industrial centre. It produces cameras, aeroplanes and fibres.

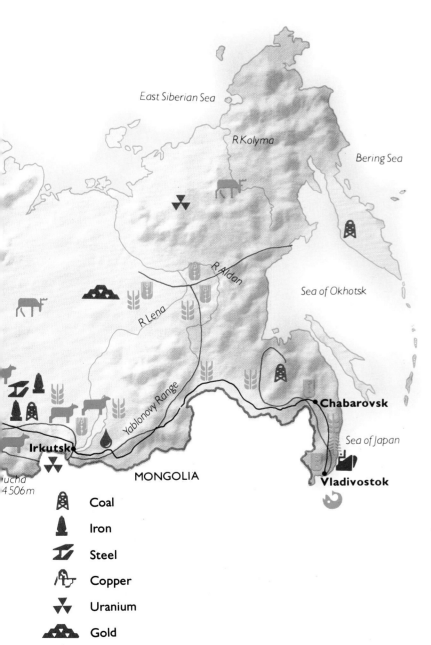

East Siberian Sea

R Kolyma

Bering Sea

R Aldan

R Lena

Sea of Okhotsk

Yablonovy Range

Chabarovsk

Sea of Japan

Irkutsk

ucha
4 506 m

MONGOLIA

Vladivostok

🛢 Coal

🔺 Iron

⚡ Steel

♻ Copper

☢ Uranium

⛰ Gold

🛢 Oil

▲ Tashkent, the capital of Uzbekistan, is one of the oldest cities in central Asia. The town has many houses of historic interest. It also has many modern buildings now and is a scientific and industrial centre. It is sometimes called the city of white gold because cotton is the main crop in Uzbekistan. Tashkent has a population of 1.5 million and is the fourth largest city in the USSR.

South-west Asia

The countries in south-west Asia are Afghanistan, Iran, Turkey, Iraq, Syria, Jordan, Lebanon, Israel, Saudi Arabia, Kuwait and the countries of southern Arabia. The seas around this area are the Arabian Gulf, Red Sea and the Gulf of Aden in the south. In the north is the Caspian Sea which is an inland sea. Here too is the Black Sea which is joined to the Mediterranean Sea by the Dardanelles and the Bosporus. The large Turkish city of Istanbul is on the Bosporus and a bridge across the Bosporus links Europe and Asia.

The Suez Canal connects the Mediterranean with the Red Sea. This is an artificial waterway which was opened in 1869. It is important because the only other way ships can travel from the east to Europe is around the southern tip of Africa which is called the Cape of Good Hope.

Much of south-west Asia is desert country and has a hot climate. There are many high mountains, especially in Turkey, Iran and Afghanistan. Water is scarce and many of the rivers run dry. The main rivers are the Tigris and Euphrates. They flow from the high mountains in eastern Turkey through Syria and Iraq to the Arabian Gulf which lies between Saudi Arabia and Iran.

Farming is a major activity, but water is always needed and so oases are important. There are many sheep, goat and camel herders in south-west Asia. This area is one of the world's main producers of oil. Saudi Arabia, Iraq, Iran and Kuwait are the most important countries for this. The oil flows by pipeline to the ports and tankers on the coasts of the Mediterranean and the Gulf.

Saudi Arabia is the centre of the religion called Islam. People who believe in Islam are called Moslems. Mecca is an important place for Moslem pilgrims. The main language in south-west Asia is Arabic. Israel has a different religion and language. Most of the people are Jewish and speak Hebrew. Farsi is spoken in Iran.

The island of Cyprus is also part of south-west Asia. The population is made up of both Greeks and Turks. The capital is Nicosia and Famagusta is an important port. The country's main export is citrus fruit.

◀ The mosque of Sultan Ahmed I is one of several beautiful temples in Istanbul. A mosque is a temple where Moslems gather to pray. They kneel in the direction of Mecca, birthplace of the prophet Mohammed. The towers at the side are called minarets.

▼ Cotton pickers gather their crop in Turkey. The raw cotton grows as a downy fibre around the seed-head. The fibre is twisted and woven to form cloth. The hulls of the seeds are used in fertilizers. Cardboard can be made out of part of the stalks.

▼ An oil rig rises above the desert landscape of Abu Dhabi. Abu Dhabi is one of the main Arab states on the Persian Gulf. Oil was first discovered in Abu Dhabi in 1960. All of the states are hot, barren lands. Oil now brings them great wealth and power. They have few other products.

Facts and Figures

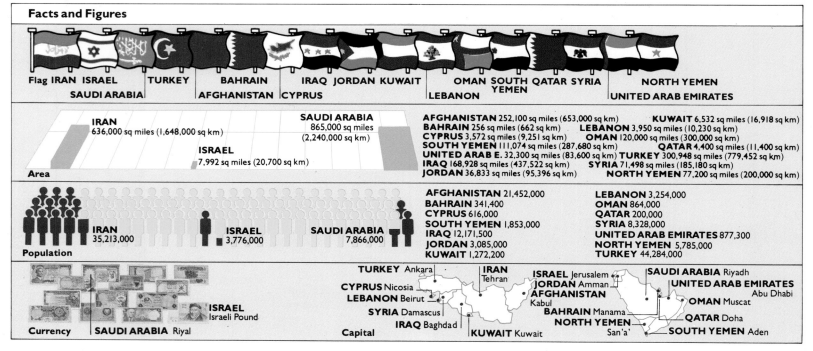

Flag	IRAN	ISRAEL		TURKEY		BAHRAIN		IRAQ	JORDAN	KUWAIT		OMAN	SOUTH	QATAR	SYRIA		NORTH YEMEN	
	SAUDI ARABIA			AFGHANISTAN	CYPRUS						LEBANON		YEMEN				UNITED ARAB EMIRATES	

Area

IRAN 636,000 sq miles (1,648,000 sq km)	**SAUDI ARABIA** 865,000 sq miles (2,240,000 sq km)
	ISRAEL 7,992 sq miles (20,700 sq km)

AFGHANISTAN 252,100 sq miles (653,000 sq km)
BAHRAIN 256 sq miles (662 sq km)
CYPRUS 3,572 sq miles (9,251 sq km)
SOUTH YEMEN 111,074 sq miles (287,680 sq km)
UNITED ARAB E. 32,300 sq miles (83,600 sq km)
IRAQ 168,928 sq miles (437,522 sq km)
JORDAN 36,833 sq miles (95,396 sq km)
KUWAIT 6,532 sq miles (16,918 sq km)
LEBANON 3,950 sq miles (10,230 sq km)
OMAN 120,000 sq miles (300,000 sq km)
QATAR 4,400 sq miles (11,400 sq km)
TURKEY 300,948 sq miles (779,452 sq km)
SYRIA 71,498 sq miles (185,180 sq km)
NORTH YEMEN 77,200 sq miles (200,000 sq km)

Population

IRAN 35,213,000	**ISRAEL** 3,776,000	**SAUDI ARABIA** 7,866,000

AFGHANISTAN 21,452,000
BAHRAIN 341,400
CYPRUS 616,000
SOUTH YEMEN 1,853,000
IRAQ 12,171,500
JORDAN 3,085,000
KUWAIT 1,272,200
LEBANON 3,254,000
OMAN 864,000
QATAR 200,000
SYRIA 8,328,000
UNITED ARAB EMIRATES 877,300
NORTH YEMEN 5,785,000
TURKEY 44,284,000

Currency

ISRAEL Israeli Pound
SAUDI ARABIA Riyal

Capital

TURKEY Ankara
CYPRUS Nicosia
LEBANON Beirut
SYRIA Damascus
IRAQ Baghdad
IRAN Tehran
ISRAEL Jerusalem
JORDAN Amman
AFGHANISTAN Kabul
BAHRAIN Manama
NORTH YEMEN San'a'
KUWAIT Kuwait
SAUDI ARABIA Riyadh
UNITED ARAB EMIRATES Abu Dhabi
OMAN Muscat
QATAR Doha
SOUTH YEMEN Aden

Black Sea

Istanbul
Samsun
Bursa
Ankara
TURKEY
Erzurum
Izmir
Caspian Sea
SOVIET UNION
Adana
Tabriz
Gaziantep
Qolleh-ye Damavand
(18369ft/5599m)
Mashhad
Mediterranean Sea
Halab
Kirkuk
Tehran
Kabul
Levkosia (Nicosia)
CYPRUS
SYRIA
IRAN
Herat
AFGHANISTAN
Tripoli
LEBANON
Dimashq
(Damascus)
Baghdad
Beirut
Haifa
IRAQ
Dezful
Kandahar
ISRAEL
Tel Aviv
Esfahan
Tel Aviv
Jerusalem
'Amman
Kerman
R Helmond
JORDAN
PAKISTAN
EGYPT
KUWAIT
Abadan
Kuwait
Shiraz
Al-Hufuf
Al-Manamah
BAHRAIN
Doha
Red Sea
Al-Madinah
(Medina)
Ar-Riyad
(Riyadh)
QATAR
Dubai
Abu Dhabi
Gulf of Oman
UNITED ARAB
EMIRATES
Muscat
Persian Gulf
Juddah
(Jiddah)
Makkah
(Mecca)
SAUDI ARABIA
OMAN
Arabian Sea
SOUTH YEMEN
Sana'
NORTH YEMEN
Aden
Gulf of Aden

▼ A girl from Kermanshah in Iran sits in a field of raw wool. The province is a flourishing centre for farming and making textiles.

◄ A camel train approaches a village in north-western Iran. The region lies on the ancient trade routes which once linked Asia with Europe.

▼ A bargeman transports rush matting throught a marshy estuary of the Tigris and Euphrates rivers. In ancient times the people of the area made huge boats from rushes and sailed them out to sea.

▶Women of Shiraz in Iran weave at their loom. Iran produces some of the most beautiful carpets in the world.

Scale
0   200 km
0   200 miles

Key

Olives		Cattle	
Grapes/Wine		Goats	
Wheat		Sheep	
Vegetables		Farming	
Tobacco		Fishing	
Rice		Animal Farming	
Citrus fruit		Coal	
Cotton		Iron	
Fruit		Minerals	
Cereals		Copper	
Port		Oil	
Industry		Gold	

The Indian Subcontinent

More people live in India than in any other country in the world except China. The high Himalayan Mountains separate India from the rest of Asia. There are two small countries – Nepal and Bhutan – in these mountains. To the south of the Himalayas in India many people live on the plain of the River Ganges. The main upland area of India is called the Deccan.

India has a tropical climate. Most of the country's rain falls during the monsoon which takes place from June to September.

Farming is very important in India. But India still has to import much of its food as it cannot grow enough to feed everyone. Wheat, millet, rice and cotton are the main crops. Tea is grown in Assam province and exported to many countries. There are a large number of cows in India which are used for pulling ploughs and carts. They are not killed because the main religion of India forbids the killing of cows as they are sacred.

Cotton and textiles are important industries. India also has many iron ore and coal mines. India's largest cities are Calcutta, Madras and Bombay, which are all ports, and Delhi, which is the capital.

Pakistan became a separate state in 1947. Most of its people are Moslems. Karachi, which is at the mouth of the River Indus, is Pakistan's largest city and its port. The capital is a new city called Islamabad. Bangladesh separated from Pakistan in 1971. Its capital is Dacca and its people are also Moslem.

Sri Lanka is an island country which lies off the southeast coast of India. Its old name was Ceylon. Tea, rubber and coconuts are its products. Colombo is the capital.

▲ Benares (now called Varanasi) is one of the world's oldest cities and an important religious centre in India. Hindu pilgrims come from all over the country to bathe here in the sacred waters of the Ganges.

▶ Yaks graze in the foothills of the Himalayas, in Nepal. This immense mountain range includes Mount Everest, the highest peak in the world (29,028 feet, 8,848 metres).

◀ Islamabad – the city of Islam – was built to replace Karachi as Pakistan's capital. Building work started in 1960.

▶ The Taj Mahal in India is one of the world's most beautiful buildings. It was built by a Mogul emperor as a memorial to his favourite wife.

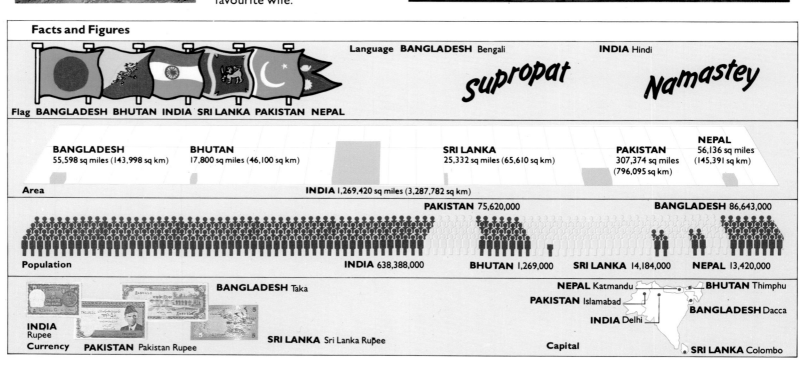

Facts and Figures

Language		
BANGLADESH Bengali		INDIA Hindi

Supropat   Namastey

Flag BANGLADESH BHUTAN INDIA SRI LANKA PAKISTAN NEPAL

BANGLADESH 55,598 sq miles (143,998 sq km)	**BHUTAN** 17,800 sq miles (46,100 sq km)		**SRI LANKA** 25,332 sq miles (65,610 sq km)	**PAKISTAN** 307,374 sq miles (796,095 sq km)	**NEPAL** 56,136 sq miles (145,391 sq km)

Area INDIA 1,269,420 sq miles (3,287,782 sq km)

PAKISTAN 75,620,000   BANGLADESH 86,643,000

Population INDIA 638,388,000   BHUTAN 1,269,000   SRI LANKA 14,184,000   NEPAL 13,420,000

INDIA Rupee	**BANGLADESH** Taka	**NEPAL** Katmandu — **BHUTAN** Thimphu
		PAKISTAN Islamabad
		INDIA Delhi
		BANGLADESH Dacca
Currency PAKISTAN Pakistan Rupee	SRI LANKA Sri Lanka Rupee	**Capital** SRI LANKA Colombo

▶ Tea pluckers gather their crop in Darjeeling, India. The leaves are picked by hand and heated to dry them out. Brands of tea are named according to the region they come from.

▼ Sacred cows wander freely through a poor district of Calcutta. Killing them is forbidden, although their milk can be drunk.

▶ Sikhs are members of a religious community which grew up in the Punjab in northern India. Sikh men wear turbans, and are supposed never to cut their hair or beards. However, many sikhs prefer to remain clean shaven and do not grow a beard.

▲ This Indian girl is dancing in bare feet, as is customary. She uses her hands to express feelings.

▼ Villagers shop in a vegetable market near Delhi, India. Food is generally bought in open markets.

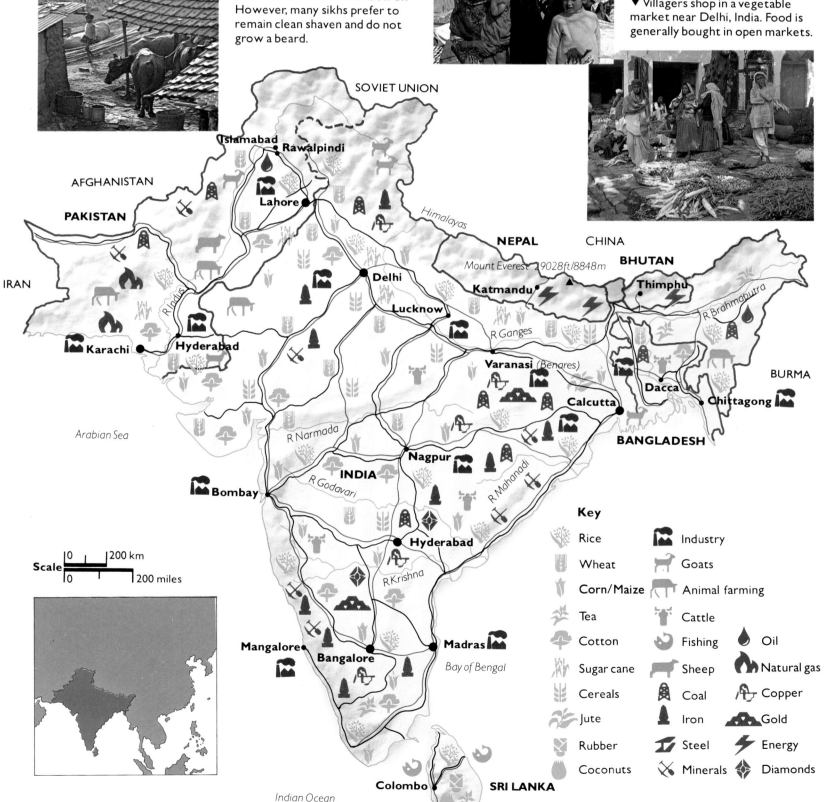

SOVIET UNION

AFGHANISTAN

PAKISTAN

IRAN

Islamabad • Rawalpindi

Lahore

Karachi Hyderabad

Arabian Sea

INDIA

Bombay R Godavari R Narmada

Mangalore Bangalore

Himalayas

NEPAL CHINA

Delhi BHUTAN

Mount Everest 29028ft/8848m

Katmandu Thimphu

Lucknow

R Ganges

Varanasi (Benares)

Dacca Chittagong BURMA

Calcutta

BANGLADESH

Nagpur

R Mahanadi

Hyderabad

R Krishna

Madras

Bay of Bengal

Colombo SRI LANKA

Indian Ocean

Scale
0 | 200 km
0 | 200 miles

Key

	Rice		Industry
	Wheat		Goats
	Corn/Maize		Animal farming
	Tea		Cattle
	Cotton		Fishing		Oil
	Sugar cane		Sheep		Natural gas
	Cereals		Coal		Copper
	Jute		Iron		Gold
	Rubber		Steel		Energy
	Coconuts		Minerals		Diamonds

China

More people live in China than in any other country in the world. Its population is over 950 million. Only the Soviet Union and Canada are larger in area than China. The correct name for the country since 1949 has been the Chinese People's Republic. This includes Manchuria, Inner Mongolia, Sinkiang and Tibet. Taiwan, which used to be called Formosa, is a separate country. The small area of Hong Kong in the south is British. Macao, which is even smaller, is controlled by Portugal.

In China many people live in the valley of the Yangtse Kiang, the hill country of the south, and in the plain of the Hwang Ho or Yellow River. These are also important farming areas. In the cooler areas of the north, wheat, cotton, maize and tobacco grow. In the hotter south, rice, sugar cane and soya beans are the main crops.

There are over 20 cities in China with populations of over a million people. These include Shanghai which is a large port and Beijing, which is the capital.

The Chinese are famous for their porcelain, silk and paper-making. Mining is also important. In Manchuria, coal and steel are the main industries.

Mongolia, North Korea and South Korea lie to the north and east of China. Herding cattle is Mongolia's main type of farming. The capital is Ulan Bator. North Korea has large deposits of iron ore and other minerals. The capital is Pyongyang. South Korea grows rice and produces silk, fruit and wine. Seoul is the capital.

▲ The Great Wall of China stretches 1500 miles (2400 km) across northern China. It was built in ancient times to keep out nomadic peoples from the north. Many tourists now visit the Great Wall each year.

► The Chinese grow rice in fields known as paddy fields. First, the paddy is ploughed over. Water buffalo are often used to do this work. Then the field is fertilized, smoothed and flooded.

► People grow the seedlings elsewhere. Then they plant the seedlings by hand in neat rows in the flooded paddy. The plants grow in the water. The paddy is drained before harvesting. Rice is a very important crop in China.

NEPAL

Mount Everest 29028

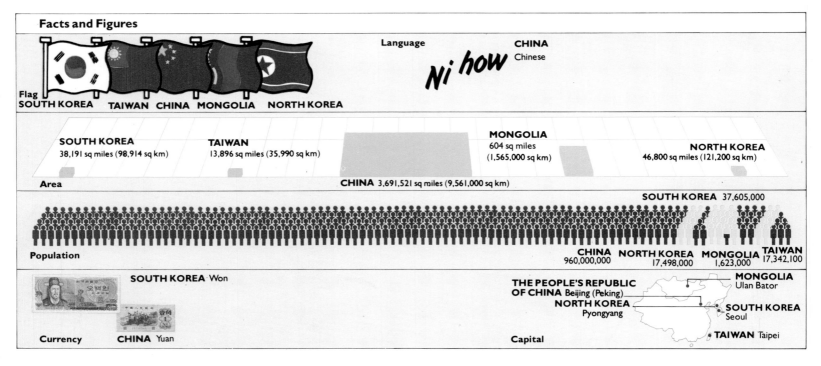

Facts and Figures

Language   Ni how   **CHINA** Chinese

Flag
SOUTH KOREA   TAIWAN   CHINA   MONGOLIA   NORTH KOREA

SOUTH KOREA 38,191 sq miles (98,914 sq km)	**TAIWAN** 13,896 sq miles (35,990 sq km)	**MONGOLIA** 604 sq miles (1,565,000 sq km)	**NORTH KOREA** 46,800 sq miles (121,200 sq km)

Area   CHINA 3,691,521 sq miles (9,561,000 sq km)

Population

SOUTH KOREA 37,605,000

CHINA 960,000,000   NORTH KOREA 17,498,000   MONGOLIA 1,623,000   TAIWAN 17,342,100

SOUTH KOREA Won

CHINA Yuan

Currency

THE PEOPLE'S REPUBLIC OF CHINA Beijing (Peking)
NORTH KOREA Pyongyang
MONGOLIA Ulan Bator
SOUTH KOREA Seoul
TAIWAN Taipei

Capital

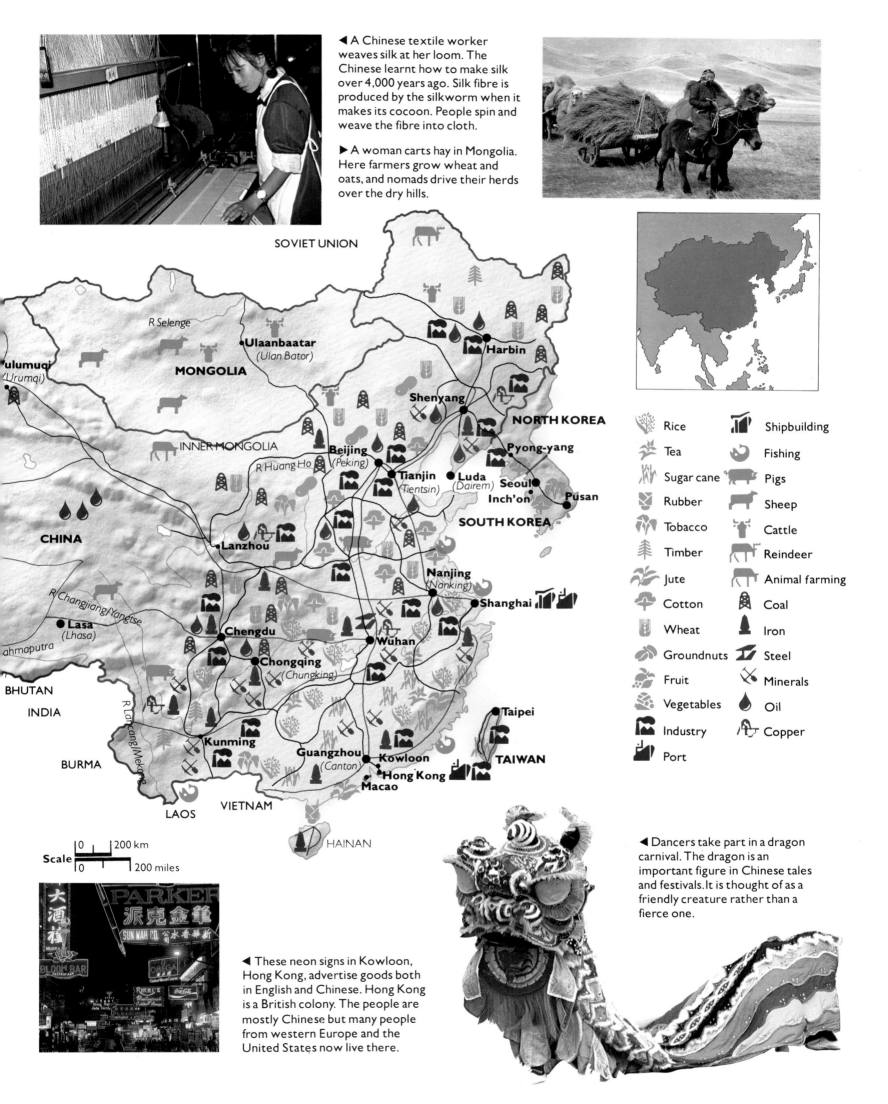

◀ A Chinese textile worker weaves silk at her loom. The Chinese learnt how to make silk over 4,000 years ago. Silk fibre is produced by the silkworm when it makes its cocoon. People spin and weave the fibre into cloth.

▶ A woman carts hay in Mongolia. Here farmers grow wheat and oats, and nomads drive their herds over the dry hills.

SOVIET UNION

R Selenge

Ulaanbaatar
(Ulan Bator)

MONGOLIA

ulumuqi
(Urumqi)

INNER MONGOLIA

CHINA

R Huang Ho

Beijing
(Peking)

Lanzhou

Tianjin
(Tientsin)

Harbin

Shenyang

NORTH KOREA

Pyong-yang

Luda
(Dairem)

Seoul

Inch'on

Pusan

SOUTH KOREA

R Changjiang/Yangtse

Lasa
(Lhasa)

ahmaputra

Chengdu

Nanjing
(Nanking)

Shanghai

BHUTAN

INDIA

R Lancang/Mekong

Chongqing
(Chungking)

Wuhan

Taipei

Kunming

BURMA

Guangzhou
(Canton)

Kowloon

Hong Kong

Macao

TAIWAN

VIETNAM

LAOS

HAINAN

Scale
0 — 200 km
0 — 200 miles

Symbol		Symbol	
Rice		Shipbuilding	
Tea		Fishing	
Sugar cane		Pigs	
Rubber		Sheep	
Tobacco		Cattle	
Timber		Reindeer	
Jute		Animal farming	
Cotton		Coal	
Wheat		Iron	
Groundnuts		Steel	
Fruit		Minerals	
Vegetables		Oil	
Industry		Copper	
Port			

◀ These neon signs in Kowloon, Hong Kong, advertise goods both in English and Chinese. Hong Kong is a British colony. The people are mostly Chinese but many people from western Europe and the United States now live there.

◀ Dancers take part in a dragon carnival. The dragon is an important figure in Chinese tales and festivals. It is thought of as a friendly creature rather than a fierce one.

Japan

Japan is a group of islands lying off the coast of northeast Asia. The Sea of Japan separates them from the mainland. The four main islands are called Honshu, Shikoku, Kyushu and Hokkaido. Honshu is the largest – it is almost as large as England, Scotland and Wales put together. There are also hundreds of small islands, many of which are uninhabited.

More than three quarters of Japan is mountainous. Many of the mountains are volcanoes. The most famous is Mount Fujiyama, which is the highest in the country. Earthquakes and earth tremors occur often. Japan has a jagged coastline and there are many natural harbours.

Japan is a very crowded country. Most of the people live in the plains along the coast and in the large cities such as Tokyo, the capital, Osaka and Yokohama.

Japan is known throughout the world for its industry. Although it must import oil, coal and iron ore, Japan manufactures ships, cars, motorbicycles, radios, televisions and cameras. Rice is Japan's main food crop. Other crops are tea and tobacco. Fishing, silkworm farming and pearl diving are also important.

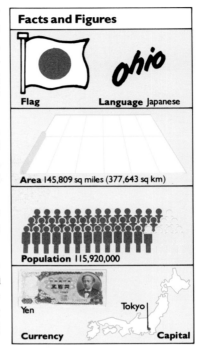

Facts and Figures

Flag   Language Japanese

ohio

Area 145,809 sq miles (377,643 sq km)

Population 115,920,000

Yen   Tokyo

Currency   Capital

▲ Flying kites is a national pastime in Japan. By tradition, kites flying over a house at night will ward off evil spirits.

▶ Japan has a thriving motor industry. The names of firms such as Datsun, Honda, Toyota and Suzuki are well known throughout the world. Japanese cars, motorcycles and trucks have a reputation for low prices and running costs.
Other important exports include high precision instruments such as computers, wristwatches and hi-fi equipment. Nikon cameras are famous. The girl (far right) is working at the factory in Tokyo.

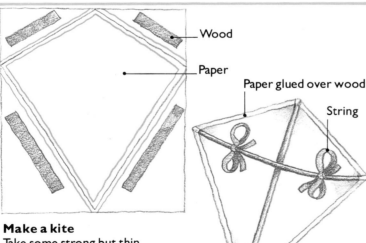

Wood

Paper

Paper glued over wood

String

Make a kite
Take some strong but thin paper (about 1 yard/metre square). Draw a diamond shape as in the picture and cut it out. Fit four pieces of light wood along the sides of the kite for the frame. Glue the ends together and then glue the paper over the frame. Glue two more pieces of wood across the centre of the kite to strengthen the frame. Attach a string for flying the kite. Finally, add a tail made from string and tissue paper.

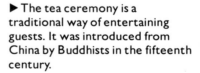

▶ The tea ceremony is a traditional way of entertaining guests. It was introduced from China by Buddhists in the fifteenth century.

▼ Ancient and modern exist side by side in Japan. Here, the 'bullet train' speeds past Mount Fujiyama. The line runs between Tokyo and Osaka. It provides the fastest train service in the world.

▲ Pearl fishers in Japan wear face masks and white clothing. The cultivation of pearls is a major industry.

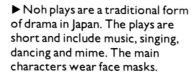
▶ Noh plays are a traditional form of drama in Japan. The plays are short and include music, singing, dancing and mime. The main characters wear face masks.

◀ Shoppers throng the streets of Tokyo. This is the capital of Japan and a seaport. The total population of this city is over 9 million people.

▲ A girl presents herself at a Shinto temple. Children are supposed to do this at the ages of three, five and seven. She is dressed in a silk kimono.

Key

Timber		Coal	
Vegetables		Minerals	
Fruit		Iron	
Cereals		Gold	
Rice		Copper	
Potatoes		Steel	
Port			
Shipbuilding			
Industry			
Fishing			
Dairy			
Cattle			
Farming			

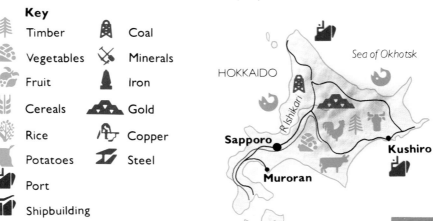

▲ Many Japanese make regular pilgrimages to Shinto shrines like this one in Kyoto. Shinto is Japan's national faith. It stresses reverence for ancestors, family virtues and cleanliness.

Scale

0	200 km
0	200 miles

South-east Asia

The countries in south-east Asia are Malaysia, Singapore, Brunei, Kampuchea, Thailand, Laos, Vietnam and Burma.

Malaysia includes Malaya which is the southern part of the Kra or Malay peninsula and the areas of Sabah and Sarawak in northern Borneo. Rubber plantations cover over half of Malaya which is the largest producer of rubber in the world. Tin is also very important here. The capital of Malaysia is Kuala Lumpur.

Singapore is a small island off the southern coast of Malaya. The Straits of Johore separate Singapore from the mainland although there is a causeway link across the straits. The city of Singapore is a great trading centre of south-east Asia. The port of Singapore handles most of Malaysia's foreign trade.

On the island of Borneo the small country of Brunei lies between Sabah and Sarawak. Brunei's main source of wealth is oil. Thailand is an important rice producing country. It also produces rubber and tin. In the northern hills elephants are used to bring teak and other kinds of wood out of the forests. The capital of Thailand is Bangkok at the mouth of the Chao Phraya river. The city has many temples and canals which in Thailand are called klongs.

Kampuchea (which used to be called Cambodia), Laos and Vietnam also grow rice. Rice grows in paddy fields and there are many in the Red River valley in northern Vietnam and along the Mekong which runs through Kampuchea and Vietnam. But the country which grows more rice than any other in the world is Burma. There are many paddy fields around the mouth of the Irrawaddy river.

◀ These women are crossing a field of young rice in Thailand. The country's central region is a flat and fertile plain, ideal for rice-growing. The crop needs both warmth and moisture to flourish. Thailand's paddy fields are irrigated by rivers and specially dug canals. Rice makes up a large part of the Thai diet.

▶ Elephants are often used to carry logs of teak from the forested mountains of northern Thailand. Although they are huge animals they are easy to train. Here, as in India, elephants have proved highly intelligent beasts of burden. They can learn to obey many different commands and perform a wide variety of tasks.

▶ This pump is at the Seria oil field in Brunei. The country has other oil fields beneath the sea, which are being worked offshore. Oil and natural gas are Brunei's main exports; rubber is also produced. The main food crops that are grown here are cassava and rice.

▲ Basketware is on display at this floating market in Bangkok. Thailand's capital is a great trading centre. Many of its people live in boats, or in waterside houses on stilts. People have used the klongs – or canals – as a way of getting about for many centuries.

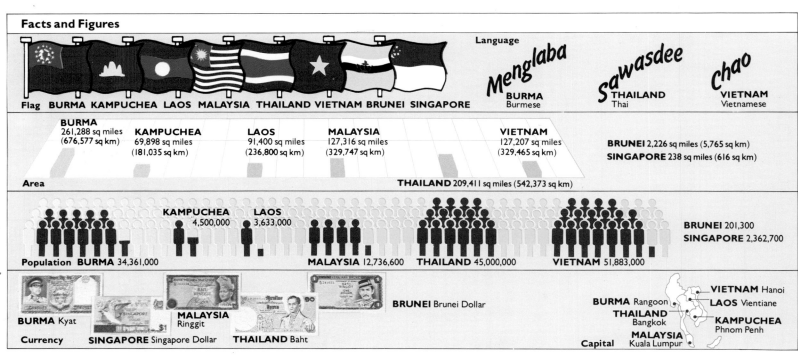

Facts and Figures

Flag BURMA KAMPUCHEA LAOS MALAYSIA THAILAND VIETNAM BRUNEI SINGAPORE

Language
Menglaba BURMA Burmese
Sawasdee THAILAND Thai
Chao VIETNAM Vietnamese

Area

BURMA 261,288 sq miles (676,577 sq km)	
KAMPUCHEA 69,898 sq miles (181,035 sq km)	
LAOS 91,400 sq miles (236,800 sq km)	
MALAYSIA 127,316 sq miles (329,747 sq km)	
VIETNAM 127,207 sq miles (329,465 sq km)	**BRUNEI** 2,226 sq miles (5,765 sq km)
	SINGAPORE 238 sq miles (616 sq km)

THAILAND 209,411 sq miles (542,373 sq km)

Population BURMA 34,361,000 · KAMPUCHEA 4,500,000 · LAOS 3,633,000 · MALAYSIA 12,736,600 · THAILAND 45,000,000 · VIETNAM 51,883,000 · BRUNEI 201,300 · SINGAPORE 2,362,700

Currency BURMA Kyat · MALAYSIA Ringgit · SINGAPORE Singapore Dollar · THAILAND Baht · BRUNEI Brunei Dollar

Capital VIETNAM Hanoi · LAOS Vientiane · BURMA Rangoon · THAILAND Bangkok · KAMPUCHEA Phnom Penh · MALAYSIA Kuala Lumpur

◄A woman taps a rubber tree on a Malayan plantation. Diagonal cuts are made in the trees, and the sap is collected in small bowls. The sap contains a substance called latex which is treated, dried and pressed into sheets of rubber for export.

►The Shwee Dragon pagoda is a Buddhist temple in Rangoon, capital of Burma. Most Burmese people are Buddhists. The monks wear saffron-coloured robes called pongyis.

▲ Much of Malaysia is bordered by the sea, and fish is an important part of the people's diet. It is generally brought ashore in slender sailing boats like these. As most of the fish that is caught is eaten by the Malaysians themselves, very little is exported.

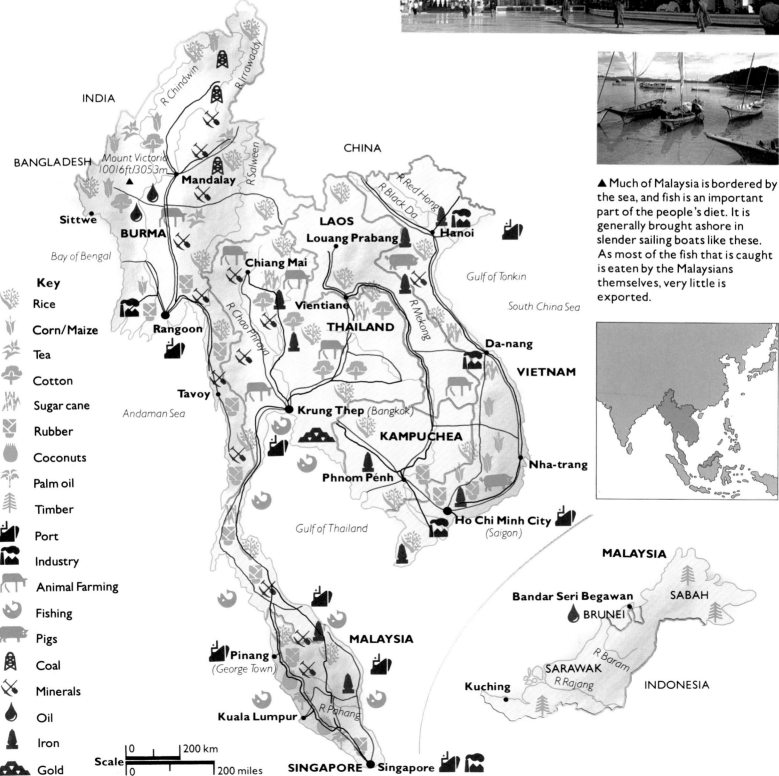

Key

Rice
Corn/Maize
Tea
Cotton
Sugar cane
Rubber
Coconuts
Palm oil
Timber
Port
Industry
Animal Farming
Fishing
Pigs
Coal
Minerals
Oil
Iron
Gold

INDIA
BANGLADESH
BURMA
Mount Victoria 10016ft/3053m
Mandalay
Sittwe
Bay of Bengal
Rangoon
Tavoy
Andaman Sea
R Chindwin
R Irrawaddy
R Salween
R Chao Phraya
CHINA
LAOS
Louang Prabang
Chiang Mai
Vientiane
THAILAND
Krung Thep (Bangkok)
KAMPUCHEA
Phnom Pénh
Gulf of Thailand
R Red Hong
R Black Da
Hanoi
Gulf of Tonkin
South China Sea
R Mekong
Da-nang
VIETNAM
Nha-trang
Ho Chi Minh City (Saigon)
MALAYSIA
Pinang (George Town)
Kuala Lumpur
R Pahang
SINGAPORE Singapore

MALAYSIA
Bandar Seri Begawan
BRUNEI
SABAH
SARAWAK
Kuching
R Baram
R Rajang
INDONESIA

Scale 0 200 km   0 200 miles

Indonesia and the Philippines

Indonesia is a large country in south-east Asia. There are more than 13,600 islands in Indonesia which lies between the Pacific and Indian Oceans. Over 900 of the islands have no-one living on them. The main islands are Java, Sumatra, Kalimantan and Celebes. Djakarta on the island of Java is the capital of Indonesia.

The islands of Indonesia lie on both sides of the Equator and they have a hot, wet climate. The country is mountainous and there are many volcanoes. The most famous of these is Krakatoa which is in the Sunda Straits between Java and Sumatra.

There are large plantations where the tropical forests have been cleared. Here rubber, tea, coffee, tobacco and sugar cane grow. Rice and cassava are important types of food in Indonesia. These crops grow on the coastal plains. Spices, copra and palm oil are also important.

Many teak and ebony trees grow in the forests of Indonesia. The wood is used to make expensive furniture. Indonesia also has many oil wells and tin mines.

The Philippines is a group of 7,000 islands to the north of Indonesia. The largest islands are Luzon and Mindanao. The capital is Manila which is on the island of Luzon. The islands are mountainous and volcanic eruptions and earthquakes are common. The main products are tobacco, timber, pineapples, palm oil and sugar cane.

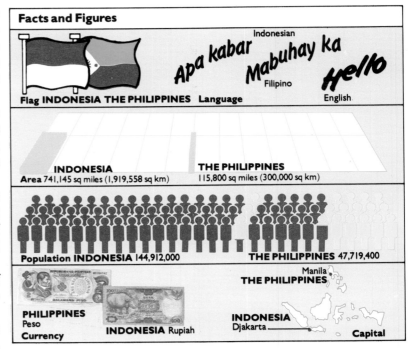

Facts and Figures

Flag INDONESIA THE PHILIPPINES | Language: *Apa kabar* (Indonesian), *Mabuhay ka* (Filipino), *Hello* (English)

INDONESIA Area 741,145 sq miles (1,919,558 sq km) | **THE PHILIPPINES** 115,800 sq miles (300,000 sq km)

Population INDONESIA 144,912,000 | THE PHILIPPINES 47,719,400

PHILIPPINES Peso | INDONESIA Rupiah — Currency

THE PHILIPPINES Manila | INDONESIA Djakarta — Capital

▲ A clothworker makes batik in Djakarta. This way of making patterned material is a speciality of Indonesia. Wax protects the pattern when the fabric is dyed.

▲ The Javanese are famous for their traditional wooden puppets. They are worked by rods from below. The puppeteer hides behind a screen, twisting and tilting the rods to achieve a wide variety of movements.

◄ Bell-shaped stone carvings decorate the steps of the great temple of Borobudur in central Java. The temple was built as a Buddhist shrine more than a thousand years ago. Today, most of Indonesia's people are Moslems.

▲Djakarta is at the mouth of the Chiliwong river. Many canals and waterways run through the city. Some houses are built on stilts. However, Djakarta is also a modern capital, with many car factories and textile mills. Its port handles most of Indonesia's foreign trade.

► Dancing girls perform in traditional costume on the island of Bali. The island people have developed high forms of music, dancing, theatre and architecture. Bali also has great natural beauty. It is now one of Indonesia's main tourist centres.

▲ The Dyaks of Borneo are a very primitive people. The interior has many regions of jungle and mountain which have never been fully explored by outsiders. Wars still break out between tribes, and headhunters still exist. Some Dyaks live along the coast as well.

▲ Dyak villages are made up of long houses. Many families may live in one long house, and each has its own chief. The people live by fishing and hunting. They also grow crops such as rice and yams.

▲ On the Philippine island of Luzon there are ancient rice terraces. The system of paddies and channels is over 2,000 years old. It was built by the primitive Igorot people. Most of the islanders are of Malay origin. They are known as Filipinos.

▲ Villagers dry peanuts on Bali. The island has volcanoes, but there is also a fertile plain. Here, rice, fruit, coffee and vegetables are grown. Pigs and cattle are also raised for sale abroad.

Key

🌿	Tobacco	🥜	Groundnuts
🌽	Corn/Maize	🌱	Spices
🌾	Rice	🏭	Industry
🥥	Coconuts	🏭	Port
🌲	Timber	🐟	Fishing
🎋	Sugar cane	⛰️	Gold
🌴	Palm oil	⛏️	Coal
☕	Coffee	⚒️	Minerals
🌼	Rubber	💧	Oil

LUZON
PHILIPPINES

South China Sea

Manila **Quezon City**

Iloilo
Cebu

Pacific Ocean

Davao

Medan

SUMATRA

MALAYSIA

Padang

Pontianak

BORNEO
(KALIMANTAN)

Palembang

SULAWESI (CELEBES)

Indian Ocean

Bandjarmasin

Java Sea

**WEST IRIAN
(NEW GUINEA)**

Djakarta

Semarang

Ujung Pandang

Bandung

R Digul

INDONESIA

JAVA

Surabaja

Scale 0 — 200 km
       0 — 200 miles

TIMOR

Timor Sea

Looking at Africa

Africa is the world's second largest continent. Only Asia is larger. It is over 5,000 miles (8,000 km) from Cape Vert in the west to Cape Guardafui in the east. This is almost as far as the greatest length of the continent from Tangier in the north to Cape Agulhas in the south.

Unlike the coasts of Europe and Asia, Africa has few large bays or gulfs and its shape is fairly regular. Off the coasts of Africa are some small, volcanic islands. These include the Canary Islands in the north and St Helena in the south. Madagascar is off the east coast. It is one of the world's largest islands.

The Equator passes through the centre of Africa. It is the only continent which both the Tropic of Cancer and Tropic of Capricorn pass through.

The main mountain ranges are the Atlas Mountains in the north-west, the Drakensberg Mountains in the south-east and the highlands of East Africa. The rest of the continent is made up of plateaus with a narrow plain around the coast.

The River Nile flows north from the highlands of East Africa to the Mediterranean Sea. It is the longest river in Africa and one of the longest in the world. The River Zaire is the second longest in Africa.

In East Africa the Great Rift Valley stretches for thousands of kilometres. Africa's largest lake is Lake Victoria in East Africa. The Sahara Desert separates northern from central and southern Africa. The people in the north are mainly Arabs and in the south they are mainly negroes.

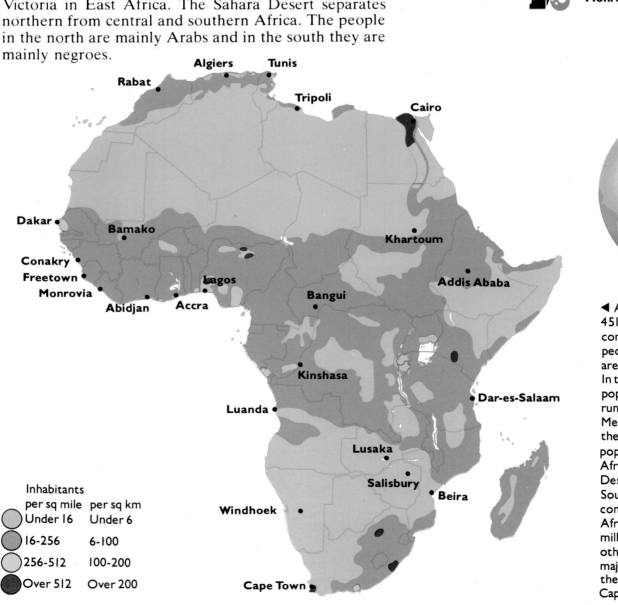

Inhabitants

per sq mile	per sq km
Under 16	Under 6
16-256	6-100
256-512	100-200
Over 512	Over 200

◀ Africa has a total population of 451 million people. Much of the continent is thinly populated. The people live mostly in a few major areas of settlement.

In the north, the main centre of population is a narrow strip running along the coast of the Mediterranean Sea. The valley of the lower Nile is also thickly populated. The rest of North Africa is covered by the Sahara Desert where few people live. South of the Sahara, the main concentration of people is in West Africa. Nigeria holds about 75 million people — far more than any other African country. Other major population centres include the East African coast and plateau, Cape Town and Johannesburg.

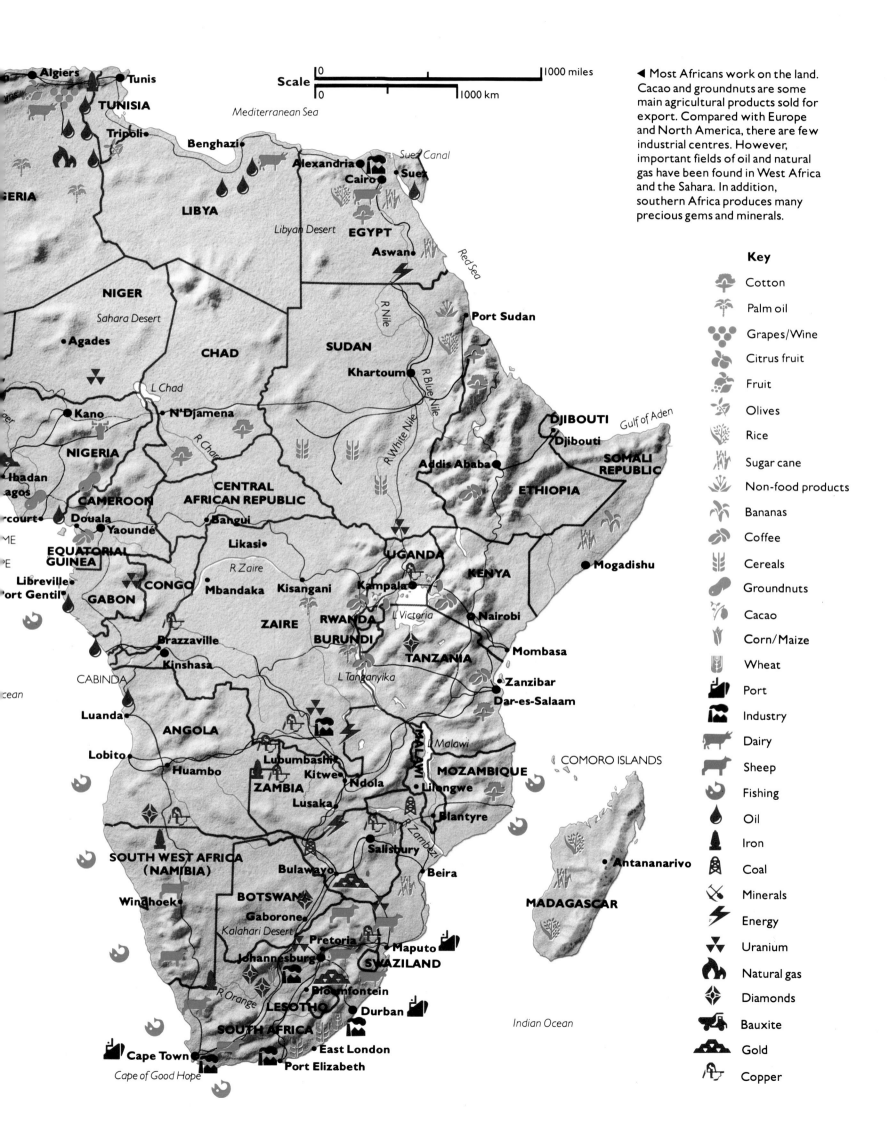

◄ Most Africans work on the land. Cacao and groundnuts are some main agricultural products sold for export. Compared with Europe and North America, there are few industrial centres. However, important fields of oil and natural gas have been found in West Africa and the Sahara. In addition, southern Africa produces many precious gems and minerals.

Scale

0 — 1000 miles
0 — 1000 km

Key

Cotton
Palm oil
Grapes/Wine
Citrus fruit
Fruit
Olives
Rice
Sugar cane
Non-food products
Bananas
Coffee
Cereals
Groundnuts
Cacao
Corn/Maize
Wheat
Port
Industry
Dairy
Sheep
Fishing
Oil
Iron
Coal
Minerals
Energy
Uranium
Natural gas
Diamonds
Bauxite
Gold
Copper

Mediterranean Sea

Algiers
Tunis
TUNISIA
Tripoli
Benghazi
LIBYA
Alexandria
Cairo
Suez
Suez Canal
EGYPT
Aswan
Libyan Desert
NIGERIA
NIGER
Sahara Desert
Agades
CHAD
L Chad
Kano
N'Djamena
R Chari
SUDAN
Khartoum
R Nile
R Blue Nile
R White Nile
Red Sea
Port Sudan
DJIBOUTI
Gulf of Aden
Djibouti
Addis Ababa
SOMALI REPUBLIC
ETHIOPIA
NIGERIA
Ibadan
Lagos
CAMEROON
Douala
Yaoundé
EQUATORIAL GUINEA
CENTRAL AFRICAN REPUBLIC
Bangui
Likasi
Libreville
Port Gentil
GABON
CONGO
Mbandaka
Kisangani
R Zaire
ZAIRE
RWANDA
BURUNDI
UGANDA
Kampala
L Victoria
KENYA
Nairobi
Mogadishu
Mombasa
TANZANIA
Zanzibar
Dar-es-Salaam
Brazzaville
Kinshasa
CABINDA
Luanda
ANGOLA
Lobito
Huambo
Lubumbashi
Kitwe
Ndola
ZAMBIA
Lusaka
L Tanganyika
L Malawi
MALAWI
Lilongwe
MOZAMBIQUE
COMORO ISLANDS
Blantyre
R Zambezi
Salisbury
SOUTH WEST AFRICA (NAMIBIA)
Bulawayo
Beira
Windhoek
BOTSWANA
Kalahari Desert
Gaborone
Pretoria
Johannesburg
Maputo
SWAZILAND
R Orange
Bloemfontein
LESOTHO
Durban
SOUTH AFRICA
East London
Cape Town
Port Elizabeth
Cape of Good Hope
Indian Ocean
Antananarivo
MADAGASCAR
Ocean

Northern Africa

The large Sahara Desert stretches across northern Africa. It is the largest desert in the world and covers over 3,500,000 square miles (9,100,000 sq km). The Sahara takes up over one quarter of Africa and is almost as big as the United States of America.

Sand dunes cover only a small part of the Sahara. Most of the ground is rocky. A hot, dusty wind called the khamsin blows from the desert to the Mediterranean. Khamsin is the Arabic for 50. The Arabs say that this wind blows for 50 days from April to June.

The camel is still an important type of transport in the Sahara. Some roads now also cross the desert. In the past, the trip from Morocco to West Africa by camel took two months. Today you can cross the desert by car or bus in five days. There are many fertile oases in the Sahara where crops, like dates, grow. It is also rich in iron ore, petroleum and natural gas.

The high Atlas Mountains are found in Morocco, Algeria and Tunisia. There is farming along the coasts as well as large cities and ports such as Casablanca, Oran, Algiers and Tunis.

Libya and Egypt lie to the east of Tunisia and Algeria. They also have Mediterranean coastlines. Most of Libya is desert and the country is rich in oil. The population of Libya is only 2.5 million. Egypt is also a desert country but its population is much bigger. Over 35 million people live there, mainly along the river Nile. Cairo is the capital of Egypt and the largest city in Africa.

The main countries of the southern Sahara are Mauritania, Mali, Niger, Chad and the Sudan. Except for the Sudan, their populations are very small. They export groundnuts. Groundnut is another name for peanut.

▲ An ancient desert settlement sprawls down a hillside in the Algerian Sahara. A district or settlement is known as a Beni.

◄ A Moroccan woman passes a stall selling vegetables, in Marrakesh near the Atlas Mountains. She is veiled according to Moslem custom. Marrakesh is a historic trading centre.

◄ Youngsters herd cattle and goats near Tenes in northern Algeria. Many Algerians are of mixed Arab and Berber origins. Most are Moslems. Algeria has two main regions: north and south. The north is more fertile. The south is a large, thinly populated desert region.

▲ Marrakesh is famous for its leatherwork. Here, skins are tanned in vats to make leather.

◄ The Tuareg are a proud Berber people of the Sahara. Unlike other Moslems, the men wear veils and the women do not.

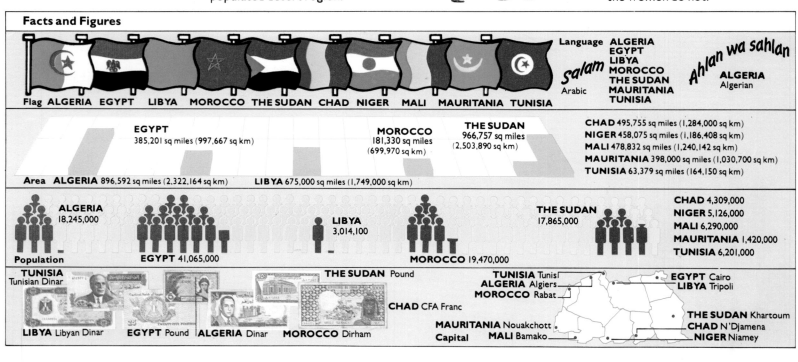

Facts and Figures

Flag ALGERIA EGYPT LIBYA MOROCCO THE SUDAN CHAD NIGER MALI MAURITANIA TUNISIA	**Language** ALGERIA EGYPT LIBYA MOROCCO THE SUDAN MAURITANIA TUNISIA — *salam* Arabic — *Ahlan wa sahlan* ALGERIA Algerian

Area
ALGERIA 896,592 sq miles (2,322,164 sq km)
EGYPT 385,201 sq miles (997,667 sq km)
MOROCCO 181,330 sq miles (699,970 sq km)
THE SUDAN 966,757 sq miles (2,503,890 sq km)
LIBYA 675,000 sq miles (1,749,000 sq km)
CHAD 495,755 sq miles (1,284,000 sq km)
NIGER 458,075 sq miles (1,186,408 sq km)
MALI 478,832 sq miles (1,240,142 sq km)
MAURITANIA 398,000 sq miles (1,030,700 sq km)
TUNISIA 63,379 sq miles (164,150 sq km)

Population
ALGERIA 18,245,000
EGYPT 41,065,000
LIBYA 3,014,100
MOROCCO 19,470,000
THE SUDAN 17,865,000
CHAD 4,309,000
NIGER 5,126,000
MALI 6,290,000
MAURITANIA 1,420,000
TUNISIA 6,201,000

Capital
TUNISIA Tunisian Dinar
LIBYA Libyan Dinar
EGYPT Pound
ALGERIA Dinar
MOROCCO Dirham
THE SUDAN Pound
CHAD CFA Franc
TUNISIA Tunis
ALGERIA Algiers
MOROCCO Rabat
MAURITANIA Nouakchott
MALI Bamako
EGYPT Cairo
LIBYA Tripoli
THE SUDAN Khartoum
CHAD N'Djamena
NIGER Niamey

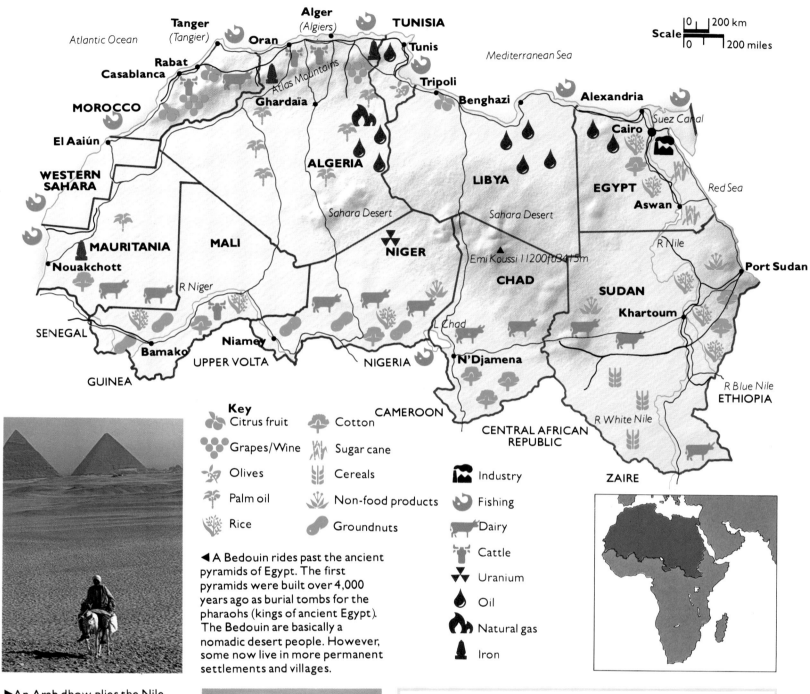

Atlantic Ocean

Tanger
(Tangier)

Alger
(Algiers)

TUNISIA

Mediterranean Sea

Scale
|0 | 200 km
|0 | 200 miles

Oran

Tunis

Rabat

Casablanca

Tripoli

Benghazi

Alexandria

MOROCCO

Ghardaïa

Suez Canal

El Aaiún

ALGERIA

LIBYA

Cairo

WESTERN
SAHARA

EGYPT

Red Sea

Aswan

Sahara Desert

Sahara Desert

R Nile

MAURITANIA

MALI

NIGER

Emi Koussi 11200ft/3415m

CHAD

Port Sudan

Nouakchott

SUDAN

R Niger

Khartoum

SENEGAL

L Chad

Niamey

UPPER VOLTA

Bamako

N'Djamena

R Blue Nile

GUINEA

NIGERIA

ETHIOPIA

Key

🫐 Citrus fruit

🍇 Grapes/Wine

🌿 Olives

🌴 Palm oil

🌾 Rice

🌿 Cotton

🌾 Sugar cane

🌾 Cereals

🌾 Non-food products

🥜 Groundnuts

CAMEROON

CENTRAL AFRICAN
REPUBLIC

ZAIRE

🏭 Industry

🐚 Fishing

🐄 Dairy

🐂 Cattle

⚛ Uranium

🛢 Oil

🔥 Natural gas

⚒ Iron

◀ A Bedouin rides past the ancient pyramids of Egypt. The first pyramids were built over 4,000 years ago as burial tombs for the pharaohs (kings of ancient Egypt). The Bedouin are basically a nomadic desert people. However, some now live in more permanent settlements and villages.

▶An Arab dhow plies the Nile near Aswan in Egypt. Dhows are vessels with triangular sails. Two great dams near Aswan store water for irrigation and hydro-electricity.

◀ A village woman of Egypt draws water from the Nile. The great river's banks have been cultivated for thousands of years. Regular flooding provides irrigation . The waters also bring down sediment which enriches the land. Many crops are grown along the Nile's fertile banks. These include cotton, rice, wheat and dates.

Making a headdress
In very hot climates people have to protect themselves from the powerful rays of the sun. This is why many people who live in such climates wear loose-fitting, flowing clothes which help to keep them cool. Many types of headdress are worn in northern Africa to shade people's heads and necks from the sun. You can make your own Arab-style headdress with a piece of cloth, such as a tea cloth. Put it on your head so that one side comes over your forehead and the rest hangs over your shoulders. Tie a cord or thin belt around your forehead to secure the cloth.

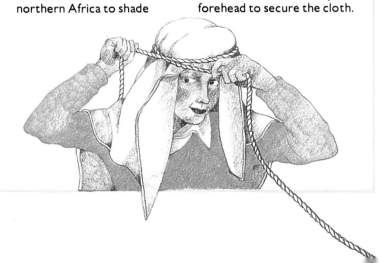

West and Central Africa

There are many countries in West and Central Africa. The largest are Ghana, Nigeria, Ivory Coast, Cameroon and Zaire. All the countries except Upper Volta and the Central African Republic have coastlines on the Atlantic. Gambia, Benin and Togo are long and narrow in shape. All the countries are tropical and have equatorial forests and grasslands.

Zaire is the largest of these countries. The River Zaire flows through it. Tropical rain forests cover most of Zaire and the Congo Republic. This area also has many copper, diamond, gold and uranium mines. But most of the people still keep to their old way of life and work as farmers. In the rain forest about 100,000 pygmies live. Pygmies have a primitive way of life.

There are hot humid rain forests along the coast of the Gulf of Guinea. This coast has many different names – the Grain Coast, Ivory Coast, Gold Coast and Slave Coast. These names refer to the products which Europeans and Arabs have taken from this coast in the past.

Away from the coasts there are grasslands called savanna. Unlike the rain forests, the grasslands have a dry season. Nearer to the Sahara, in the north, thorn bushes and scrub vegetation grow.

The Niger is the second largest river in West Africa. It enters the sea in Nigeria. Nigeria has many tin mines. It also produces palm oil and cacao from which cocoa and chocolate are made.

The largest producer of cacao in the world is Ghana. In Ghana there are also many bauxite mines. The metal aluminium is made from bauxite.

◄ A woman from Bida decorates pottery. Bida is a town lying in the west of central Nigeria. It has long been famous for its local crafts. Like other Nigerian towns, it was visited by Arab traders long ago, who introduced the Moslem religion.

▼ A pygmy family poses in a rain-forest clearing in Zaire. They hunt game with spears and nets. Their hut is made from dried banana fronds.

▼ These are ancient dye pits in Kano, Nigeria. The mud-walled city has been a trading centre for centuries. Modern Kano is a thriving commercial city with around 500,000 inhabitants.

◄ The great Akosombo Dam in Ghana has helped to create an immense artificial lake. The dam was completed in 1965, and blocks the Volta river in the Ajena gorge. Water is stored here to irrigate the land. It also produces hydro-electricity for the aluminium industry, one of the most important in Ghana.

Atlantic Ocean

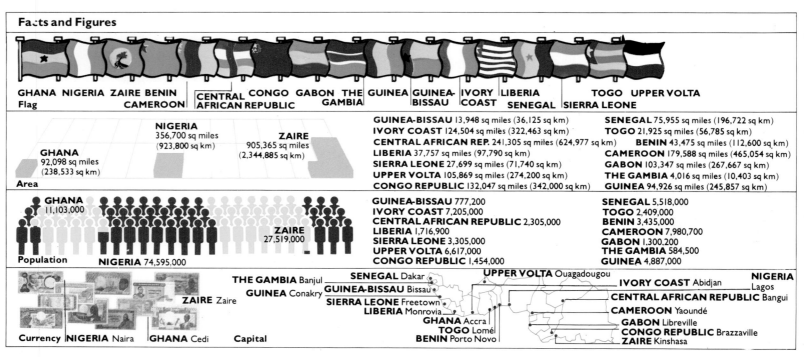

Facts and Figures

Flag: GHANA, NIGERIA, ZAIRE, BENIN, CAMEROON, CENTRAL AFRICAN REPUBLIC, CONGO, GABON, THE GAMBIA, GUINEA, GUINEA-BISSAU, IVORY COAST, LIBERIA, SENEGAL, SIERRA LEONE, TOGO, UPPER VOLTA

Area:
NIGERIA 356,700 sq miles (923,800 sq km)
ZAIRE 905,365 sq miles (2,344,885 sq km)
GHANA 92,098 sq miles (238,533 sq km)
GUINEA-BISSAU 13,948 sq miles (36,125 sq km)
IVORY COAST 124,504 sq miles (322,463 sq km)
CENTRAL AFRICAN REP. 241,305 sq miles (624,977 sq km)
LIBERIA 37,757 sq miles (97,790 sq km)
SIERRA LEONE 27,699 sq miles (71,740 sq km)
UPPER VOLTA 105,869 sq miles (274,200 sq km)
CONGO REPUBLIC 132,047 sq miles (342,000 sq km)
SENEGAL 75,955 sq miles (196,722 sq km)
TOGO 21,925 sq miles (56,785 sq km)
BENIN 43,475 sq miles (112,600 sq km)
CAMEROON 179,588 sq miles (465,054 sq km)
GABON 103,347 sq miles (267,667 sq km)
THE GAMBIA 4,016 sq miles (10,403 sq km)
GUINEA 94,926 sq miles (245,857 sq km)

Population:
GHANA 11,103,000
ZAIRE 27,519,000
NIGERIA 74,595,000
GUINEA-BISSAU 777,200
IVORY COAST 7,205,000
CENTRAL AFRICAN REPUBLIC 2,305,000
LIBERIA 1,716,900
SIERRA LEONE 3,305,000
UPPER VOLTA 6,617,000
CONGO REPUBLIC 1,454,000
SENEGAL 5,518,000
TOGO 2,409,000
BENIN 3,435,000
CAMEROON 7,980,700
GABON 1,300.200
THE GAMBIA 584,500
GUINEA 4,887,000

Currency: ZAIRE Zaire, NIGERIA Naira, GHANA Cedi

Capital:
THE GAMBIA Banjul
GUINEA Conakry
SENEGAL Dakar
GUINEA-BISSAU Bissau
SIERRA LEONE Freetown
LIBERIA Monrovia
GHANA Accra
TOGO Lomé
BENIN Porto Novo
UPPER VOLTA Ouagadougou
IVORY COAST Abidjan
CENTRAL AFRICAN REPUBLIC Bangui
CAMEROON Yaoundé
GABON Libreville
CONGO REPUBLIC Brazzaville
ZAIRE Kinshasa
NIGERIA Lagos

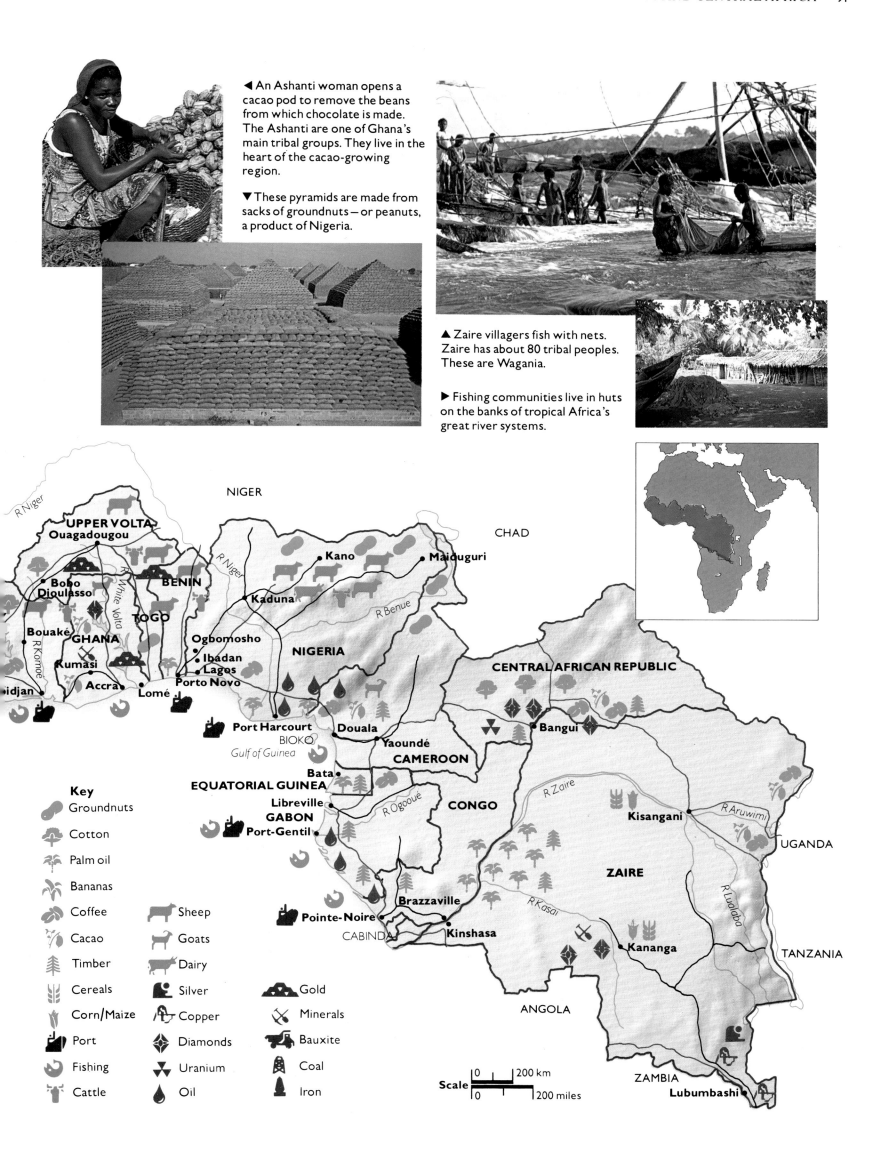

◀ An Ashanti woman opens a cacao pod to remove the beans from which chocolate is made. The Ashanti are one of Ghana's main tribal groups. They live in the heart of the cacao-growing region.

▼ These pyramids are made from sacks of groundnuts — or peanuts, a product of Nigeria.

▲ Zaire villagers fish with nets. Zaire has about 80 tribal peoples. These are Wagania.

▶ Fishing communities live in huts on the banks of tropical Africa's great river systems.

Key

- Groundnuts
- Cotton
- Palm oil
- Bananas
- Coffee
- Cacao
- Timber
- Cereals
- Corn/Maize
- Port
- Fishing
- Cattle
- Sheep
- Goats
- Dairy
- Silver
- Copper
- Diamonds
- Uranium
- Oil
- Gold
- Minerals
- Bauxite
- Coal
- Iron

Scale 0 — 200 km
0 — 200 miles

NIGER

CHAD

UPPER VOLTA
Ouagadougou

Bobo Dioulasso

BENIN

TOGO

GHANA

Bouaké

Kumasi

Accra

idjan

Lomé

Porto Novo

Kano

Maiduguri

Kaduna

R Niger

R Benue

Ogbomosho

Ibadan

Lagos

NIGERIA

Port Harcourt

Douala

BIOKO

Gulf of Guinea

Yaoundé

CAMEROON

Bata

EQUATORIAL GUINEA

Libreville

GABON

Port-Gentil

CENTRAL AFRICAN REPUBLIC

Bangui

CONGO

R Ogooué

R Zaire

Kisangani

R Aruwimi

UGANDA

ZAIRE

R Kasai

R Lualaba

Brazzaville

Pointe-Noire

CABINDA

Kinshasa

Kananga

TANZANIA

ANGOLA

ZAMBIA

Lubumbashi

Eastern Africa

The main countries in East Africa are Kenya, Uganda, Tanzania, Ethiopia, and Somalia. Smaller countries in this area are Rwanda, Burundi and Djibouti.

All of East Africa is in the tropics. The Equator passes through Kenya and Uganda. However, most of the countries are high and mountainous and so they have cooler climates than in West Africa. The two highest African mountains are in East Africa, Mount Kilimanjaro and Mount Kenya. Mount Kilimanjaro is 19,340 feet (5,895 metres) high and it lies in Tanzania.

The people of Kenya and most of eastern and southern Africa are called the Bantu. The population of Kenya is over 15 million and it includes many Asian, Arab and European people. Coffee, tea, cotton and sisal grow in Kenya. Nairobi is the capital. The main port is Mombasa. Kenya has many good beaches and famous wildlife parks which many visitors go to each year.

Uganda is an inland country. Its capital is Kampala. It produces cotton, sisal, tobacco and copper. A railway line runs from Kampala to Nairobi and Mombasa. The old countries Tanganyika and Zanzibar together form Tanzania. The capital and port of Tanzania is Dar-es-Salaam. It is a farming country and its main crops are cassava, yams, wheat and spices such as cloves.

Rwanda and Burundi are small farming countries. Ethiopia is Africa's most mountainous country. Many rivers, such as the Blue Nile, flow from these mountains. The capital is Addis Ababa. Somalia is a desert land. Cotton growing and fishing for tunny and mother-of-pearl are important industries. The capital is Mogadishu.

▲ Mount Kilimanjaro towers above the surrounding countryside. It has two peaks which are linked by a sloping ridge. The graceful animals are impala, part of the antelope family.

▶ The giraffe, lion, elephant, gazelle and zebra are just some of the animals native to Africa which are now in danger of becoming extinct. Game and Safari parks have been set up to protect these animals from hunters. Elephants are most often hunted for their ivory tusks. Ivory traders sell them for vast sums of money. Other animals are hunted for their skins.

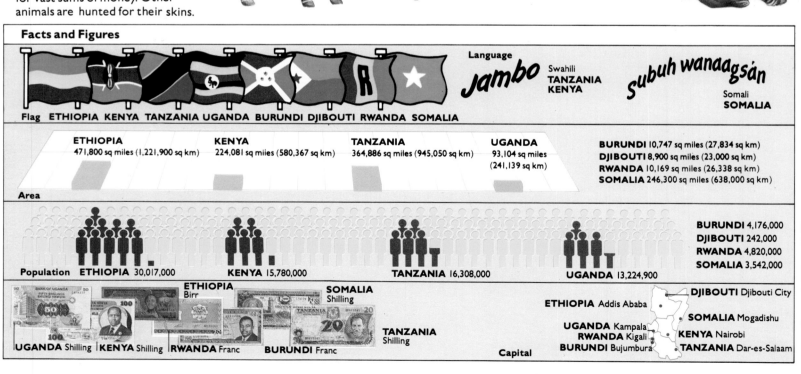

Facts and Figures

Language

Jambo Swahili TANZANIA KENYA

subuh wanaagsán Somali SOMALIA

Flag ETHIOPIA KENYA TANZANIA UGANDA BURUNDI DJIBOUTI RWANDA SOMALIA

ETHIOPIA	KENYA	TANZANIA	UGANDA	
471,800 sq miles (1,221,900 sq km)	224,081 sq miles (580,367 sq km)	364,886 sq miles (945,050 sq km)	93,104 sq miles (241,139 sq km)	BURUNDI 10,747 sq miles (27,834 sq km) DJIBOUTI 8,900 sq miles (23,000 sq km) RWANDA 10,169 sq miles (26,338 sq km) SOMALIA 246,300 sq miles (638,000 sq km)

Area

Population ETHIOPIA 30,017,000	KENYA 15,780,000	TANZANIA 16,308,000	UGANDA 13,224,900	BURUNDI 4,176,000 DJIBOUTI 242,000 RWANDA 4,820,000 SOMALIA 3,542,000

ETHIOPIA Birr

SOMALIA Shilling

TANZANIA Shilling

UGANDA Shilling KENYA Shilling RWANDA Franc BURUNDI Franc

Capital

DJIBOUTI Djibouti City
ETHIOPIA Addis Ababa
SOMALIA Mogadishu
UGANDA Kampala
RWANDA Kigali
BURUNDI Bujumbura
KENYA Nairobi
TANZANIA Dar-es-Salaam

▶A labourer cuts sisal in Kenya. Sisal is a type of hemp. Cords and twine are made from the leaves, most of this is exported.

▼ A ploughman drives his team in the highlands of Ethiopia. Few trees are left in these regions. Many of the forests have been cleared by farmers working the poor soil.

◀ A doctor treats Masai in a mobile clinic. The Masai are a proud, nomadic people who drive their herds across the bushlands of Kenya and Tanzania. They live off the meat and milk of their livestock.

▲ Kenyan fishermen use basketwork traps to catch their fish. The traps have tapering entrances, so the fish cannot get out again.

🌿 Cotton		🐄 Dairy	
☕ Coffee		🐂 Cattle	
🌽 Corn/Maize		🐑 Sheep	
🌾 Wheat		🐐 Goats	
🌾 Sugar cane		❖ Diamonds	
🌿 Tea		⚒ Copper	
🌿 Tobacco			
🌾 Rice			
🌷 Coconuts			
🌴 Bananas			
🌾 Cereals			

▲ A woman pounds maize in Rwanda. The country is poor and most people live in small villages. Maize is the basic diet of many villagers. Cassava, sweet potatoes and pulses are also grown here.

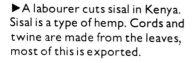

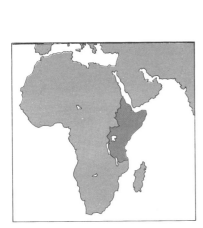

▶A Masai woman prepares to take part in a dance called the muchungwa. She wears traditional ear-rings, necklace and make-up.

Scale
0 — 200 km
0 — 200 miles

Southern Africa

The main countries in southern Africa are Angola, Zambia, Zimbabwe, Botswana, Mozambique, South-West Africa and the Republic of South Africa.

In the north of the area, there are tropical grasslands. In Zimbabwe cattle rearing is important. There are also many mineral mines. Zimbabwe exports gold and asbestos. In Zambia there are large copper and zinc mines. An important railway runs through Angola. It takes the copper from the mines in Shaba province in Zaire to the port of Lobito on the coast.

South-West Africa, which is also called Namibia, and Botswana are much drier countries. The long and narrow Kalahari Desert is in Botswana. There are many mines in Botswana and South-West Africa which produce diamonds, nickel and tin.

The Republic of South Africa is the most southerly country in Africa. The population is about 24 million. Of these over 15 million are Bantu Africans, 4 million are Europeans and over 5 million are Asians. There are many racial problems in South Africa.

Farming and cattle raising are important in South Africa, but it is also a mining country. Gold mines around Johannesburg employ many people. Diamonds are exported from Kimberley. There are also iron, copper, and asbestos mines. Johannesburg is the largest city in South Africa.

▲ Smoke rises from a Bantu village in Lesotho. The round huts are a traditional kind of dwelling.

▶ The Victoria Falls are on the border between Zambia and Zimbabwe. This great cascade is formed as the Zambezi river plunges over a great gorge one mile (1.6 km) wide.

▲ South Africa produces more gold than any other country. Its annual production accounts for about two thirds of the world's total. The gold is cast in bars like these.

◀ These Zambian miners work in a copper mine. Copper is Zambia's main export. The country is poor and depends heavily on the copper industry. But many Zambians work the land. They live on small farms, growing just enough food to feed themselves and their families. This is called subsistence farming.

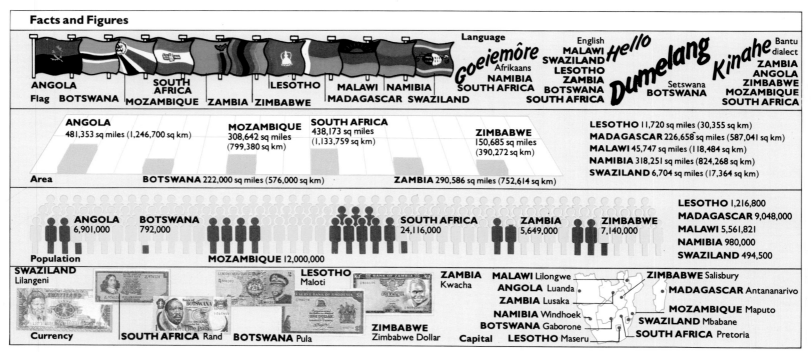

Facts and Figures

Flag										
ANGOLA	BOTSWANA	SOUTH AFRICA	MOZAMBIQUE	ZAMBIA	ZIMBABWE	LESOTHO	MALAWI	NAMIBIA MADAGASCAR	SWAZILAND	

Language

Goeiemôre Afrikaans NAMIBIA SOUTH AFRICA — English MALAWI SWAZILAND LESOTHO ZAMBIA BOTSWANA SOUTH AFRICA — Hello — Dumelang Setswana BOTSWANA — Kinahe Bantu dialect ZAMBIA ANGOLA ZIMBABWE MOZAMBIQUE SOUTH AFRICA

Area

ANGOLA 481,353 sq miles (1,246,700 sq km)

MOZAMBIQUE 308,642 sq miles (799,380 sq km)

SOUTH AFRICA 438,173 sq miles (1,133,759 sq km)

ZIMBABWE 150,685 sq miles (390,272 sq km)

LESOTHO 11,720 sq miles (30,355 sq km)
MADAGASCAR 226,658 sq miles (587,041 sq km)
MALAWI 45,747 sq miles (118,484 sq km)
NAMIBIA 318,251 sq miles (824,268 sq km)
SWAZILAND 6,704 sq miles (17,364 sq km)

BOTSWANA 222,000 sq miles (576,000 sq km)

ZAMBIA 290,586 sq miles (752,614 sq km)

Population

ANGOLA 6,901,000
BOTSWANA 792,000
SOUTH AFRICA 24,116,000
ZAMBIA 5,649,000
ZIMBABWE 7,140,000
MOZAMBIQUE 12,000,000

LESOTHO 1,216,800
MADAGASCAR 9,048,000
MALAWI 5,561,821
NAMIBIA 980,000
SWAZILAND 494,500

Currency

SWAZILAND Lilangeni
LESOTHO Maloti
ZAMBIA Kwacha
SOUTH AFRICA Rand
BOTSWANA Pula
ZIMBABWE Zimbabwe Dollar

Capital

MALAWI Lilongwe
ANGOLA Luanda
ZAMBIA Lusaka
NAMIBIA Windhoek
BOTSWANA Gaborone
LESOTHO Maseru
ZIMBABWE Salisbury
MADAGASCAR Antananarivo
MOZAMBIQUE Maputo
SWAZILAND Mbabane
SOUTH AFRICA Pretoria

► A river San lays his net in Botswana. The San are a people of southern Africa, known to whites as Bushmen. The San are basically a nomadic people. Some now live in settlements, but others still roam the bushlands in small hunting bands.

▼ The great Table Mountain dominates the skyline of Cape Town. You can reach the top by cable car. There is a very good view of the cape from the summit.

▲ A San tribesman hunts with bow and arrow in Namibia. The arrow is tipped with poison. The San have learnt to survive in the Kalahari Desert. They camp in rock shelters and kill what game they can find.

▲ Herero women pose for a photograph in Botswana. The Herero are a Bantu people famous for their great cattle herds. Many still live in small farming communities, but others are now living in larger settlements.

Scale
0 — 200 km
0 — 200 miles

Key

- Coffee
- Corn/Maize
- Cotton
- Vegetables
- Non-food products
- Tobacco
- Tea
- Rice
- Wheat
- Fruit
- Grapes/Wine
- Sugar cane
- Industry
- Port
- Fishing
- Dairy
- Cattle
- Sheep
- Goats
- Oil
- Diamonds
- Iron
- Copper
- Coal
- Gold
- Uranium

ZAIRE

ANGOLA
Luanda
Lobito
Huambo
R Kwanza

ZAMBIA
Ndola
Lusaka
Livingstone
R Luangwa
R Zambezi

MALAWI
TANZANIA
Lilongwe
Blantyre
R Lugenda

MOZAMBIQUE

SOUTH-WEST AFRICA (NAMIBIA)
Windhoek

BOTSWANA
Kalahari Desert
Gaborone

ZIMBABWE
Salisbury
Bulawayo
Beira
R Limpopo

Pretoria
Johannesburg
Maputo
SWAZILAND
Bloemfontein
Maseru
Kimberley
LESOTHO
SOUTH AFRICA
Durban
Orange River
East London
Port Elizabeth
Cape Town

MADAGASCAR
Mahajanga
Antananarivo
R Betsiboka
Toliary

Looking at Australasia

Australasia is made up of Australia, New Zealand and the islands of the southern and western pacific. It would fit into Asia almost seven times and it is the only continent which is made up entirely of islands. It is also the only continent in the world that does not join directly onto the mainland of any other continent.

Australasia lies on the opposite side of the globe from Europe and the eastern United States. Because of this Australia is sometimes nick-named the 'down-under' country.

The largest island in the continent is Australia which is also the world's largest island. The rest of Australasia is made up of New Zealand, the many small islands in the Pacific Ocean and the eastern half of New Guinea. The islands in the Pacific Ocean are called Oceania. The islands are extremely scattered. This means that air and sea transport are very important.

European settlers went to live in Australia and New Zealand in the eighteenth and nineteenth centuries. There are fewer European settlers in Oceania. The native people of Australia are called Aborigines. In New Zealand the native people are the Maoris.

The whole continent has a small population. It has only 0.02% of the world's population but covers 6% of the world's land surface. In Australia there are only 2 people to every square kilometre. In the United States there are 23 and in Britain 230 people to the same area.

▼ Australasia is a continent of sharp contrasts. The populated regions of Australia and New Zealand are highly industrialized. Their farming is efficient, and the two countries export meat, grain and dairy produce on a world scale. The other Pacific islands are not so developed and they produce little for export. Distances between the islands are immense. Some have become centres for international air travel. The Pacific islanders are great sea-farers themselves. They have travelled a very long way in their wooden boats.

▲ The total population of Australasia is 22 million. Australia is the largest country with a population of 14 million people. Next come New Zealand and Papua New Guinea, with populations of about 3 million each. None of the other islands holds even a million people. Many of the smallest islands have not been given a name.
The interior of Australia is mostly flat, dry and barren. Few people live in this desert region. Most Australians live in cities, many in the fertile regions of the south-eastern seaboard. The main cities here are Sydney and Melbourne. Each has a population of over 2 million people. There is also a fertile area around Perth in the south-west.
New Zealand is made up of two main islands. Most people live on the North Island. Wellington and Auckland are the main cities. The South Island includes the important coastal cities of Christchurch and Dunedin. However, the interior is mountainous and more thinly populated.

Inhabitants
per sq mile	per sq km
Under 16	Under 6
16-256	6-100
256-512	100-200
Over 512	Over 200

Key

Fruit		Fishing	
Wheat		Sheep	
Vegetables		Cattle	
Cereals		Dairy	
Grapes/Wine		Coal	
Citrus fruit		Iron	
Timber		Minerals	
Bananas		Oil	
Sugar cane		Bauxite	
Coconuts		Gold	
Palm oil		Natural gas	
Port		Copper	
Industry			

KIRIBATI

Pacific Ocean

A

SOLOMON
ISLANDS

esby

PHOENIX ISLANDS

Coral Sea

TUVALU

ier
f

MARQUESAS ISLANDS

VANUATU

WESTERN
SAMOA

FIJI

COOK ISLANDS

NEW
CALEDONIA

Brisbane

dney

erra

Auckland

Tasman Sea

Cook Strait

Wellington

Southern Alps

NEW
ZEALAND

Australia

Australia has six states and two territories. The states are Western Australia, Queensland, South Australia, New South Wales, Victoria, and the island of Tasmania. The two territories are the Australian Capital Territory, with the nation's capital, Canberra, and the Northern Territory whose main town is Darwin.

Australia is a fairly level land mass. A low-lying, dry, flat area called the Western Shield covers almost half of Australia. The name for this type of flat country is a plateau. Much of the Western Shield is desert. The main lake in the Western Shield is called Lake Disappointment. It is not a real lake but an area of salt marsh. Very few people live in the Western Shield except around Perth in the south-west.

East of the Western Shield, three large basins run from north to south. A basin is a large flat, lowland area surrounded by hills so that is is shaped like a bowl. The Carpentaria Basin is a southern extension of the Gulf of Carpentaria. Further south is the Great Artesian Basin. The isolated town of Alice Springs is in this region. South again, the third basin is around the Murray river and its main tributaries, the Darling and the Murrumbidgee rivers.

Along the eastern coast of Australia is the Great Dividing Range. These mountains separate the wetter coastal areas from the dry interior. Most Australians live in the cities, towns and farmlands between these mountains and the Pacific coast. The five largest cities in Australia are also the main ports. Sydney has a population of almost 3 million. Melbourne, Brisbane, Adelaide and Perth are the other large cities.

Sheep-raising is very important in Australia and there are many more sheep than people. The country exports wool and lamb. Mining for silver, gold and other metals are important Australian industries.

The climate of Australia is varied. Much of the centre is hot desert. In the north the climate is tropical but in the south and south-east the climate is milder. Fruit such as apples and peaches are some of the crops grown.

Facts and Figures

Flag

Good day

Language English

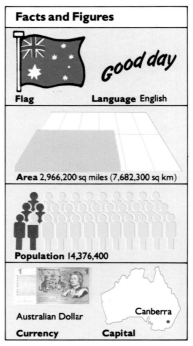

Area 2,966,200 sq miles (7,682,300 sq km)

Population 14,376,400

Australian Dollar
Currency

Canberra
Capital

▲ This map shows the states and territories in Australia. The largest state is Western Australia and the smallest territory is the tiny Australian Capital Territory.

▲ The Great Barrier Reef, along the coast of north-east Australia, is the largest coral reef in the world. It is 1,250 miles (2,000 km) long. Coral is a small marine animal related to the sea anemone. There are over 200 coral species here.

▶ Sheep stations cover huge areas of land. The heavy-coated merino sheep, which is raised for its wool, is suited to areas with little rain. Sheep for meat are raised on the wetter coastal areas.

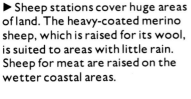

▼ Kangaroos and koalas carry their young in pouches. Koalas live in trees, feeding on leaves and shoots. Kangaroos have powerful hind legs for leaping.

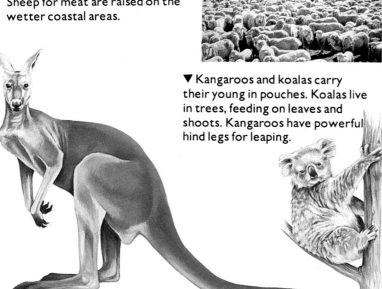

Making an Australian hat
1. Take an old felt hat with a brim, string, about 20 corks, scissors and a thick needle.

2. Cut one piece of string about 4in (10cm) long for each cork. Tie one end of the string tightly around the cork. With the needle, make a hole carefully through the hat brim about ½in (1cm) from the edge. Thread a piece of the string through the hole.
3. Repeat until the corks go around the whole brim. The hat will help protect you from the sun and keep flies out of your eyes.

▲ Australia is the largest producer of bauxite in the world. This mine is in Gove Peninsula in the north. Australia also exports lead, iron ore, nickel and zinc. Oil has been discovered in Bass Strait, south Australia. This is a valuable addition to Australia's resources.

► The famous Opera House, overlooking Sydney Harbour, was opened in 1974. Sydney is the largest city in Australia and is its chief port. Its main exports are wool, wheat, flour, sheepskins and meat. There are also shipyards and oil refineries.

◄ The Flying Doctor service was introduced for people living on sheep and cattle stations, long distances from the nearest town and doctor. Aeroplanes are an important means of transport for everyone who lives in the Australian outback.

Key

Timber	Fishing
Sugar cane	Coal
Fruit	Iron
Wheat	Minerals
Cereals	Silver
Vegetables	Gold
Bananas	Natural gas
Citrus fruit	Oil
Grapes/Wine	Bauxite
Port	
Industry	
Sheep	
Dairy	
Cattle	

Scale
0 200 km
0 200 miles

► An aborigine plays the didgeridoo, a traditional instrument. There are about 125,000 aborigines, mostly living in the semi-desert of the northern region.

New Zealand

New Zealand is a group of islands in the south-west Pacific midway between the Equator and the South Pole. The main islands are the North and South Islands. New Zealand also includes Stewart Island and some other small islands. New Zealand is about the same size as Britain or Japan. It is 930 miles (1,500 km) away from Australia and 6,580 miles (10,600 km) away from South America.

New Zealand is a mountainous country and North Island has many volcanoes. The main active volcanoes are Ruapehu and Ngauruhoe. Ruapehu is 9,175 feet (2,797 metres) high. Ngauruhoe is 7,515 feet (2,290 metres high. The North Island has pools of boiling mud.

The main mountains in South Island are the Southern Alps. There are 19 mountains over 9,000 feet (3,000 metres) high. New Zealand's highest mountain is Mount Cook in the centre of South Island. It is 12,349 feet (3,764 metres) high. In and around the Southern Alps are glaciers, lakes and large inlets called 'sounds'. South and east of the Southern Alps are the Canterbury Plains.

New Zealand is the world's largest exporter of dairy products and lamb. It is the second largest exporter of wool. Sheep farming is important on the Canterbury Plains. Cattle are raised in the North Island.

Facts and Figures

Flag   Language   English   Kiaora Maori

Area 103,747 sq miles (268,704 sc km)

Population 3,105,800

New Zealand Dollar
Currency

Wellington

Capital

▼ New Zealand has 12 land districts. On the North Island are North Auckland, South Auckland, Hawke's Bay, Gisborne, Taranaki and Wellington. The South Island has Canterbury and Marlborough. Nelson, Otago, Southland and Westland.

◀ The kiwi is a small bird which cannot fly and is found only in New Zealand. It's the symbol of New Zealand and appears on coins and stamps.

▶ The Canterbury Plains, South Island, are a very fertile area. The land is used for sheep farming and growing wheat.

▼ Nelson district, South Island, produces many tons of apples and pears for export. There is a sunny climate, transport is good and there are modern well-equipped packing stations.

▼ The Canterbury area in the South Island is known for its production of lamb. New Zealand was the first country to begin exporting frozen lamb.

▶ Farming accounts for three quarters of New Zealand's exports. Wool and lamb make up 40 per cent of exports and dairy products make up 15 per cent. This dairy herd is at South Auckland, North Island.

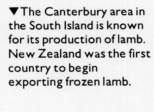

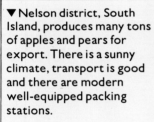

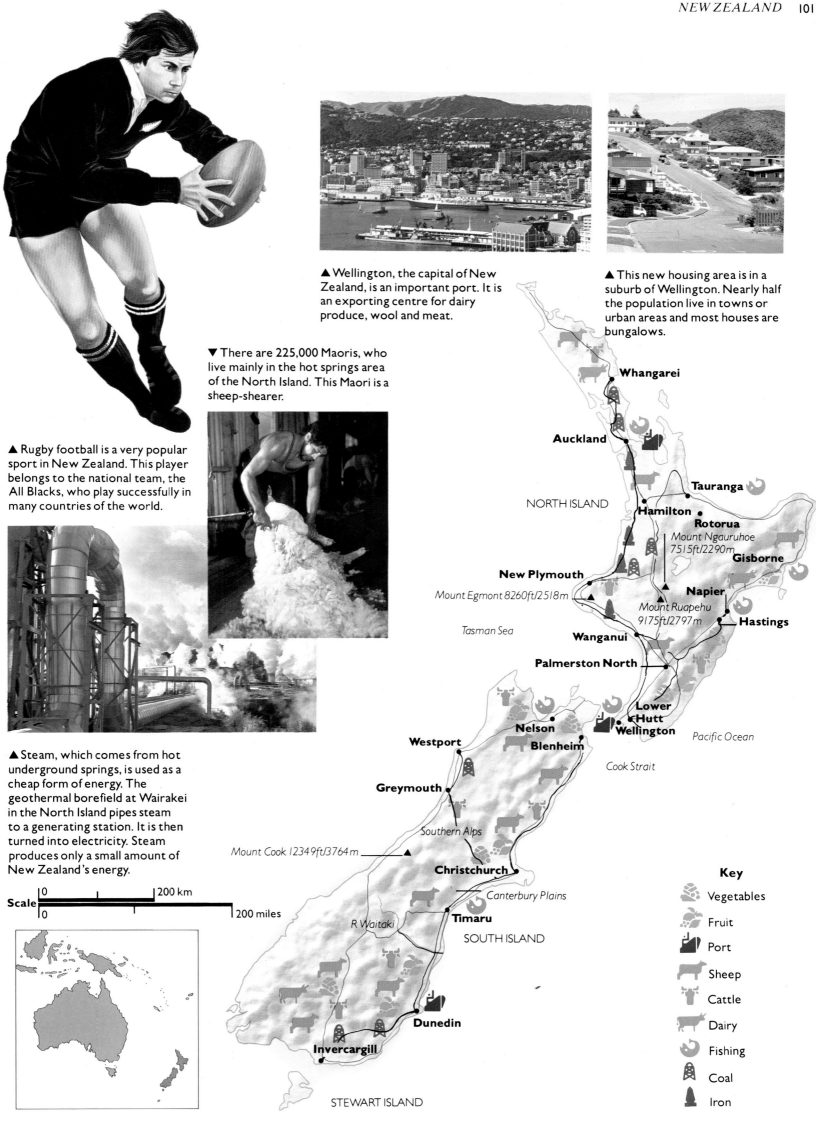

▲ Wellington, the capital of New Zealand, is an important port. It is an exporting centre for dairy produce, wool and meat.

▲ This new housing area is in a suburb of Wellington. Nearly half the population live in towns or urban areas and most houses are bungalows.

▼ There are 225,000 Maoris, who live mainly in the hot springs area of the North Island. This Maori is a sheep-shearer.

▲ Rugby football is a very popular sport in New Zealand. This player belongs to the national team, the All Blacks, who play successfully in many countries of the world.

▲ Steam, which comes from hot underground springs, is used as a cheap form of energy. The geothermal borefield at Wairakei in the North Island pipes steam to a generating station. It is then turned into electricity. Steam produces only a small amount of New Zealand's energy.

Scale

0   200 km
0   200 miles

Whangarei

Auckland

Tauranga

NORTH ISLAND

Hamilton

Rotorua

Mount Ngauruhoe 7515ft/2290m

Gisborne

New Plymouth

Mount Egmont 8260ft/2518m

Napier

Mount Ruapehu 9175ft/2797m

Hastings

Tasman Sea

Wanganui

Palmerston North

Nelson

Lower Hutt

Westport

Blenheim

Wellington

Pacific Ocean

Cook Strait

Greymouth

Southern Alps

Mount Cook 12349ft/3764m

Christchurch

Canterbury Plains

Timaru

R Waitaki

SOUTH ISLAND

Dunedin

Invercargill

STEWART ISLAND

Key

🪨 Vegetables

🍏 Fruit

🏭 Port

🐑 Sheep

🐂 Cattle

🐄 Dairy

🐦 Fishing

⛏ Coal

⛰ Iron

Oceania

Oceania is the name of the many islands in the southern Pacific Ocean. There are three main groups called Polynesia, Micronesia and Melanesia. Most of the Pacific islands are either volcanic islands or coral islands. The coral islands are usually atolls. An atoll is a coral reef shaped like a ring or a horseshoe. Inside the reef is an area of shallow water called a lagoon. Coral reefs are made from the skeletons of tiny creatures like sea anemones. When the animal dies, a skeleton is left behind. Millions and millions of these skeletons gradually build up into reefs and islands.

The Polynesian islands are to the north-east of New Zealand. The main island groups are Samoa, Tonga, the Cook Islands and Marquesas. The Hawaiian Islands are in Polynesia, too, but they now belong to the United States. The Polynesians are great boatbuilding people.

The islands of Micronesia lie to the east of the Philippines and north of New Guinea. The largest groups of islands in Micronesia are called the Marshall, Caroline and Mariana islands. Tuvalu and Kiribati are also in Micronesia.

The island region of Melanesia curves around northeast Australia. Melanesia includes some of the largest Pacific islands such as New Guinea, the Solomon Islands, New Caledonia and Fiji.

The coconut palm is the most important plant in Oceania. It provides the island people with food, drink, and building materials. When the inside of the coconut is dried it is called copra. Coconut oil comes from this.

◄ A boy displays his catch at a quayside market on the island of Tonga. The Pacific islands produce copra and bananas for export. Pineapples are grown in all parts of Polynesia.

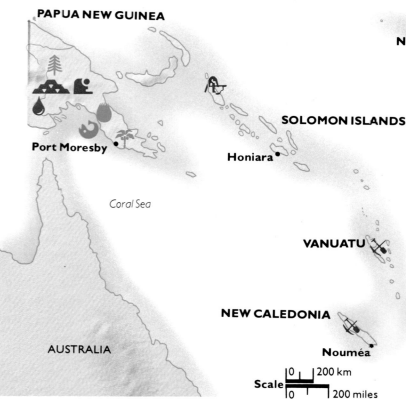

PAPUA NEW GUINEA

Port Moresby

Coral Sea

SOLOMON ISLANDS

Honiara

VANUATU

NEW CALEDONIA

AUSTRALIA

Nouméa

Scale
0   200 km
0   200 miles

NA

Facts and Figures

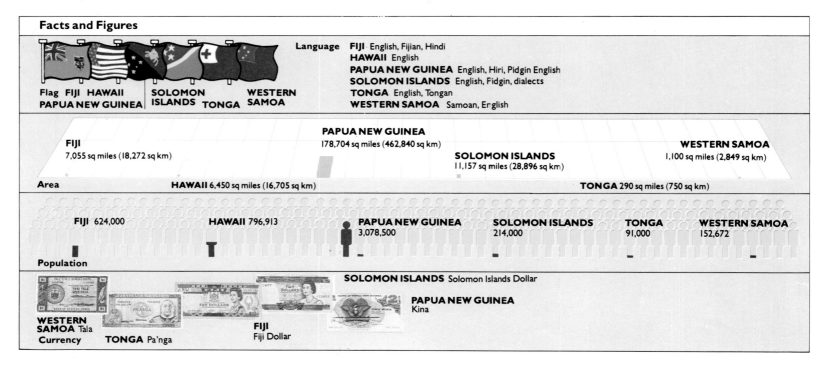

Flag	FIJI	HAWAII	SOLOMON ISLANDS	TONGA	WESTERN SAMOA
	PAPUA NEW GUINEA				

Language
FIJI English, Fijian, Hindi
HAWAII English
PAPUA NEW GUINEA English, Hiri, Pidgin English
SOLOMON ISLANDS English, Fidgin, dialects
TONGA English, Tongan
WESTERN SAMOA Samoan, English

		PAPUA NEW GUINEA 178,704 sq miles (462,840 sq km)			
FIJI 7,055 sq miles (18,272 sq km)			**SOLOMON ISLANDS** 11,157 sq miles (28,896 sq km)		**WESTERN SAMOA** 1,100 sq miles (2,849 sq km)

Area   **HAWAII** 6,450 sq miles (16,705 sq km)   **TONGA** 290 sq miles (750 sq km)

FIJI 624,000	HAWAII 796,913	**PAPUA NEW GUINEA** 3,078,500	**SOLOMON ISLANDS** 214,000	**TONGA** 91,000	**WESTERN SAMOA** 152,672

Population

SOLOMON ISLANDS Solomon Islands Dollar

PAPUA NEW GUINEA Kina

WESTERN SAMOA Tala
TONGA Pa'nga
FIJI Fiji Dollar
Currency

▼ Nobody knows who carved the ancient stone heads on Easter Island. The people are Polynesian, but the island belongs to Chile.

▲ A girl sells fabrics at a shop in Nukualofa in the Tonga Islands. The material is distinctive and colourful. Women generally make up their dresses for themselves.

▲ These women of Nukualofa are carrying food in baskets woven from coconut fronds. This is the usual way to carry things around.

Pacific Ocean

ARSHALL ISLANDS

KIRIBATI

PHOENIX ISLANDS

◄ This coral atoll is in Tahiti. The island is one of the most beautiful in the southern Pacific. It produces fruit, copra and pearls which are all exported.

TUVALU

WESTERN SAMOA
● Apia

Nukualofa

FIJI
● Suva

SOCIETY ISLANDS

MARQUESAS ISLANDS

COOK ISLANDS

TAHITI

◄ Young men of Papua New Guinea have been harvesting yams. This food is an important part of the local diet.

Key

🌲 Timber

🥥 Coconuts

🌴 Palm oil

🌾 Sugar cane

🍓 Fruit   💰 Silver

🍌 Bananas   ⛏ Copper

🐟 Fishing   🛢 Oil

⛏ Gold   ⚒ Minerals

◄ In western New Guinea the jungle is dense and the people are primitive. This village is in the middle of tropical forest.

▼ Coconuts are the fruit of coco palms which grow throughout the Pacific islands. The white flesh is called copra. Palm oil comes from this. Desiccated coconut is shredded copra, which is used in all kinds of food.

Looking at North America

North America is shaped like a huge triangle. The largest countries in this continent are Canada, the United States and Mexico. The coasts of North America touch three oceans – the Arctic, the Pacific and the Atlantic. Its northern lands are less than 500 miles (800 km) away from the North Pole. The southern part of North America is 500 miles (800km) from the Equator. The continent is so wide that it has eight time zones. This means that when it is noon at St John's in Newfoundland it is only 5am at Anchorage in Alaska.

Cape Morris Jessup in Greenland is the most northerly tip of land in the world. Although Greenland is in North America it belongs to Denmark. The Arctic Circle passes through southern Greenland, northern Canada and Alaska. The Bering Strait separates Alaska from Siberia in Asia. This narrow sea passage is only 55 miles (88 km) wide. It joins the Arctic and the Pacific oceans.

In the south of the North American continent the Tropic of Cancer passes through Mexico and the West Indies. The isthmus of Panama joins North America to South America. The Panama Canal crosses this isthmus and links the Caribbean part of the Atlantic with the Pacific Ocean.

There are three main regions in North America. In the west a chain of high mountains stretches from Alaska to Mexico. The main range is called the Rocky Mountains. Along the eastern side of the continent is another chain which includes the Appalachian Mountains. Between them lies a huge central area which extends from north to south for nearly 3,000 miles (4,800 km). This is the area of the Great Plains and the valley of the Mississippi, North America's longest river.

To the south of Mexico there are several small countries which make up Central America. The islands of the West Indies lie off the coasts of Central America and the south-eastern part of the United States.

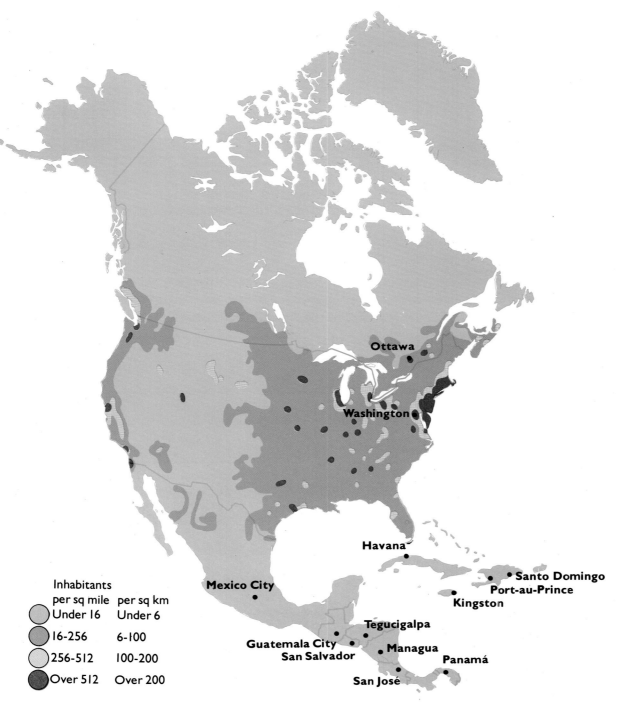

Inhabitants
per sq mile / per sq km
- Under 16 / Under 6
- 16-256 / 6-100
- 256-512 / 100-200
- Over 512 / Over 200

Ottawa
Washington
Havana
Mexico City
Santo Domingo
Port-au-Prince
Kingston
Tegucigalpa
Guatemala City
San Salvador
Managua
Panamá
San José

◀The total population of North America is 358 million people. Most of these are of European or African origin.

The United States has the largest population, with about 220 million people. Mexico comes next with 66 million. Canada is the third most populated country with 23 million people. In fact, Canada is slightly larger than the United States. However, much of its land mass falls inside, or near, the Arctic Circle. Most Canadians live in a few populated areas around the southern border.

The main centres of population in the United States are along the eastern seaboard. New York State alone contains 16 million people – an average of over 3,000 people per square mile (2,500 people per square kilometre).

The midwestern plains are less densely populated, and there are many desert areas in parts of the Rocky Mountains and the Great Salt Basin.

The western seaboard includes the urban sprawls of Los Angeles and San Francisco. Altogether, the United States has 16 cities with populations of more than 2 million people. Its vast urban population produces many industrial goods.

▼The United States is the world's leading industrial nation, and also the main producer of maize, tobacco and other agricultural goods. It is rich in coal, oil and natural gas, and it is the world's main producer of nuclear energy.

Scale

0   1000 miles

0   1000 km

Arctic Ocean

GREENLAND

Bering Strait

Brook's Range

ALASKA

Beaufort Sea

Baffin Bay

● **Anchorage** ● **Dawson**

R. Mackenzie

VICTORIA ISLAND

BAFFIN ISLAND

● **Godthaab**

Prince Rupert ●

Hudson Bay

CANADA

● **St John's**

Vancouver ●
Seattle ●

Rocky Mountains

Winnipeg

R. St Lawrence
Gulf of St Lawrence

Quebec

● **Portland**

Montreal

Pacific Ocean

Minneapolis ● ● **St Paul**
Milwaukee

R. Missouri

Toronto
Detroit

Ottawa
● **Boston**
New York City

Great Lakes

San Francisco

Salt Lake City
● **Denver**

R. Colorado

Chicago
Pittsburgh

Philadelphia
Baltimore
Washington DC

UNITED STATES

Appalachian Mts

Los Angeles ●

Cuidad Juárez **El Paso**

Dallas

R. Mississippi

Atlanta

Atlantic Ocean

Key

🌲 Timber

🌾 Wheat

🌿 Cereals

🍊 Citrus fruit

🍇 Fruit

🍇 Grapes/Wine

🌱 Cotton

🌽 Corn/Maize

🥬 Vegetables

🍌 Bananas

🌾 Sugar cane

🥜 Groundnuts

🌿 Tobacco

🏭 Port

🏭 Industry

🐂 Cattle

🐄 Dairy

⛏ Gold

🐑 Sheep

⚡ Copper

🐟 Fishing

💧 Oil

⚡ Energy

⛏ Minerals

🔥 Iron

🏭 Coal

🔥 Natural gas

🚂 Steel

MEXICO

Monterrey ●

Gulf of Mexico

Houston

New Orleans

Miami ●

BAHAMAS

WEST INDIES

Tampico

Mérida

Havana ●

CUBA

PUERTO RICO

DOMINICAN REPUBLIC

HAITI

Guadalajara ●
Mexico City ●

Veracruz

JAMAICA ● **Kingston**

Port-au-Prince

BELIZE

Caribbean Sea

GUATEMALA ● **San Pedro Sula**

Guatemala City ● **HONDURAS**

EL SALVADOR **NICARAGUA**

Managua ● *L. Nicaragua*

San José ● **Panamá**

COSTA RICA

PANAMA *Gulf of Panama*

Canada, Alaska and Greenland

Canada is in the northern part of the North American continent and it is the second largest country in the world. It extends from the Atlantic in the east to the Pacific in the west, and from the Arctic Ocean in the north to the United States in the south. This boundary follows the St Lawrence River, the Great Lakes and the 49th Parallel which is a line of latitude. In the north-west, Canada also has a border with Alaska which is part of the United States.

Canada consists of the Arctic regions in the north, the Rocky Mountains in the west, the Laurentian Plateau in the east and the vast central prairies. The St Lawrence River is part of a seaway which connects the five great lakes of Canada and the United States with the Atlantic Ocean. The island of Newfoundland lies to the north of the Gulf of St Lawrence.

Most Canadians live in the provinces of Ontario and Quebec in the south-east. Central Ontario is one of the world's important mining areas. The southern part of the province, surrounded by the lakes, is a farming area famous for its fruit. Toronto is the capital of Ontario.

The province of Quebec is French speaking. It contains Montreal which is Canada's largest city and one of the busiest ports in North America. The historic city of Quebec is the provincial capital. Canada's main capital city is Ottawa which is in Ontario on the border with Quebec.

The prairie provinces of Manitoba, Saskatchewan and Alberta all produce wheat. Alberta also has oilfields, coal mines and valuable mineral resources. British Columbia is Canada's mountainous state in the west. Its main city is Vancouver which is Canada's largest port on the Pacific. Canada is one of the world's main industrial countries. Most of its trade is with the United States. Timber, oil, natural gas and cereals are all exported.

Very few people live in the cold north of Canada apart from the Eskimos. However, there are mining camps, weather and defence stations and fur-trading posts where people buy and sell fur.

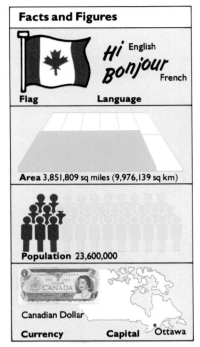

Facts and Figures

Flag | Language

Hi English
Bonjour French

Area 3,851,809 sq miles (9,976,139 sq km)

Population 23,600,000

Canadian Dollar

Currency | **Capital** Ottawa

▲ The city of Quebec has many fortifications. In 1759, a young man named General James Wolfe led British troops to victory in their battle against the French. He landed his troops in a cove at the bottom of the Heights of Abraham. The men scaled the cliffs to reach the city.

▲ Canada is made up of ten provinces: Newfoundland, Nova Scotia, New Brunswick, Prince Edward Island, Quebec, Ontario, Manitoba, Saskatchewan, Alberta and British Columbia. In addition, Canada includes vast Arctic regions where few people live. These are the Yukon Territory and North-west Territories.

▼ The Indians of north-western Canada have carved totem poles for hundreds of years. The totem is a ritual bond between members of a community.

▲ The Welland Ship Canal is on the St Lawrence Seaway. It links Lake Ontario with Lake Erie. The lakes are on different levels, so the canal includes a system of locks. It was opened in 1959 to connect the lakes but avoid the Niagara Falls.

▶ Mount Robson is the highest peak in the Canadian Rocky Mountains. The summit is 12,972 feet/3,954 metres above sea level. It stands in a vast forest reserve of mountains, falls and glaciers, which is popular with visitors.

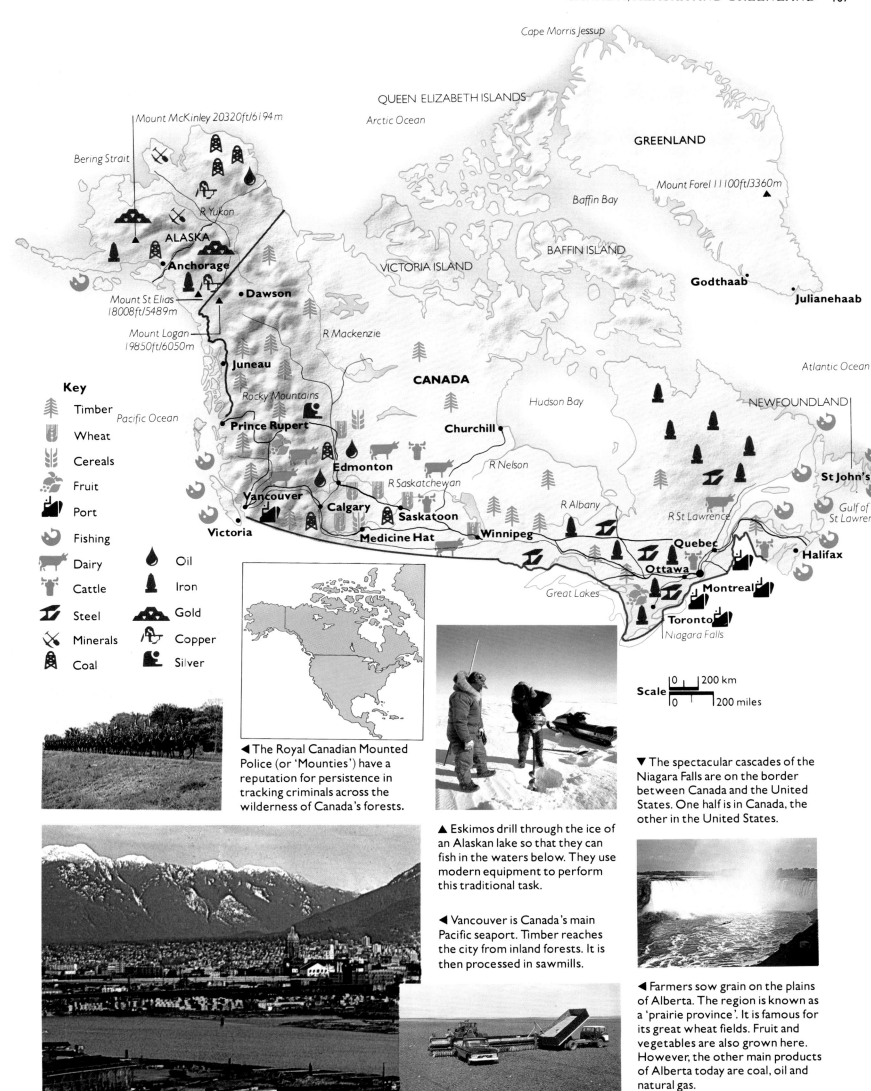

Cape Morris Jessup

QUEEN ELIZABETH ISLANDS

Arctic Ocean

GREENLAND

Mount McKinley 20320ft/6194m

Bering Strait

Baffin Bay

Mount Forel 11100ft/3360m

R Yukon

ALASKA

VICTORIA ISLAND

BAFFIN ISLAND

Anchorage

Mount St Elias
18008ft/5489m

Dawson

Godthaab

Julianehaab

Mount Logan
19850ft/6050m

R Mackenzie

Juneau

Atlantic Ocean

CANADA

Rocky Mountains

Pacific Ocean

Hudson Bay

NEWFOUNDLAND

Prince Rupert

Churchill

Key

Timber

Wheat

Cereals

Fruit

Port

Fishing

Dairy

Cattle

Steel

Minerals

Coal

Oil

Iron

Gold

Copper

Silver

Edmonton

R Nelson

St John's

Vancouver

Calgary

R Saskatchewan

R Albany

Gulf of
St Lawrence

Saskatoon

R St Lawrence

Victoria

Medicine Hat

Winnipeg

Quebec

Halifax

Ottawa

Montreal

Great Lakes

Toronto

Niagara Falls

Scale

0   200 km

0   200 miles

◀ The Royal Canadian Mounted
Police (or 'Mounties') have a
reputation for persistence in
tracking criminals across the
wilderness of Canada's forests.

▲ Eskimos drill through the ice of
an Alaskan lake so that they can
fish in the waters below. They use
modern equipment to perform
this traditional task.

◀ Vancouver is Canada's main
Pacific seaport. Timber reaches
the city from inland forests. It is
then processed in sawmills.

▼ The spectacular cascades of the
Niagara Falls are on the border
between Canada and the United
States. One half is in Canada, the
other in the United States.

◀ Farmers sow grain on the plains
of Alberta. The region is known as
a 'prairie province'. It is famous for
its great wheat fields. Fruit and
vegetables are also grown here.
However, the other main products
of Alberta today are coal, oil and
natural gas.

United States

The United States of America is one of the world's largest countries in both size and population. The country is in the central part of the North American continent between Canada and Mexico. It extends from the Atlantic Ocean in the east to the Pacific Ocean in the west.

Within these boundaries are 48 states which each have their own government and capital city. The capital of the United States is Washington DC. DC stands for District of Columbia. Alaska, in the north-west of the continent, and Hawaii, a group of islands in the central Pacific, are also states of the union. This makes a total of 50 states. The United States flag is called the 'stars and stripes'. There are 50 stars on the flag, one for each state.

The United States has a wide variety of land forms including mountains, plateau lands, hot desert basins, plains, lowlands, coastal swamps and wooded uplands. Its climate also varies from very hot in the south to much colder weather along the Canadian border and in the Rocky Mountains.

Between the Rocky and the Appalachian Mountains lie the Great Plains and the Mississippi basin. This is some of the richest farmland in the world. Cotton, wheat, maize and tobacco are all important farm products. Beef and dairy cattle, pigs and sheep are reared in parts of the Great Plains. The United States is also a major industrial country. It is the world's largest producer of both coal and petroleum products and it has many mines and oil wells.

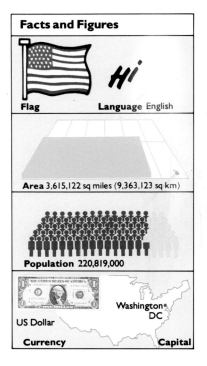

Facts and Figures

Flag　　　　　Language English

Area 3,615,122 sq miles (9,363,123 sq km)

Population 220,819,000

US Dollar　　　　　Washington DC

Currency　　　　**Capital**

▲ On 21 July, 1969, the Apollo II lifted off with three astronauts and landed on the moon. Neil Armstrong called this "a giant leap for mankind."

▲ The United States is made up of 50 states. Forty-nine of these are on the continent and the fiftieth, Hawaii, is a group of islands in the Pacific Ocean.
Washington DC is the capital.

▼ New York City is the largest city in the United States and the third largest in the world. It is the trading centre of the country.

Mount Rainier 14408ft/4392m　　　Seattle　　　CANADA

Portland

R Columbia　　R Snake

R Yellowstone

Salt Lake City　　R Pla

Denver
Mount Elbert 14431ft/4399m

San Francisco
Mount Whitney 14495ft/4418m
R Colorado　　Rocky Mountains

Los Angeles

Pacific Ocean

El Paso

MEXICO

◄ American food and drink is famous all over the world. One of the advantages of the hamburger is that it can be served to customers in a very short time.

► The Grand Canyon runs along the River Colorado and is from 4 to 18 miles (6.4 to 29 kms) wide and 217 miles (349 kms) long. Many visitors go there each year.

◄ The Everglades are a marshy, tropical area in Florida. The National Park is the third largest in the world.

◄ Baseball is one of the most popular sports in the United States. It comes from the English game of rounders.

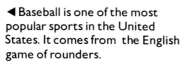

► The Walt Disney cartoon characters Mickey and Minnie Mouse are known all over the world. Disneyworld in Florida and Disneyland in California are major tourist attractions.

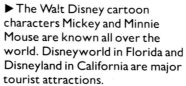

◄ Many Indians still live in the western part of the United States. These are Navajo Indians of Arizona. They are the largest tribe in America.

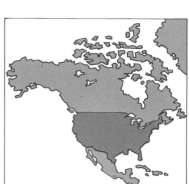

◄ Las Vegas, Nevada is a popular gambling and nightclub resort. Its bright lights and famous actors and singers attract people from far and wide.

Key

Wheat		Port		Coal	
Corn/Maize		Industry		Minerals	
Cotton		Cattle		Oil	
Fruit		Dairy		Natural gas	
Groundnuts		Fishing		Iron	
Tobacco		Sheep		Steel	
Grapes/Wine		Pigs		Uranium	

▲ The River Mississippi is the principal river of the United States. Steamer and paddle boats were common in the nineteenth century.

► These musicians are in St Louis, Missouri, which is on the Mississippi. Jazz music is very popular and many groups are formed here.

Scale 0 | 200 km
0 | 200 miles

Central America

Mexico is between the United States and the Central American republics of Guatemala and Honduras. The Rio Grande forms the north-eastern border with the United States. This river also divides the mainly English speaking part of the Americas (Anglo-America) from the Spanish and Portuguese speaking part to the south (Latin America).

The eastern and western Sierra Madre, two mountain ranges, run through Mexico. Between them is a plateau. The highest peaks in Mexico are Citlaltepetl (18,700 feet/5,700 metres) and Popocatepetl (17,887 feet/5,452 metres). Both are snow-covered volcanoes which have erupted in the past.

The Tropic of Cancer crosses the centre of Mexico. The country's climate is tropical in the south and more temperate in the north and in the highlands. There is dense tropical forest in the south, especially in Yucatan, which is Mexico's largest lowland area.

Maize, coffee, cotton, sugar cane, sisal and chicle are Mexico's main farming products. Sisal is the fibre from which ropes are made and chicle is used in making chewing gum. Mexico's wealth comes from minerals and from oil and natural gas wells along the Gulf coast. Mexico City, the capital, is one of the world's largest cities.

Central America is made up of the countries of Guatemala, Honduras, El Salvador, Belize, Nicaragua, Costa Rica, Panama and the Panama Canal Zone. Compared to Mexico, they are small countries. They all have tropical climates. The important products of Central America are coffee, bananas, sugar and cotton. Some minerals and oil products are also exported.

▲ The peak of Popocatepetl is covered with snow all the year round. It has not erupted for many years. However, sometimes smoke billows from the crater.

▶ The Latin American building in Mexico City is 43 floors high. Mexico's sprawling capital contains over 15 million people.

◀ Indians tend their coffee crop in the highlands of Guatemala. The Fuego volcano is in the background.

▶ A Mexican girl has a haircut. In small villages, many craftsmen work in the open air. The shop's plaster walls are typical of much building in Mexico.

Facts and Figures

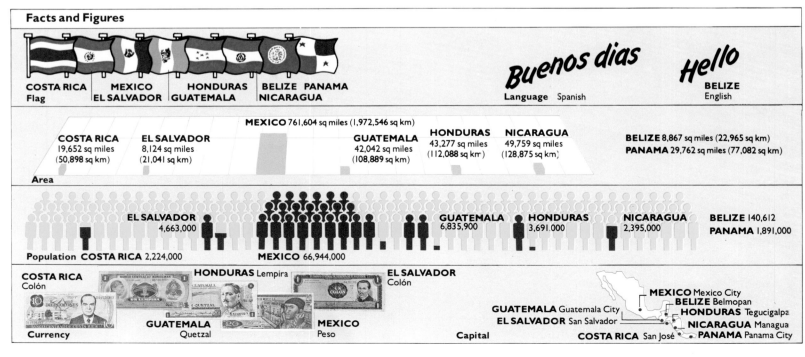

Flag				
COSTA RICA	MEXICO EL SALVADOR	HONDURAS GUATEMALA	BELIZE PANAMA NICARAGUA	

Language Spanish — *Buenos dias*

BELIZE English — *Hello*

Area

MEXICO 761,604 sq miles (1,972,546 sq km)

COSTA RICA 19,652 sq miles (50,898 sq km)	EL SALVADOR 8,124 sq miles (21,041 sq km)	GUATEMALA 42,042 sq miles (108,889 sq km)	HONDURAS 43,277 sq miles (112,088 sq km)	NICARAGUA 49,759 sq miles (128,875 sq km)

BELIZE 8,867 sq miles (22,965 sq km)
PANAMA 29,762 sq miles (77,082 sq km)

Population

EL SALVADOR 4,663,000
GUATEMALA 6,835,900
HONDURAS 3,691,000
NICARAGUA 2,395,000
BELIZE 140,612
PANAMA 1,891,000
COSTA RICA 2,224,000
MEXICO 66,944,000

Currency

COSTA RICA Colón
HONDURAS Lempira
EL SALVADOR Colón
GUATEMALA Quetzal
MEXICO Peso

Capital

MEXICO Mexico City
BELIZE Belmopan
GUATEMALA Guatemala City
HONDURAS Tegucigalpa
EL SALVADOR San Salvador
NICARAGUA Managua
COSTA RICA San José
PANAMA Panama City

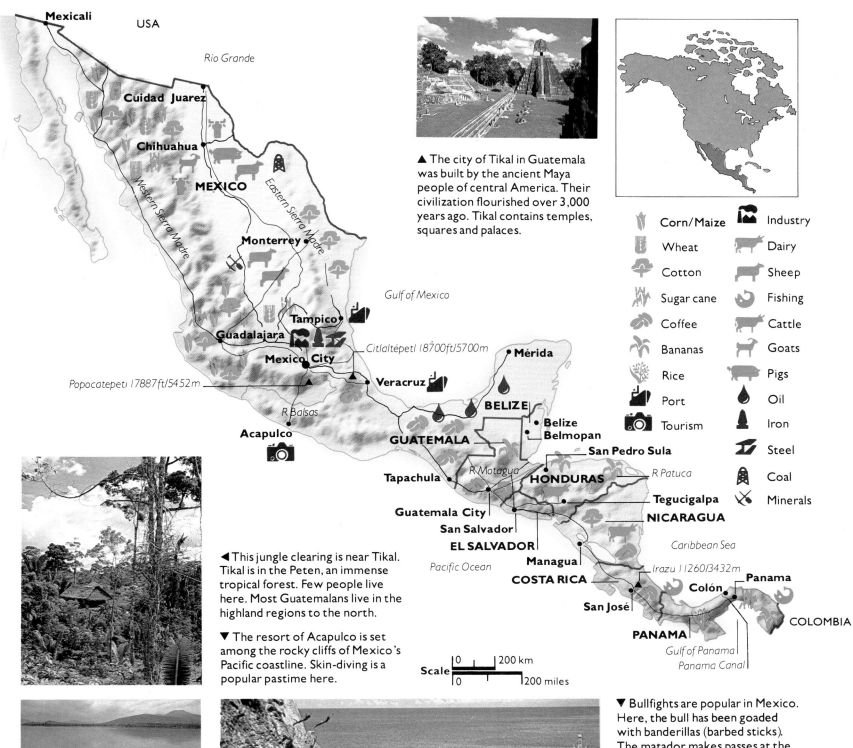

Map labels:

Mexicali
USA
Río Grande
Cuidad Juarez
Chihuahua
MEXICO
Eastern Sierra Madre
Western Sierra Madre
Monterrey
Gulf of Mexico
Tampico
Guadalajara
Citlaltépetl 18700ft/5700m
Mexico City
Mérida
Popocatepeti 17887ft/5452m
Veracruz
R Balsas
Acapulco
BELIZE
Belize
Belmopan
GUATEMALA
San Pedro Sula
Tapachula
R Motagua
HONDURAS
R Patuca
Guatemala City
Tegucigalpa
San Salvador
NICARAGUA
EL SALVADOR
Caribbean Sea
Managua
Pacific Ocean
Irazu 11260/3432m
COSTA RICA
Colón
Panama
San José
COLOMBIA
PANAMA
Gulf of Panama
Panama Canal

The city of Tikal in Guatemala was built by the ancient Maya people of central America. Their civilization flourished over 3,000 years ago. Tikal contains temples, squares and palaces.

Key:

- Corn/Maize
- Wheat
- Cotton
- Sugar cane
- Coffee
- Bananas
- Rice
- Port
- Tourism
- Industry
- Dairy
- Sheep
- Fishing
- Cattle
- Goats
- Pigs
- Oil
- Iron
- Steel
- Coal
- Minerals

◄ This jungle clearing is near Tikal. Tikal is in the Peten, an immense tropical forest. Few people live here. Most Guatemalans live in the highland regions to the north.

▼ The resort of Acapulco is set among the rocky cliffs of Mexico's Pacific coastline. Skin-diving is a popular pastime here.

Scale
0 ——— 200 km
0 ——— 200 miles

▼ Bullfights are popular in Mexico. Here, the bull has been goaded with banderillas (barbed sticks). The matador makes passes at the bull with his cape. He prepares himself for the kill.

▲ Indians fish on Lake Patzcuaro in western Mexico. The 'butterfly' shape of their nets is typical of the local fishermen. The people are Tarascan Indians. The scenery makes Patzcuaro a popular resort.

◄ The town of Antigua in Guatemala lies on an earthquake belt. It has often been hit by earthquakes and floods. Many historic buildings have been destroyed. Here, Indians sell fruit and vegetables in a market in the ruins of a Jesuit monastery.

◄ A Mexican woman weaves serapes at her loom in Oaxaca. A serape is a woollen blanket. Oaxaca is a state in southern Mexico, and most of its people are Indians. It is famous for its handicrafts which include fine pottery and leatherwork.

The Caribbean

The West Indies or Antilles are made up of many islands which form a chain over 2,500 miles (4,000 km) long stretching from Yucatan and Florida to the north coast of South America.

The islands can be divided into three groups. The first group is the Bahama Islands off the coast of Florida. Here there are over 700 islands and reefs, but only 20 are populated. Andros is the largest island but Nassau, the capital of the Bahamas, is on the small island of New Providence. Fruits and vegetables are the main products of the Bahamas.

The Greater Antilles form the second group of islands and include Cuba, Jamaica, Hispaniola and Puerto Rico. Cuba is larger than all the other West Indian Islands combined. It is famous for its tobacco, and it also produces sugar. The capital of Cuba is Havana which is a major port and the largest city in the West Indies.

The island of Hispaniola belongs to both Haiti and the Dominican Republic. Puerto Rico is associated with the United States and many of its people now live and work in American cities. Jamaica is famous for crops such as sugar cane and bananas. Kingston is its capital.

The Lesser Antilles make up the third group of West Indian islands. They extend in a curve from Puerto Rico to the coast of Venezuela. The largest island is Trinidad which is also famous for its sugar crop. Other islands in this group include Barbados, Tobago, Martinique, Guadaloupe, Dominica and Grenada. Britain, France and the Netherlands still have West Indian colonies.

The West Indies suffer from hurricanes which are strong, destructive winds. Many tourists visit the islands because of the hot summers and the mild winters.

▲ This 'shanty' town is in Dominica. Poverty is a problem throughout the West Indies. Many people live in townships known as 'shanties' built from any material available.

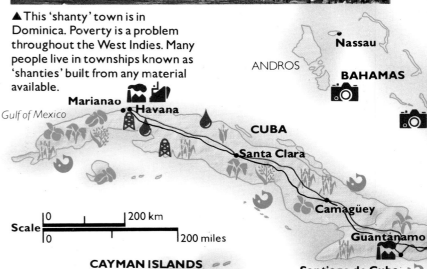

◄ Fishing nets are being hung out to dry in the hot sun on a beach in St Lucia. In the background, the Pitons are visible. These are cone-shaped peaks which are produced by volcanic action. Most of the island's soil is volcanic and fertile. Forests, lush vegetation and tropical fruit grow well here.

◄ A Cuban woman rolls a Havana cigar. Tobacco is one of Cuba's main exports. The fine leaves of Havana cigars are highly prized. The inner leaves are pressed, and the outer ones wrapped spirally around them.

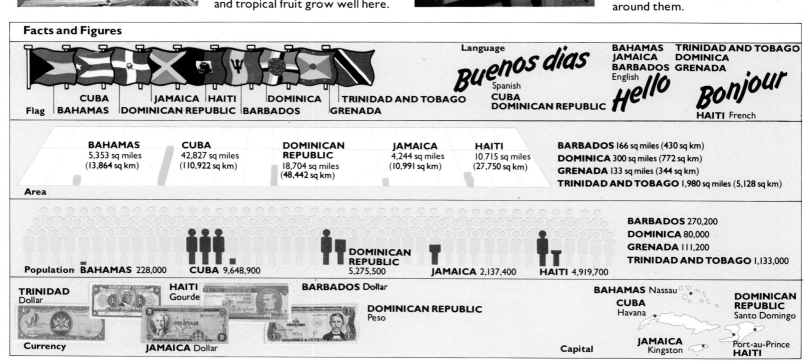

Facts and Figures

Flag | CUBA | BAHAMAS | JAMAICA | DOMINICAN REPUBLIC | HAITI | DOMINICA | BARBADOS | TRINIDAD AND TOBAGO | GRENADA

Language
Buenos días Spanish — CUBA, DOMINICAN REPUBLIC
Hello English — BAHAMAS, JAMAICA, BARBADOS, TRINIDAD AND TOBAGO, DOMINICA, GRENADA
Bonjour HAITI French

Area

BAHAMAS	CUBA	DOMINICAN REPUBLIC	JAMAICA	HAITI	
5,353 sq miles (13,864 sq km)	42,827 sq miles (110,922 sq km)	18,704 sq miles (48,442 sq km)	4,244 sq miles (10,991 sq km)	10,715 sq miles (27,750 sq km)	BARBADOS 166 sq miles (430 sq km) DOMINICA 300 sq miles (772 sq km) GRENADA 133 sq miles (344 sq km) TRINIDAD AND TOBAGO 1,980 sq miles (5,128 sq km)

Population BAHAMAS 228,000 CUBA 9,648,900 DOMINICAN REPUBLIC 5,275,500 JAMAICA 2,137,400 HAITI 4,919,700

BARBADOS 270,200
DOMINICA 80,000
GRENADA 111,200
TRINIDAD AND TOBAGO 1,133,000

Currency
TRINIDAD Dollar
HAITI Gourde
BARBADOS Dollar
DOMINICAN REPUBLIC Peso
JAMAICA Dollar

Capital
BAHAMAS Nassau
CUBA Havana
DOMINICAN REPUBLIC Santo Domingo
JAMAICA Kingston
HAITI Port-au-Prince

◄ A banana grower brings in his crop on the Leeward island of Montserrat. Bananas are grown throughout the West Indies. The clusters grow upwards. They are picked while green.

▼ Workmen cut sugar cane in Cuba. It is hard work, carried out by hand with a heavy knife called a machete. Sugar is Cuba's main export.

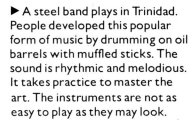

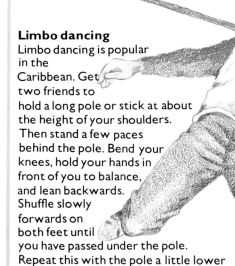

Limbo dancing
Limbo dancing is popular in the Caribbean. Get two friends to hold a long pole or stick at about the height of your shoulders. Then stand a few paces behind the pole. Bend your knees, hold your hands in front of you to balance, and lean backwards. Shuffle slowly forwards on both feet until you have passed under the pole. Repeat this with the pole a little lower each time. Be careful not to fall backwards as you might hurt yourself.

► A steel band plays in Trinidad. People developed this popular form of music by drumming on oil barrels with muffled sticks. The sound is rhythmic and melodious. It takes practice to master the art. The instruments are not as easy to play as they may look.

Pico Duarte 10200ft/3175m

HAITI

Port-au-Prince

Atlantic Ocean

Santo Domingo
DOMINICAN REPUBLIC

Caribbean Sea

PUERTO RICO
San Juan

Ponce

⌐ **ANGUILLA**

ST CHRISTOPHER
NEVIS
MONTSERRAT

ANTIGUA
• **St Johns**

GUADELOUPE

DOMINICA
Roseau •

MARTINIQUE
Fort-de-France

ST LUCIA

ST VINCENT

Bridgetown
BARBADOS

GRENADA
St George's •

NETHERLANDS ANTILLES

Willemstad

Coffee		Palm oil	
Citrus fruit		Corn/Maize	
Sugar cane		Tourism	
Bananas		Port	
Cacao		Industry	
Tobacco		Oil	
Rice		Coal	
		Bauxite	
		Copper	
		Minerals	

TRINIDAD AND TOBAGO
Port-of-Spain

► The main sport in the West Indies is cricket. Children often play on beaches or in the streets. Here top player Viv Richards plays a typical stroke.
◄ Deserted beaches, like this one on the island of San Andres, attract many foreign visitors. Tourism is a major industry in the West Indies.

Looking at South America

South America is the fourth largest continent in the world. The isthmus of Panama joins it to Central America. South America's shape is like a triangle which becomes very narrow towards the southern tip of Chile and Argentina. Here the Strait of Magellan separates a group of islands called Tierra del Fuego from the mainland. Cape Horn is south of these islands. The Falkland Islands are part of South America. They lie over 250 miles (400 km) off the east coast.

South America has four highland regions – the Andes, the Guiana Highlands, the Brazilian Highlands and the Patagonian uplands – and it has three lowland areas which are the Amazon basin, the Orinoco basin and the Parana-Paraguay plain. The Andes Mountains dominate the west of South America. They extend from north to south through Venezuela, Colombia, Ecuador, Peru, Bolivia, Chile and Argentina. Many of the mountains in the Andes are volcanic and are over 9,500 feet (6,000 metres high. Even at the Equator the peaks are so high that they are covered in snow. Aconcagua (22,835

feet/6,850 metres) in Argentina is the highest mountain in the western hemisphere.

The Guiana Highlands are shared by Venezuela, Brazil and Guyana. Mount Roraima (9,220 feet/2,816 metres) is its highest point. To the north is the Orinoco basin. The eastern part, called the Llanos, is a large grassland area. The vast Amazon lowlands separate the Guiana Highlands from the Brazilian Highlands. The Parana-Paraguay lowlands lie between the Brazilian Highlands and the Andes. In the north is the Gran Chaco area which is dry scrubland. The southern part is rich grassland called the Pampas. The barren tableland of Patagonia is even further south than the Pampas.

It was mainly the Spanish and the Portuguese who colonized South America so many people who now live there are of Spanish and Portuguese descent. There are also many Indians and negroes. Spanish is spoken in twelve of the countries in South America and Portuguese is spoken in Brazil. The Indians also speak many native dialects.

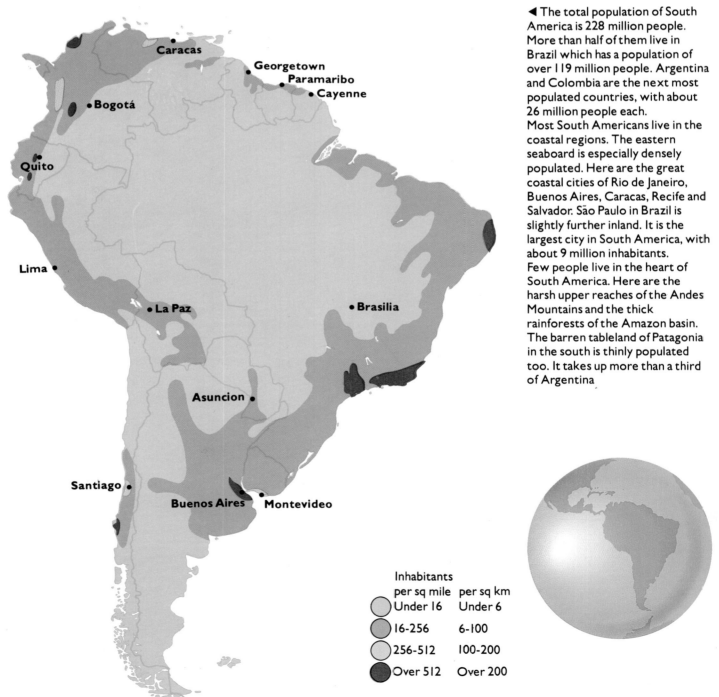

◄ The total population of South America is 228 million people. More than half of them live in Brazil which has a population of over 119 million people. Argentina and Colombia are the next most populated countries, with about 26 million people each.

Most South Americans live in the coastal regions. The eastern seaboard is especially densely populated. Here are the great coastal cities of Rio de Janeiro, Buenos Aires, Caracas, Recife and Salvador. São Paulo in Brazil is slightly further inland. It is the largest city in South America, with about 9 million inhabitants.

Few people live in the heart of South America. Here are the harsh upper reaches of the Andes Mountains and the thick rainforests of the Amazon basin. The barren tableland of Patagonia in the south is thinly populated too. It takes up more than a third of Argentina.

Inhabitants

per sq mile	per sq km
Under 16	Under 6
16-256	6-100
256-512	100-200
Over 512	Over 200

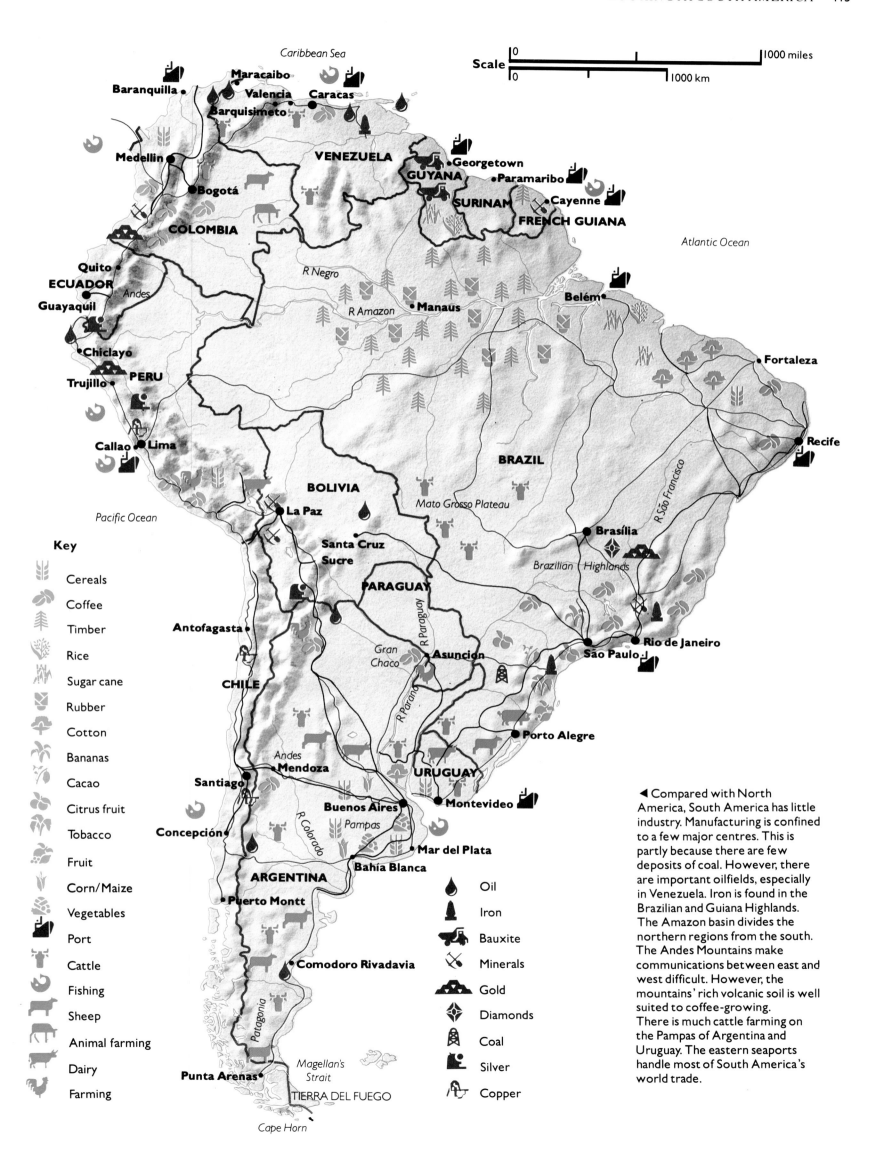

Scale

| 0 | | | 1000 miles |
| 0 | | 1000 km | |

Caribbean Sea

Barranquilla

Maracaibo
Valencia
Barquisimeto
Caracas

VENEZUELA

GUYANA
Georgetown
Paramaribo
SURINAM
Cayenne
FRENCH GUIANA

Atlantic Ocean

Medellin

Bogotá

COLOMBIA

R Negro

Quito
ECUADOR
Andes
Guayaquil

R Amazon
Manaus

Belém

Chiclayo

Fortaleza

Trujillo
PERU

BRAZIL

Callao
Lima

R São Francisco

Recife

Pacific Ocean

BOLIVIA

La Paz

Mato Grosso Plateau

Brasília

Santa Cruz
Sucre

Brazilian Highlands

PARAGUAY

Antofagasta

R Paraguay

Rio de Janeiro
São Paulo

Gran
Chaco

Asuncion

CHILE

R Paraná

Porto Alegre

Andes
Mendoza

URUGUAY

Santiago

Montevideo

Buenos Aires
Pampas

Concepción

R Colorado

Mar del Plata

Bahía Blanca

ARGENTINA

Puerto Montt

Comodoro Rivadavia

Patagonia

Punta Arenas

Magellan's
Strait

TIERRA DEL FUEGO

Cape Horn

Key

Cereals
Coffee
Timber
Rice
Sugar cane
Rubber
Cotton
Bananas
Cacao
Citrus fruit
Tobacco
Fruit
Corn/Maize
Vegetables
Port
Cattle
Fishing
Sheep
Animal farming
Dairy
Farming

Oil
Iron
Bauxite
Minerals
Gold
Diamonds
Coal
Silver
Copper

◀ Compared with North
America, South America has little
industry. Manufacturing is confined
to a few major centres. This is
partly because there are few
deposits of coal. However, there
are important oilfields, especially
in Venezuela. Iron is found in the
Brazilian and Guiana Highlands.
The Amazon basin divides the
northern regions from the south.
The Andes Mountains make
communications between east and
west difficult. However, the
mountains' rich volcanic soil is well
suited to coffee-growing.
There is much cattle farming on
the Pampas of Argentina and
Uruguay. The eastern seaports
handle most of South America's
world trade.

Brazil

Brazil, which covers half of South America, is the fifth largest country in the world. It has boundaries with all the countries in South America except Chile and Ecuador. Very few people live in the interior of Brazil. Most of its cities, industries and farmlands are in the coastal and hill country in the east.

The River Amazon, which is the largest river in the world, is just south of the Equator in Brazil. Its source is the Andes in Peru less than 100 miles (160 km) from the Pacific coast. It flows for over 4,000 miles (6,570 km) to the Atlantic in the east. The Amazon has many large tributaries which drain parts of Peru, Ecuador, Colombia and Bolivia as well as half of Brazil. The Amazon's delta is over 200 miles (320 km) wide and its muddy waters can be seen far out at sea.

The Amazon basin, or Amazonia, is a huge lowland area covered with thick equatorial forest. The Brazilian Highlands and the Mato Grosso Plateau are to the south of Amazonia. Cattle and other livestock ranching is important here. Sugar cane, cotton, rice, tobacco, oranges, pineapples and bananas are all grown in the coastal areas of the east. Coffee grows on the mountain slopes in the south-east. Brazil produces more coffee than any other country in the world. There are also large iron ore, tin, gold and diamond mines in Brazil. The capital of Brazil is a new city called Brasilia. It is to the north-west of Rio de Janeiro which was the old capital city. São Paulo is the largest city in South America and one of the largest cities in the world.

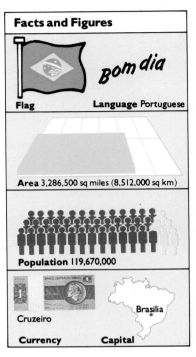

Facts and Figures

Flag　　　　　Language Portuguese

Bom dia

Area 3,286,500 sq miles (8,512,000 sq km)

Population 119,670,000

Cruzeiro

Currency

Brasilia

Capital

▼ Brasilia is a new city which was opened in 1960. It was built as Brazil's new capital to encourage people to settle in the country's central region. Many of its buildings are strikingly modern.

▼ A tributary of the River Amazon winds through the dense rain forests which cover much of the river's basin. There are many remote regions known only to the local Indian peoples.

▶ Guarani Indians like these live in village communities in many parts of northern South America. Guarani of the Amazon region are know as Tupi.

Making coffee

There are many good ways of making coffee. One of the easiest methods is to use a jug or coffee pot, ground coffee and boiling water. If you have a coffee grinder, you can grind the coffee beans freshly. However, you can use ready-ground coffee instead. Put two medium spoons of coffee for each person into the pot. Boil the water and then pour it over the coffee. Be very careful not to burn yourself. Stir the coffee once or twice and leave it for a few minutes so the grounds can settle. Put a strainer over the cup and pour the coffee through it. Take care not to spill it.

◀ A Camiura Indian of the Mato Grosso wears traditional face paint and headgear. The Mato Grosso is a plateau in west central Brazil. Its name means 'thick forest' in Portuguese. European settlers brought much cattle farming to the region in the nineteenth century. Today, modern development threatens the traditional ways of life of the native Indian peoples.

▲ Rio de Janeiro is Brazil's main seaport. Corcovado peak rises above the harbour which has an immense statue of Christ at its summit.

▶ A workman examines a pile of Brazil nuts at Manaus. The city is the main trading centre on the Amazon. The nuts are the seed pods of trees which grow along the banks of the Amazon and Orinoco.

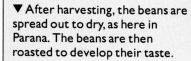

▶ Coffee workers on a plantation in Campinas tend their crop. Coffee grows well in the rich, well-drained soil of south-east Brazil.

▼ After harvesting, the beans are spread out to dry, as here in Parana. The beans are then roasted to develop their taste.

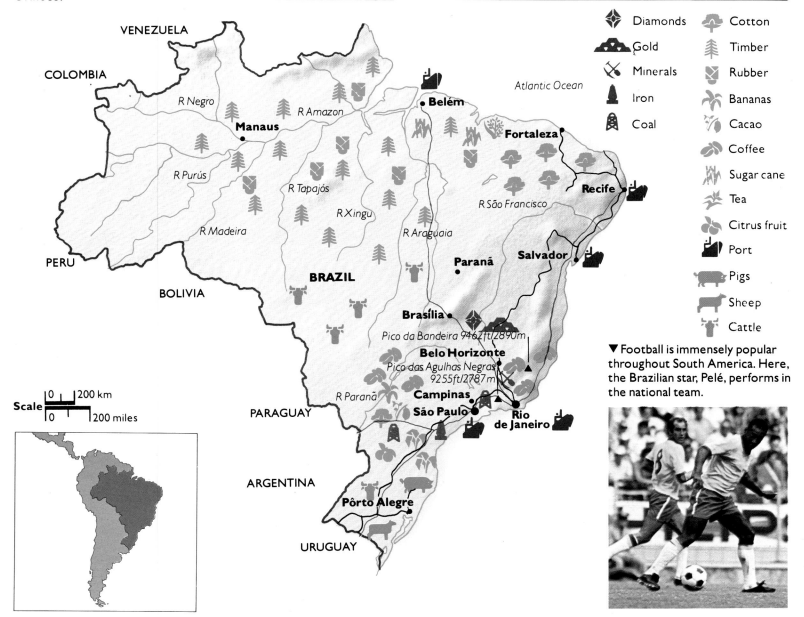

◈ Diamonds	🌿 Cotton
⛰ Gold	🌲 Timber
⚒ Minerals	🌿 Rubber
🔩 Iron	🌴 Bananas
⛽ Coal	🌿 Cacao
	🫘 Coffee
	🌾 Sugar cane
	🌿 Tea
	🍊 Citrus fruit
	🏭 Port
	🐖 Pigs
	🐑 Sheep
	🐂 Cattle

VENEZUELA

COLOMBIA

R Negro

R Amazon

Manaus

R Purús

R Tapajós

R Madeira

R Xingu

PERU

BOLIVIA

BRAZIL

R Araguaia

R São Francisco

Atlantic Ocean

Belém

Fortaleza

Recife

Salvador

Paraná

Brasília

Pico da Bandeira 9462ft/2890m

Belo Horizonte

Pico das Agulhas Negras 9255ft/2787m

R Paraná

Campinas

São Paulo

Rio de Janeiro

PARAGUAY

ARGENTINA

Pôrto Alegre

URUGUAY

Scale 0 200 km 0 200 miles

▼ Football is immensely popular throughout South America. Here, the Brazilian star, Pelé, performs in the national team.

Colombia, Venezuela and the Guianas

Colombia, Venezuela and the Guianas – which are now called Guyana, Surinam and French Guiana – are in the northern part of South America. They all have coastlines on the Caribbean Sea or the Atlantic Ocean and have boundaries with Brazil in the south. Colombia also has a coastline on the Pacific.

Colombia has a hot and swampy coastal plain. The Andes mountains separate it from the Llanos and the equatorial forests of Amazonia. On the coast there are important gold and platinum mines. Colombia's main ports are Barranquilla and Cartagena. Most Colombians live in the highlands. Bogotá, the country's capital, is 8,700 feet (2,650 metres) above sea level. The main crop in the Colombian highlands is coffee.

In Venezuela the Gulf of Venezuela and Lake Maracaibo lie in the north-west near the most northern part of the Andes. Petroleum, iron ore and coffee are the country's main products, There are thousands of oil wells in the Maracaibo lowlands. Caracas, the capital, is one of the most modern cities in South America.

Guyana is a tropical country between the deltas of the Orinoco and the Amazon. Georgetown is its capital and sugar and rice are the main crops. Guyana exports minerals such as bauxite from which aluminium is obtained. Surinam is also a major bauxite producer. Its capital is Paramaribo.

French Guiana belongs to France and is the only colonial country in South America. The country is famous for its shrimps which are sent to the United States and timber and minerals are also important. Cayenne is the capital of French Guiana.

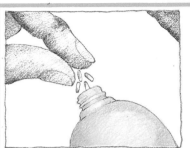

Make your own maraca
1. Take an empty plastic lemon or fruit that syrup comes in. Clean it out and put in some uncooked rice or bird seeds.

2. When enough rice is inside the lemon, fit a pencil into the opening as a handle. Use sticky tape to attach it to the lemon.

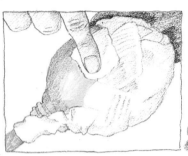

3. Now cover the lemon and pencil with small pieces of newspaper. Stick these one on top of the other either with glue or with a flour and water mixture.

4. When the maraca is a good shape, leave it to dry until it does not feel at all damp. Then paint it brightly. Now it is ready for shaking in time with music.

◄ Oil rigs rise from Venezuela's Lake Maracaibo. The surrounding region is also rich in oil, Venezuela's main export.

► The glittering sprawl of Caracas is viewed here from the south. The city has impressive new government buildings, highways and shopping centres.

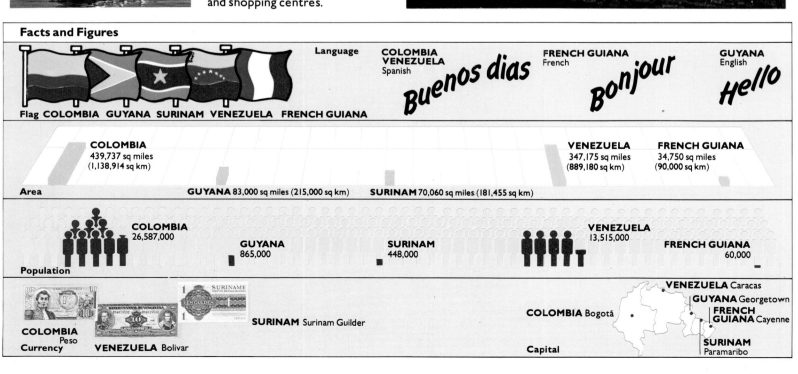

Facts and Figures

Flag COLOMBIA GUYANA SURINAM VENEZUELA FRENCH GUIANA	**Language** COLOMBIA VENEZUELA Spanish — *Buenos dias* — FRENCH GUIANA French — *Bonjour* — GUYANA English — *Hello*

Area
COLOMBIA 439,737 sq miles (1,138,914 sq km)
VENEZUELA 347,175 sq miles (889,180 sq km)
FRENCH GUIANA 34,750 sq miles (90,000 sq km)
GUYANA 83,000 sq miles (215,000 sq km)
SURINAM 70,060 sq miles (181,455 sq km)

Population
COLOMBIA 26,587,000
GUYANA 865,000
SURINAM 448,000
VENEZUELA 13,515,000
FRENCH GUIANA 60,000

Currency
COLOMBIA Peso
VENEZUELA Bolivar
SURINAM Surinam Guilder

Capital
VENEZUELA Caracas
GUYANA Georgetown
FRENCH GUIANA Cayenne
COLOMBIA Bogotá
SURINAM Paramaribo

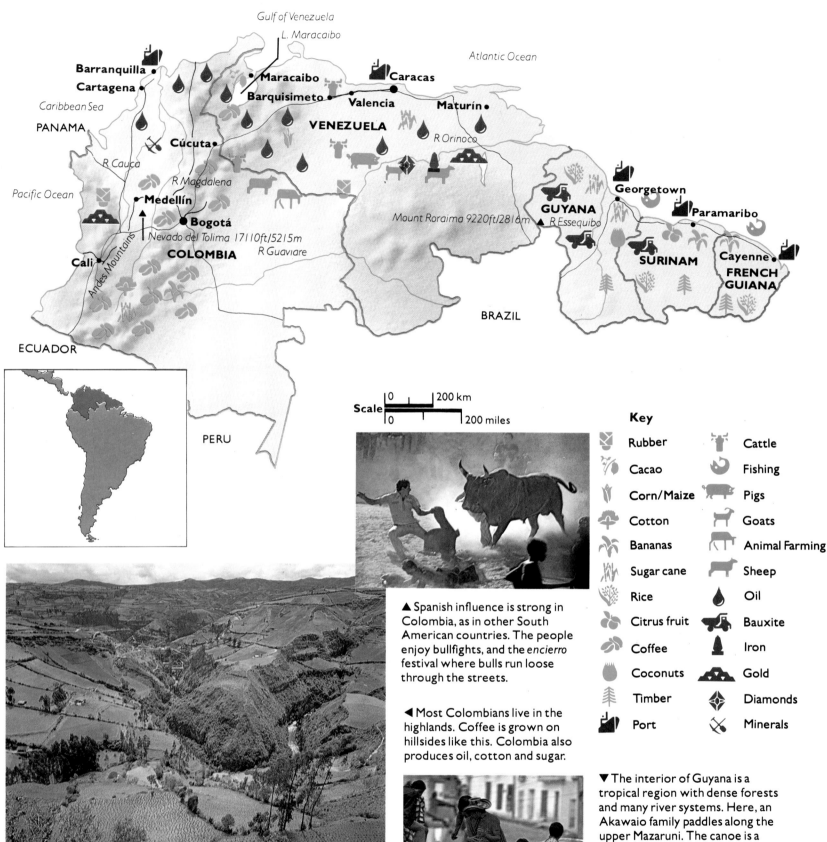

Gulf of Venezuela
L. Maracaibo
Atlantic Ocean

Barranquilla
Cartagena
Caribbean Sea
PANAMA
Maracaibo
Barquisimeto
Caracas
Valencia
Maturín
VENEZUELA
R Orinoco
Cúcuta
R Cauca
Pacific Ocean
R Magdalena
Medellín
Bogotá
Nevado del Tolima 17110ft/5215m
COLOMBIA
R Guaviare
Mount Roraima 9220ft/2816m
GUYANA
R Essequibo
Georgetown
Paramaribo
Cali
Andes Mountains
SURINAM
Cayenne
FRENCH GUIANA
BRAZIL
ECUADOR
PERU

Scale
0   200 km
0   200 miles

Key

	Rubber		Cattle
	Cacao		Fishing
	Corn/Maize		Pigs
	Cotton		Goats
	Bananas		Animal Farming
	Sugar cane		Sheep
	Rice		Oil
	Citrus fruit		Bauxite
	Coffee		Iron
	Coconuts		Gold
	Timber		Diamonds
	Port		Minerals

▲ Spanish influence is strong in Colombia, as in other South American countries. The people enjoy bullfights, and the *encierro* festival where bulls run loose through the streets.

◄ Most Colombians live in the highlands. Coffee is grown on hillsides like this. Colombia also produces oil, cotton and sugar.

▼ The interior of Guyana is a tropical region with dense forests and many river systems. Here, an Akawaio family paddles along the upper Mazaruni. The canoe is a dugout, carved from a single log.

◄ Colombian coffee workers lay out their harvest of beans to dry. The volcanic soil of the Andes Mountains is particularly good for growing the crop.

► Buses are colourful and crowded in Colombia. They are an important form of transport on the highland roads. There are few railways.

Ecuador, Peru, Bolivia and Chile

Ecuador and Peru, like Colombia, have coastal plains along the Pacific. The Andes separate these plains, which in Peru are narrow, from the Amazon forests.

The Equator passes through Ecuador and bananas and other tropical fruits grow well in the humid climate. Guayaquil, at the head of the Gulf of Guayaquil is the country's chief port. A railway from Guayaquil climbs over 9,000 feet (2,745 metres) to Quito, Ecuador's capital in the Andes. There are many volcanoes around Quito. Cotopaxi is the most active. Most of Ecuador's population live in the cooler highlands.

The Galapagos Islands belong to Ecuador. They are volcanic and they are about 650 miles (1,040 km) away from the mainland. Unusual animals such as iguanas and giant tortoises live there.

Peru is smaller than Brazil and it has a narrow coastal belt along the Pacific. The Peruvian Andes are rich in copper, lead and zinc. All the mining areas are linked to Lima, the capital, and Callao which is its port.

The highest city in South America is La Paz which is the seat of government in Bolivia. It is 12,000 feet (3,660 metres) above sea level. The capital of Bolivia is called Sucre. The Andes cover about a third of Bolivia. In the south is high tableland area called the Altiplano. This is one of the highest areas in the world where people live. Bolivia is the second largest producer of tin in the world. It also has silver, lead and tungsten mines.

Chile is a long, narrow country which stretches over 2,600 miles (4,160 km) from the Peruvian border to the southern tip of South America, Tierra del Fuego. Its widest part is only 110 miles (176 km). The Atacama Desert in the north of Chile is one of the driest places in the world and it is rich in mineral salts such as potash and iodine.

The centre of Chile, around Santiago the capital, has a climate similar to that of California. The farmers in Chile grow olives, grapes and citrus fruits.

Southern Chile is largely covered with forest. The extreme south is uninhabited. It is a land of mountains, glaciers, fjords and islands.

▶ Smoke billows from an active volcano on the border between Chile and Argentina.

▼ Volcanic mountains rise steeply from Chile's northern desert on the border with Peru.

◀ These thatched dwellings are near Pisaq in the highlands of central Peru. Three ranges of the Andes pass through the central region. Its people are mostly poor peasants. They grow just enough to feed themselves and their families. They do not sell much.

▲ The ruined city of Machu Picchu is in the mountains of Peru. The Incas once hid there from the Spanish conquerors.

▼ Llamas are creatures of the Andes. The Indians use them as beasts of burden. They also use llama wool for making clothes.

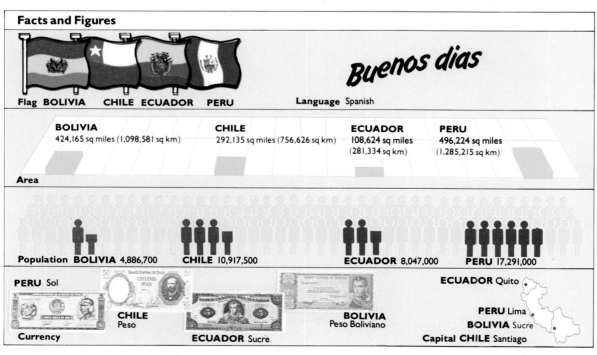

Facts and Figures

Buenos dias

Flag BOLIVIA   CHILE   ECUADOR   PERU   Language Spanish

BOLIVIA	CHILE	ECUADOR	PERU
424,165 sq miles (1,098,581 sq km)	292,135 sq miles (756,626 sq km)	108,624 sq miles (281,334 sq km)	496,224 sq miles (1,285,215 sq km)

Area

Population BOLIVIA 4,886,700   CHILE 10,917,500   ECUADOR 8,047,000   PERU 17,291,000

PERU Sol

CHILE Peso

ECUADOR Sucre

BOLIVIA Peso Boliviano

ECUADOR Quito

PERU Lima

BOLIVIA Sucre

Currency

Capital CHILE Santiago

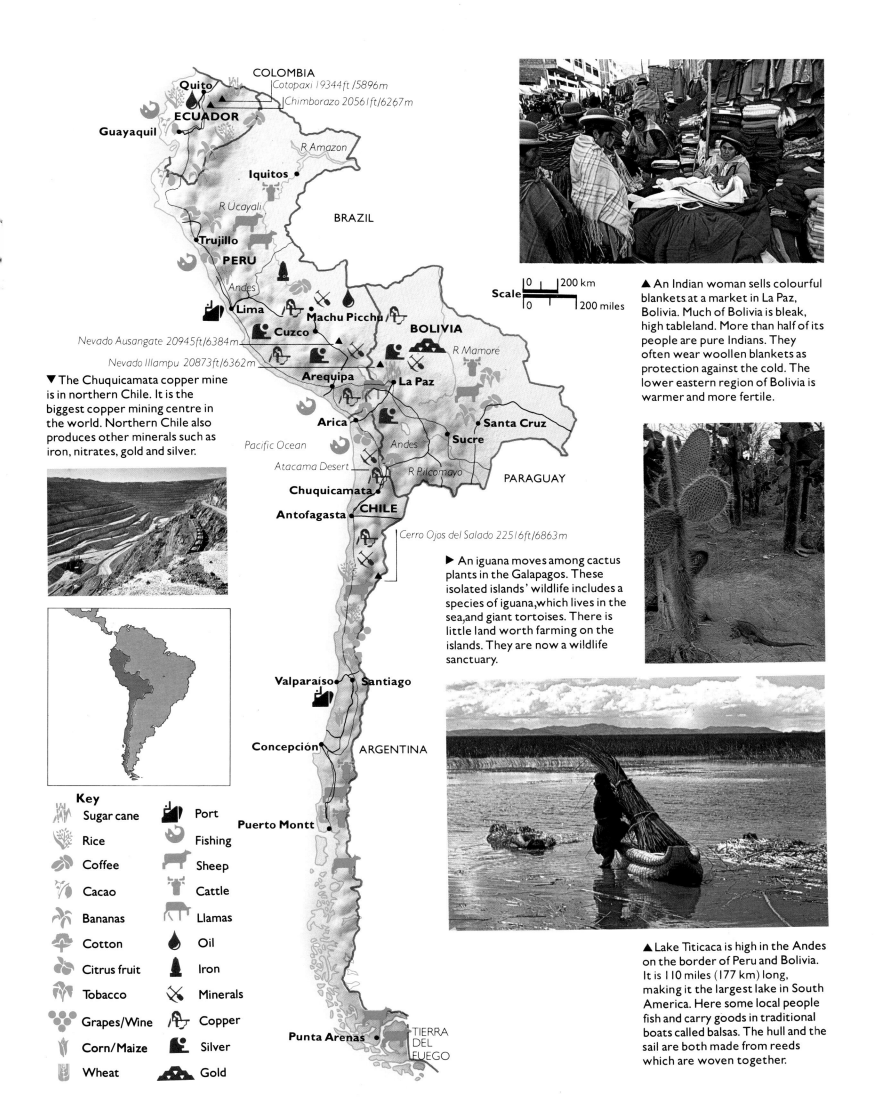

COLOMBIA

Quito
ECUADOR

Cotopaxi 19344ft /5896m
Chimborazo 20561ft/6267m

Guayaquil

R Amazon

Iquitos

R Ucayali

BRAZIL

Trujillo
PERU

Andes

Lima

Nevado Ausangate 20945ft/6384m

Machu Picchu

Cuzco

BOLIVIA

R Mamoré

Nevado Illampu 20873ft/6362m

Arequipa

La Paz

▼ The Chuquicamata copper mine is in northern Chile. It is the biggest copper mining centre in the world. Northern Chile also produces other minerals such as iron, nitrates, gold and silver.

Arica

Santa Cruz

Pacific Ocean

Sucre

Andes

Atacama Desert

R Pilcomayo

PARAGUAY

Chuquicamata

CHILE

Antofagasta

Cerro Ojos del Salado 22516ft/6863m

▲ An Indian woman sells colourful blankets at a market in La Paz, Bolivia. Much of Bolivia is bleak, high tableland. More than half of its people are pure Indians. They often wear woollen blankets as protection against the cold. The lower eastern region of Bolivia is warmer and more fertile.

Scale
0   200 km
0   200 miles

▶ An iguana moves among cactus plants in the Galapagos. These isolated islands' wildlife includes a species of iguana,which lives in the sea,and giant tortoises. There is little land worth farming on the islands. They are now a wildlife sanctuary.

Valparaíso
Santiago

Concepción
ARGENTINA

Key
〰 Sugar cane   Port
Rice   Fishing
Coffee   Sheep
Cacao   Cattle
Bananas   Llamas
Cotton   Oil
Citrus fruit   Iron
Tobacco   Minerals
Grapes/Wine   Copper
Corn/Maize   Silver
Wheat   Gold

Puerto Montt

▲ Lake Titicaca is high in the Andes on the border of Peru and Bolivia. It is 110 miles (177 km) long, making it the largest lake in South America. Here some local people fish and carry goods in traditional boats called balsas. The hull and the sail are both made from reeds which are woven together.

Punta Arenas
TIERRA DEL FUEGO

Argentina, Uruguay and Paraguay

Argentina is the second largest country in South America. It consists of four main regions. In the north there are sub-tropical plains and scrub-forests called the Gran Chaco. There are Pampas grasslands in the centre, the Andes are in the west and there is an upland plain in the south called Patagonia.

Argentina is an important meat producer. Cattle are reared on the Pampas by South American cowboys who are known as gauchos. The Pampas also grow wheat, maize, flax and cotton.

Farming is also important outside the Pampas. Cotton is grown in northern Argentina, sugar cane in the north-west and fruit trees grow in the foothills of the Andes. Patagonia is mainly a sheep rearing area, but it has oil, coal and other mineral deposits. Buenos Aires is Argentina's large capital city. It stands on the shore of the wide Rio de la Plata and is a major port. Most of Argentina's industries are in and around Buenos Aires.

Uruguay is another country of plains, low hills and plateaux. It lies on the northern shores of the Rio de la Plata. Stock-raising is the main activity in this country. Wool, animal fats, meat and leather are its chief products. Montevideo is the capital and chief port of Uruguay. It has large meat-packing stations, flour mills and textile industries. Montevideo now has a growing tourist trade from all over the world.

Paraguay has borders with Brazil, Bolivia and Argentina. It has no sea coast but the Paraguay-Parana river provides access to the Atlantic. Paraguay has very few industries and most of its people are farmers.

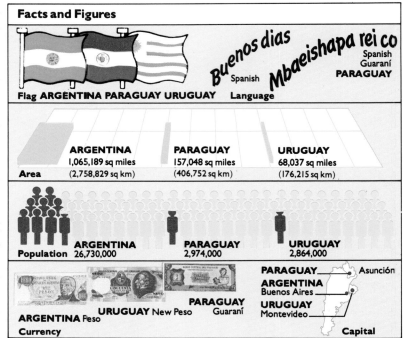

Facts and Figures

Flag ARGENTINA PARAGUAY URUGUAY

Buenos dias
Spanish
ARGENTINA

Mbaeishapa rei co
Spanish
Guaraní
PARAGUAY

Language

	ARGENTINA	PARAGUAY	URUGUAY
Area	1,065,189 sq miles (2,758,829 sq km)	157,048 sq miles (406,752 sq km)	68,037 sq miles (176,215 sq km)
Population	ARGENTINA 26,730,000	PARAGUAY 2,974,000	URUGUAY 2,864,000

Currency: ARGENTINA Peso — URUGUAY New Peso — PARAGUAY Guaraní

Capital: PARAGUAY Asunción — ARGENTINA Buenos Aires — URUGUAY Montevideo

◀ Traffic throngs down the Avenida de Corientes. This is the centre for night-life and theatre-going in Buenos Aires. Argentina's capital has a population of over 3,000,000 people. As one of the world's great ports it is constantly receiving influence from Europe, North America and elsewhere.

▶ The Chaco of Paraguay is a dry scrubland region where cactus plants grow high. There are swamps and forests too.

▼ A farm worker herds sheep in Uruguay. Over two thirds of Uruguay is given over to raising sheep and cattle.

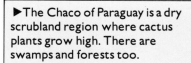

▶ Paraguayan gauchos gallop through a ranch. Gauchos pride themselves on their courage, their sense of honour and their skilful horsemanship.

◀ Paraguayan gauchos round up a herd of cattle and bring it to the ranch.

▼ Cattle are driven into pens by gauchos at a large ranch in Argentina, which exports beef.

◀ A herd of of sheep is set out to graze on the uplands of Patagonia. Sheep are raised here mainly for wool. The bare plains slope gently towards the Atlantic Ocean where the land is a bit more fertile.

▲ There are many cliffs and canyons in parts of the Argentinian Andes. These have been caused by rivers eroding rock. The steep valleys are called quebradas.

BOLIVIA

PARAGUAY

R Paraguay

●**Asunción**

San Miguel de Tucumán

R Salado

R Parana

BRAZIL

Aconcagua 22835ft/6960m

●**Córdoba**

URUGUAY

Mendoza

Tupungato 22310ft/6800m

Rosario●

Montevideo

Buenos Aires

ARGENTINA

CHILE

Mar del Plata

Bahía Blanca

R Colorado

R Negro

Atlantic Ocean

Patagonia

●**Comodoro Rivadavia**

TIERRA DEL FUEGO

Key

🌾 Rice

🌽 Corn/Maize

🍃 Tea

🌿 Cotton

🌾 Wheat

🍒 Citrus fruit

🍇 Grapes/Wine

🌾 Cereals

🍂 Fruit

📷 Tourism

🏭 Industry

⚓ Port

🐂 Cattle

🐄 Dairy

🐑 Sheep

🐟 Fishing

⛏ Coal

🔥 Natural gas

💧 Oil

Scale
0 ————— 200 km
0 ————— 200 miles

▲ A ferryboat carries a lorry on one of Paraguay's rivers. There are few good roads or railways. Paraguayan products, such as meat and timber, are often carried on the river systems.

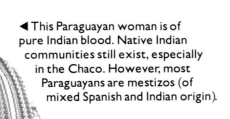

◄ This Paraguayan woman is of pure Indian blood. Native Indian communities still exist, especially in the Chaco. However, most Paraguayans are mestizos (of mixed Spanish and Indian origin).

▼ The Transandine railway runs across the Andes from Mendoza in Argentina to Santiago in Chile. Here the range is narrow but steep, and the peaks are always covered with snow.

The Arctic and the Antarctic

Antarctica lies around the South Pole and is the world's seventh continent. It is larger than both Europe and Australia and was the last continent to be discovered.

Antarctica has two deep inlets called the Ross and Weddell seas and a long, curved peninsula which is known as Graham Land. This is only 650 miles (1,040 km) away from South America. The most southern parts of the Atlantic, Pacific and Indian Oceans surround Antarctica. These seas are always stormy and are full of ice and icebergs.

For both scientific and military reasons various countries claim parts of Antarctica. Britain, France, Norway, Australia, New Zealand, Chile and Argentina all signed the Antarctic Treaty in 1959. This gave each country an area of land along the coast.

Antarctica is a plateau which rises to 10,000 feet (3,000 metres) above sea level with mountains that reach 15,000 feet (4,500 metres). Some of these are volcanic peaks. Antarctica has minerals such as copper, nickel and coal. It may have oil as well.

Very thick ice and snow cover the whole continent except for a few coastal areas in summer which are ice-free. Antarctica has the world's harshest climate and the temperature of −126°F (−88°C) has been recorded there. Like the Arctic, Antarctica has nearly 24 hours of daylight in summer and 24 hours of darkness in winter.

Unlike at the South Pole, an ocean, not a continent surrounds the North Pole. This is the Arctic Ocean and the North Pole is near its centre. The borders of this ocean are with the Arctic regions of Asia, Europe and North America. The Arctic Circle is often used as a boundary for the Arctic region. The climate at the North Pole is very cold and the temperature is nearly always below freezing point.

The Arctic Ocean flows into the Atlantic on both sides of Greenland. The Bering Strait, between Alaska and Siberia in the Soviet Union, links the Arctic with the Pacific Ocean and the Bering Sea. Compared to other oceans, the Arctic is small and because of the cold climate it is a sea of ice.

The Arctic Circle is around the North Pole. The Antarctic Circle is around the South Pole. Both are the furthest regions from the Equator so they are always cold. The Arctic is a frozen mass of water. Its shape is constantly changing as it drifts. Ice melts in some places, new ice forms in others. People can now travel under the Arctic in submarines.

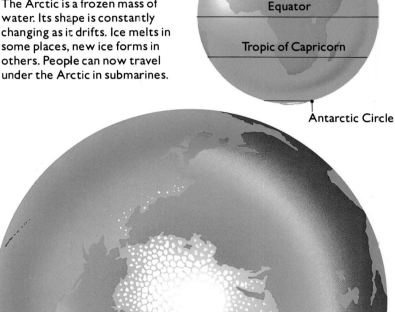

Arctic Circle

Tropic of Cancer

Equator

Tropic of Capricorn

Antarctic Circle

◀The Arctic itself is not a land mass. However, some countries have northern regions which come within the Arctic Circle. Here, melting snow forms cold streams in Norway. No trees can grow so far north. The bare landscape is known as tundra.

▲ Blizzards occur both in the Arctic and Antarctic. The high winds and driving snow make travel difficult and dangerous.

▶ Penguins are only found in the Antarctic. They live in colonies sometimes of many thousand birds.

Polar bear

Arctic tern

Penguin

Arctic fox

◀Icebreakers are ships designed for travelling through ice packs. The prow slides over the ice. The ship's weight breaks it up.

▶There are many radar stations in the Antarctic, both for scientific study and military purposes.

▶Weather stations are bases where scientists study atmospheric conditions. Results are pieced together with information from other parts of the world. Together they help to build up a total picture of the world's weather.

▲An iceberg is a block of ice that has split off from a larger mass and drifts freely in the ocean. You can see about a ninth of an iceberg on the surface. The rest is underwater. The hidden mass is dangerous to shipping.

▼The Beardmore Glacier is in Antarctica. As the glacier reaches the sea, blocks of ice break away and form icebergs.

▲The atmosphere of the Antarctic and Arctic regions can cause strange effects of light. Tiny particles of ice in the air can form

glowing shapes called parhelia. These are usually two spots which look like fake suns. They appear opposite the real sun.

▲A meteorologist checks temperatures at a weather station. The information is vital for other parts of the world. For example, if a cold air current builds up in Antarctica it will soon reach neighbouring regions.

▼The Antarctic is a true continent. Beneath the sheets of ice and snow lies a solid mass of rock. It is visible in many places.

Atlantic Ocean

QUEEN MAUD LAND

Indian Ocean

GRAHAM LAND

COATS LAND

ENDERBY LAND

Weddell Sea

Bellingshausen Sea

PRINCESS ELIZABETH LAND

Reindeer

ELLSWORTH LAND

South Pole

QUEEN MARY LAND

Beardmore Glacier

▲ Mount Markham 14270ft/435m

Pacific Ocean

BYRD LAND   Ross Ice Shelf

WILKES LAND

Seal

◀Polar bears are found on the Arctic ice cap. The Antarctic has no land animals. However, the surrounding seas are rich in fish and plankton and there are many seals and penguins. The Arctic tern migrates to the Antarctic yearly.

VICTORIA LAND

Ross Sea

Scale 0 200 km / 0 200 miles

Index

Acknowledgements

l Alan Hutchinson; 4, 6, 8 Michael Freeman; 26, 28, l, c Walter Rawlings, r Geoslides Photo Library; 29 t John Moss, c Alan Hutchinson, b South African Tourist Corp; 30 Michael Freeman; 31 t Michael Freeman, c ZEFA, b Brian Dicks; 34 Michael Freeman; 37 tl Eric Hosking, tc Oxford Scientific Films, tr J Allan Cash Ltd; 37 bl Geoslides Photo Library, bcl Walter Rawlings, bcr Barnabys Picture Library, br Michael Freeman; 41 J Allan Cash Ltd; 42 t Michael Freeman, cr British Railways Board, cl Geoslides/Peter Corrigan, b Brian Dicks; 43 t Qantas, b Alastair Campbell; 46 whole page Michael Freeman; 50 r Jon Wyand, b Irish Tourist Board; 51 tl, tc, bl Alan Hutchinson, tr, l British Tourist Authority, cr Rolls Royce, cr British Leyland, br Brian Dicks; 52 t, bl, bcl Zefa, l Alastair Campbell, tc, l Ronald Sheridan, bcr Gerald Clyde/Barnabys, br Jon Wyand; 53 l Alastair Campbell, cl Bernard Regent/Alan Hutchinson, tcr Renault, cr Citroën, r Michelin; 54 tl, br Netherlands Tourist Office, tc, tr Brian Dicks, cr Barnabys Picture Library, bc Walter Rawlings; 55 tl, tr Belgian Tourist Office, London, c, cr, bl Belgian National Tourist Office, New York; 56 ZEFA; 57 tl German National Tourist Office, tc, br ZEFA, tr Autocar, c Porsche; 58 t Johane

Berge/Norwegian Tourist Office, b ZEFA; 59 t, bl ZEFA, tr Danish Agricultural Producers, b Finnish Tourist Board; 60 t Feature-pix, tl Barnabys Picture Library rest Swiss National Tourist Office; 61 tl ZEFA, c Swiss National Tourist Office, b Austrian National Tourist Office; 62 tl Fiat, tr, c ZEFA, br J Allan Cash Ltd; 63 t ZEFA, r, br J Allan Cash Ltd, tl Italian State Tourist Office, bl Alastair Campbell; 64 tr Spanish National Tourist Office, c Brian Dicks, r Spectrum, b Ronald Sheridan; 65 t Brian Dicks, b J Allan Cash Ltd; 66 t, bc Czech Travel Bureau, tc, b ZEFA; 67 t A Jaroszewicz/D Williamson, c, b David Williamson; 68 tl Bulgarian Tourist Office, rest David Williamson; 69 tl Brian Dicks, tcl, tr, b ZEFA, tcr Michael Freeman, bc Yugoslavian National Tourist Office; 72 t A Jaroszewicz/D Williamson, c, b Novosti Press Agency; 73 tc Colorsport, br A Jaroszewicz/D Williamson, rest Novosti Press Agency; 74 t ZEFA, c J Allan Cash Ltd, b Abu Dhabi Petroleum Co; 75 tl Ann & Bury Peerless, bl Michael Freeman, rest Ann & Bury Peerless, br Michael Freeman; 77 tl Michael Freeman, tc, c Ann & Bury Peerless, tr Jesse Davis, r, b Compix; 78 t ZEFA, c, b Geoslides/Peter Corrigan; 79 tl, br Geoslides/Peter

Corrigan, tr, bl ZEFA, r Michael Freeman; 80 t Japanese Information Centre, cl Sony, c Datsun, Yamaha, r Barnabys Picture Library, br ZEFA; 81 tl, br ZEFA, tc Spectrum, tr Japanese Information Centre, bl Walter Rawlings; 82 tl Michael Freeman, tr A G Sanderson, bl Geoslides Photo Library, br ZEFA; 83 tl, cr Geoslides Photo Library, br ZEFA; 84 l, tc Alan Hutchinson, tr Hogarth Puppets, c Barnabys Picture Library, b ZEFA; 85 tl, tc, bl ZEFA, tr Alan Hutchinson; 88 t, b Walter Rawlings, c ZEFA; 89 tl John Moss, c ZEFA, b Walter Rawlings; 90 r John Moss, bl ZEFA; 91 tl ZEFA, bl John Moss, tr Alan Hutchinson, b, r Brian Dicks; 92 ZEFA; 93 tl, br John Moss, tr Compix, bl Alan Hutchinson; 94 t ZEFA, bl South African Tourist Office, bc Zambia Tourist Office, br Alan Hutchinson; 95 t Alan Hutchinson, bl John Moss; 98 t Bruce Coleman, b Australian News & Information Service; 99 Australian News & Information Service; 100 New Zealand High Commission; 101 New Zealand High Commission; 103 tl, tc, bc Barnabys Picture Library, tr, c, bl ZEFA, br Alan Hutchinson; 106 l ZEFA, c Brian Dicks, r Walter Rawlings; 107 tl, br Barnabys Picture Library, tc Brian Dicks, tr, bl ZEFA; 108 t Peter Newark's Western Americana, b Brian Dicks; 109 tl, tcr

Michael Freeman, tr, rc ZEFA, l Colorsport, br Peter Newark's Western Americana; 110 t, bl, bc ZEFA, br Spectrum; 111 tl, r Walter Rawlings, l, c ZEFA, r Mexican Government Tourist Office, b Michael Freeman; 112 t, l Stephen Benson, br ZEFA; 113 tl, cr Stephen Benson, tc ZEFA, bl Michael Freeman, br Colorsport; 116 tr Varig, r Michael Freeman, br ZEFA, b John Moss; 117 tl Pan American, r John Moss, cl Michael Freeman, b Sporting Pictures; 118 l Stephen Benson, r Michael Freeman; 119 bl ZEFA, rest Michael Freeman; 120 t Stephen Benson, tr, b Walter Rawlings, c, r John Moss; 121 t John Moss, l Stephen Benson, r Walter Rawlings; 122 tl Walter Rawlings, tc Spectrum, tr Daily Telegraph, r, bc Peter Keen/Daily Telegraph, bl ZEFA, br J Allan Cash Ltd; 123 tl Walter Rawlings, l, br Peter Keen/Daily Telegraph, bl Stephen Benson; 124 t Dr Parks/Oxford Scientific Films, l, b Geoslides/Ken Lax; 125 t, r, c Geoslides/Ken Lax, Eric Hosking FRPS; 126 bl New Zealand High Commission.

b   bottom
c   centre
l   left
r   right
t   top